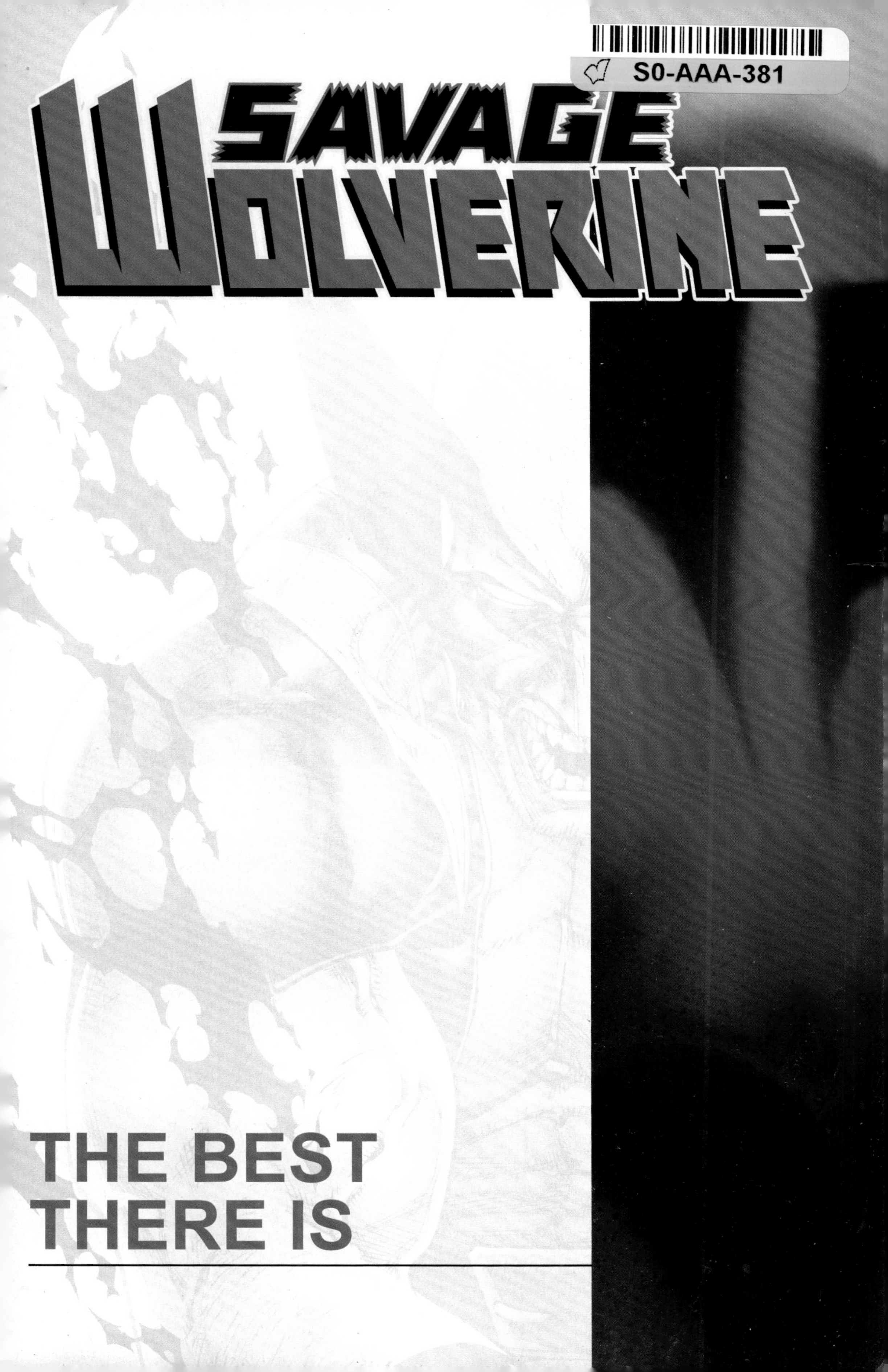

SAVAGE WOLVERINE

THE BEST THERE IS

SAVAGE WOLVERINE #18
WRITER
JEN VAN METER
ARTIST
RICH ELLIS
COLOR ARTIST
RUTH REDMOND

SAVAGE WOLVERINE #19
WRITER
GAIL SIMONE
PENCILER
NEIL EDWARDS
INKER
TERRY PALLOT
COLORIST
CHRIS SOTOMAYOR

SAVAGE WOLVERINE #20
WRITER
FRANK TIERI
ARTIST
FELIX RUIZ
COLOR ARTIST
DAN BROWN

SAVAGE WOLVERINE #21-22
WRITER
JOHN ARCUDI
ARTIST
JOE QUINONES

SAVAGE WOLVERINE #23
WRITER
DAVID MORRELL
ARTIST
JONATHAN MARKS
COLOR ARTIST
JOSE VILLARRUBIA

COVER ART
SHANE DAVIS &
MORRY HOLLOWELL;
DECLAN SHALVEY &
JORDIE BELLAIRE;
AND **KEVIN NOWLAN**
LETTERER
VC'S CORY PETIT

ASSISTANT EDITOR
FRANKIE JOHNSON
EDITORS
**JEANINE SCHAEFER,
KATIE KUBERT
& TOM BRENNAN**
X-MEN GROUP EDITOR
MIKE MARTS

COLLECTION EDITOR **ALEX STARBUCK**
ASSISTANT EDITOR **SARAH BRUNSTAD**
EDITORS, SPECIAL PROJECTS
JENNIFER GRÜNWALD & MARK D. BEAZLEY
SENIOR EDITOR, SPECIAL PROJECTS **JEFF YOUNGQUIST**
SVP PRINT, SALES & MARKETING **DAVID GABRIEL**
BOOK DESIGN **NELSON RIBEIRO**

EDITOR IN CHIEF **AXEL ALONSO**
CHIEF CREATIVE OFFICER **JOE QUESADA**
PUBLISHER **DAN BUCKLEY**
EXECUTIVE PRODUCER **ALAN FINE**

SAVAGE WOLVERINE

THE BEST THERE IS

SAVAGE WOLVERINE VOL. 4: THE BEST THERE IS. Contains material originally published in magazine form as SAVAGE WOLVERINE #18-23. First printing 2015. ISBN# 978-0-7851-8965-7. Published by MARVEL WORLDWIDE, INC., a subsidiary of MARVEL ENTERTAINMENT, LLC. OFFICE OF PUBLICATION: 135 West 50th Street, New York, NY 10020. Copyright © 2015 MARVEL No similarity between any of the names, characters, persons, and/or institutions in this magazine with those of any living or dead person or institution is intended, and any such similarity which may exist is purely coincidental. **Printed in Canada.** ALAN FINE, President, Marvel Entertainment; DAN BUCKLEY, President, TV, Publishing and Brand Management; JOE QUESADA, Chief Creative Officer; TOM BREVOORT, SVP of Publishing; DAVID BOGART, SVP of Operations & Procurement, Publishing; C.B. CEBULSKI, VP of International Development & Brand Management; DAVID GABRIEL, SVP Print, Sales & Marketing; JIM O'KEEFE, VP of Operations & Logistics; DAN CARR, Executive Director of Publishing Technology; SUSAN CRESPI, Editorial Operations Manager; ALEX MORALES, Publishing Operations Manager; STAN LEE, Chairman Emeritus. For information regarding advertising in Marvel Comics or on marvel.com, please contact Jonathan Rheingold, VP of Custom Solutions & Ad Sales, at jrheingold@marvel.com. For Marvel subscription inquiries, please call 800-217-9158. **Manufactured between 5/29/2015**

Many years ago, a secret government organization abducted the man called Logan, a mutant possessing razor-sharp bone claws and the ability to heal from any wound. In their attempt to create the perfect living weapon, the organization bonded the unbreakable metal Adamantium to his skeleton. The process was excruciating, and by the end there was little left of the man known as Logan. He had become...

SAVAGE WOLVERINE

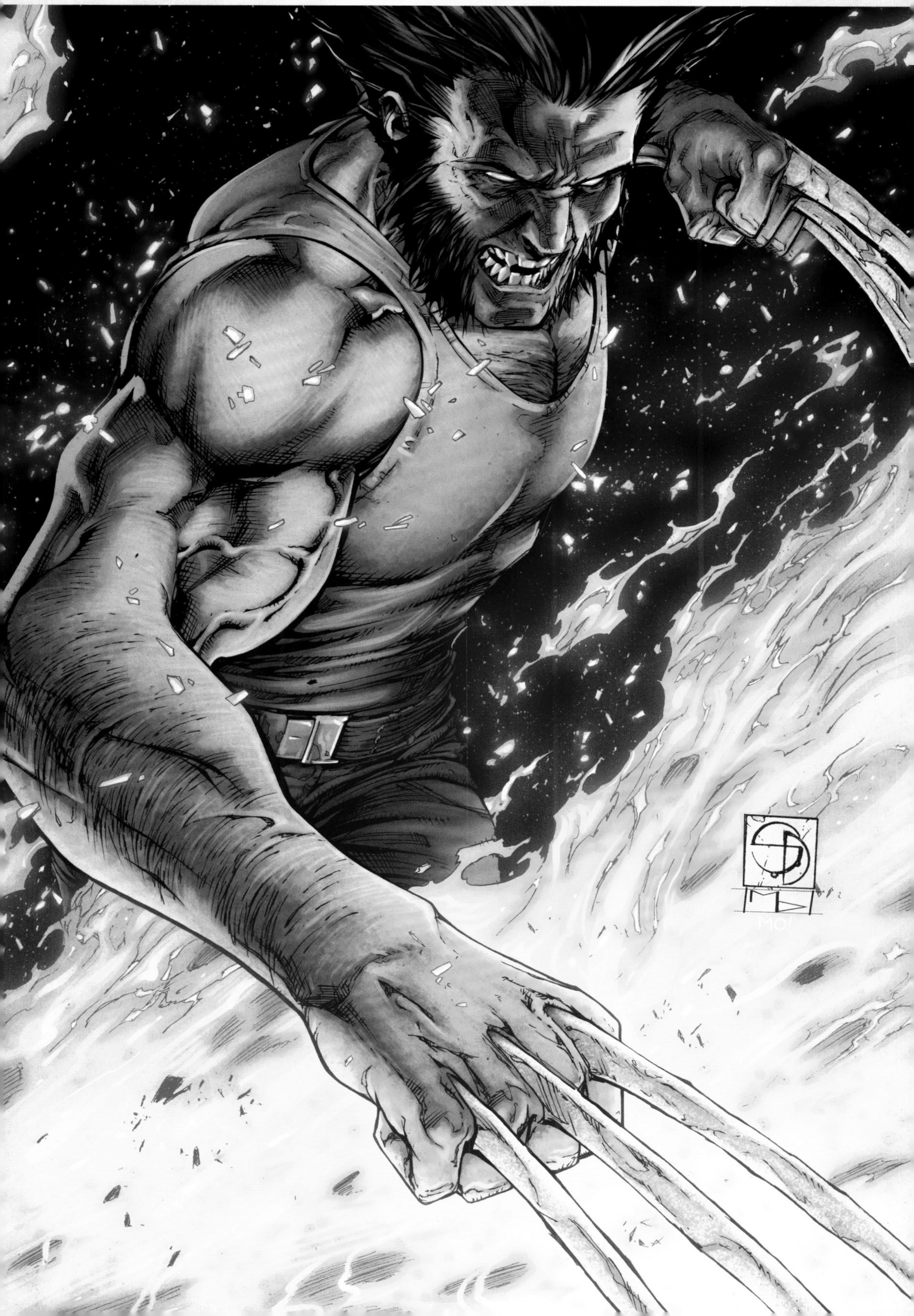

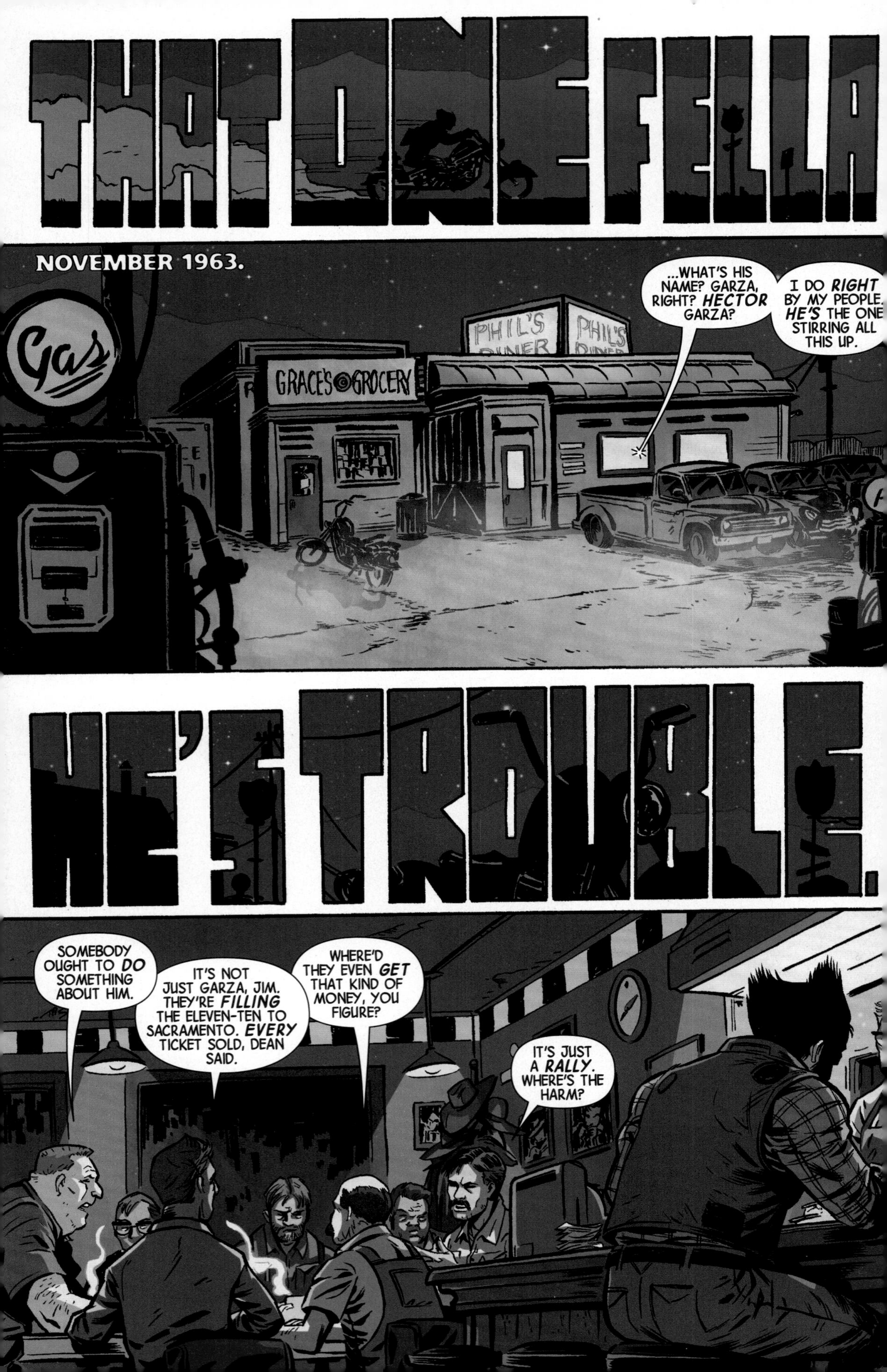
THAT ONE FELLA
NOVEMBER 1963.
...WHAT'S HIS NAME? GARZA, RIGHT? HECTOR GARZA?
I DO RIGHT BY MY PEOPLE. HE'S THE ONE STIRRING ALL THIS UP.
GAS
GRACE'S GROCERY
PHIL'S DINER
HE'S TROUBLE.
SOMEBODY OUGHT TO DO SOMETHING ABOUT HIM.
IT'S NOT JUST GARZA, JIM. THEY'RE FILLING THE ELEVEN-TEN TO SACRAMENTO. EVERY TICKET SOLD, DEAN SAID.
WHERE'D THEY EVEN GET THAT KIND OF MONEY, YOU FIGURE?
IT'S JUST A RALLY. WHERE'S THE HARM?

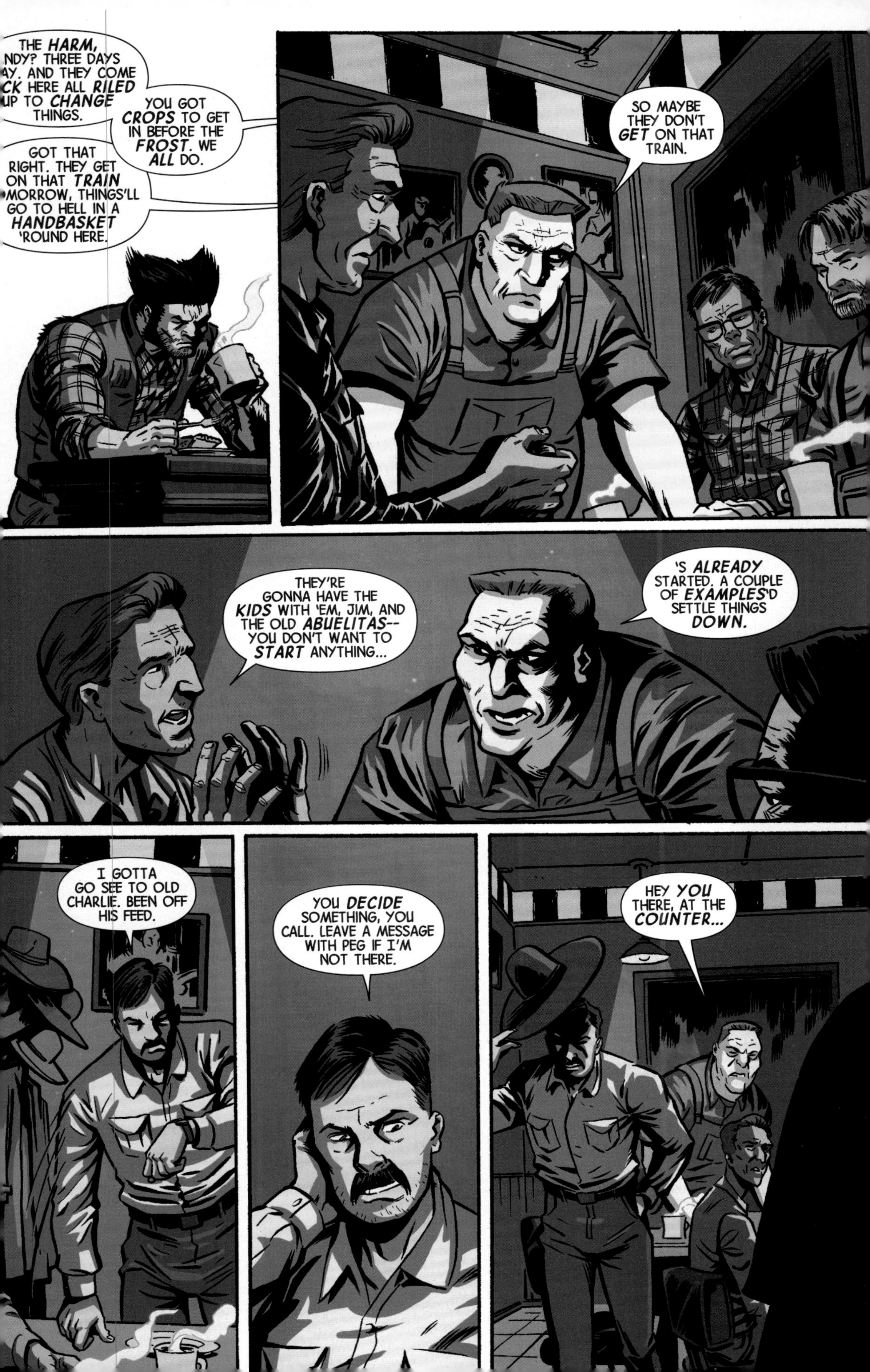
THE HARM, NDY? THREE DAYS AY. AND THEY COME CK HERE ALL RILED UP TO CHANGE THINGS.
YOU GOT CROPS TO GET IN BEFORE THE FROST. WE ALL DO.
GOT THAT RIGHT. THEY GET ON THAT TRAIN MORROW, THINGS'LL GO TO HELL IN A HANDBASKET 'ROUND HERE.
SO MAYBE THEY DON'T GET ON THAT TRAIN.
THEY'RE GONNA HAVE THE KIDS WITH 'EM, JIM, AND THE OLD ABUELITAS-- YOU DON'T WANT TO START ANYTHING...
'S ALREADY STARTED. A COUPLE OF EXAMPLES'D SETTLE THINGS DOWN.
I GOTTA GO SEE TO OLD CHARLIE. BEEN OFF HIS FEED.
YOU DECIDE SOMETHING, YOU CALL. LEAVE A MESSAGE WITH PEG IF I'M NOT THERE.
HEY YOU THERE, AT THE COUNTER...

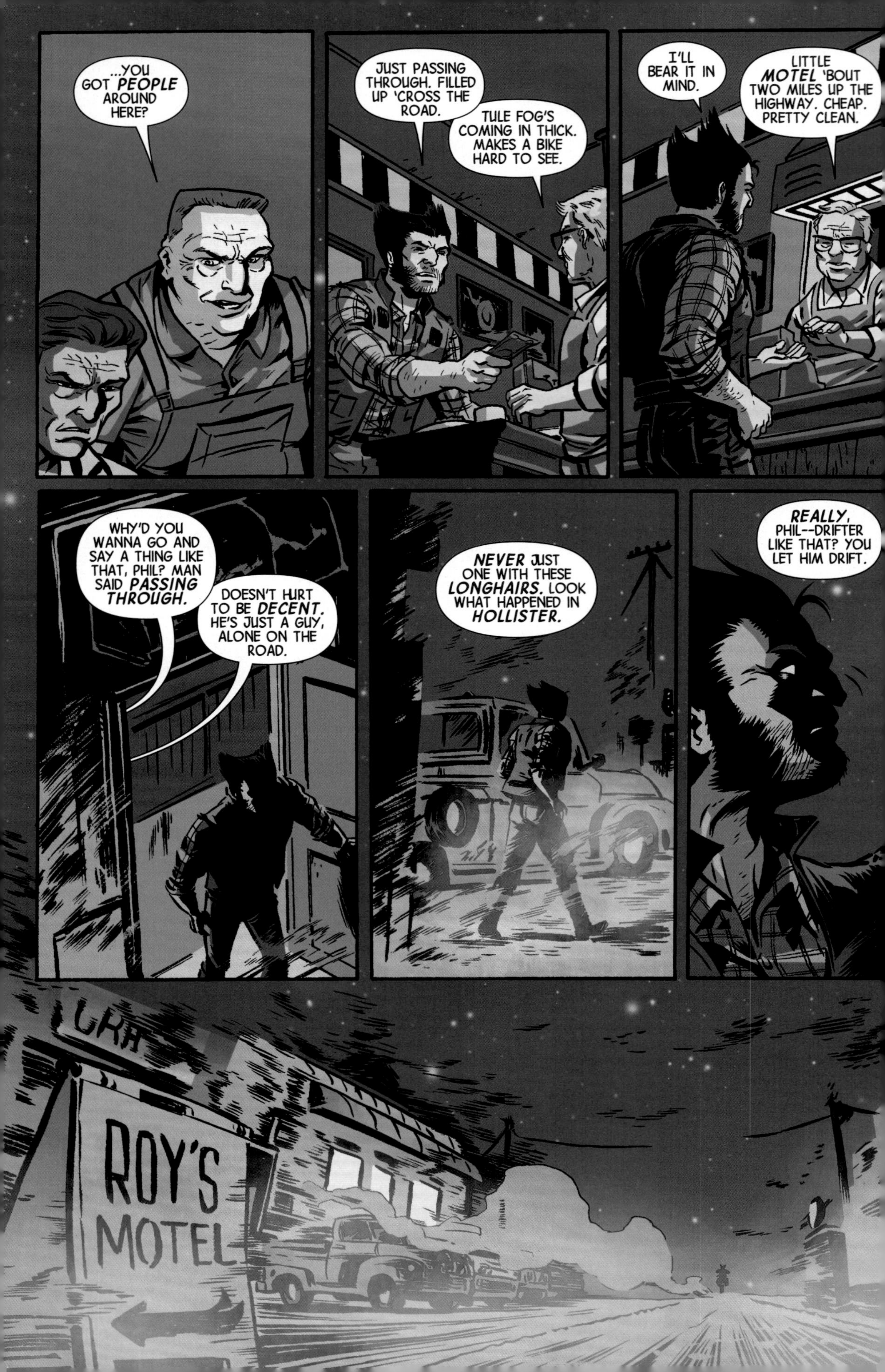
...YOU GOT PEOPLE AROUND HERE?
JUST PASSING THROUGH. FILLED UP 'CROSS THE ROAD.
TULE FOG'S COMING IN THICK. MAKES A BIKE HARD TO SEE.
I'LL BEAR IT IN MIND.
LITTLE MOTEL 'BOUT TWO MILES UP THE HIGHWAY. CHEAP. PRETTY CLEAN.
WHY'D YOU WANNA GO AND SAY A THING LIKE THAT, PHIL? MAN SAID PASSING THROUGH.
DOESN'T HURT TO BE DECENT. HE'S JUST A GUY, ALONE ON THE ROAD.
NEVER JUST ONE WITH THESE LONGHAIRS. LOOK WHAT HAPPENED IN HOLLISTER.
REALLY, PHIL--DRIFTER LIKE THAT? YOU LET HIM DRIFT.
ROY'S MOTEL

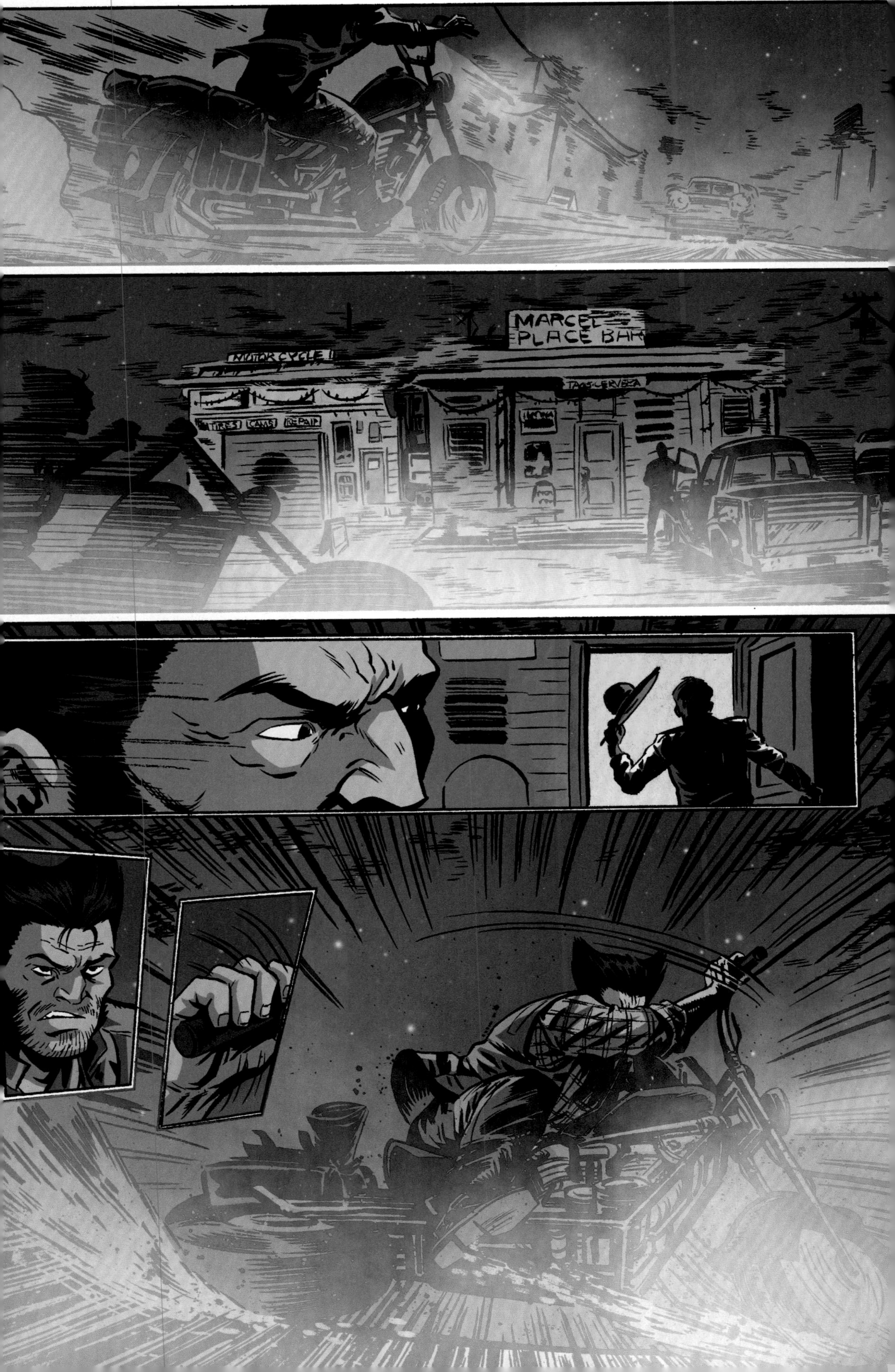
MARCEL
PLACE BAR
MOTORCYCLE
TIRES
CAMS
REPAIR

MADRE MIA. THIS *FOG.* YOU'RE PRETTY DAMN *LUCKY,* MISTER.

HEARD THAT BEFORE.

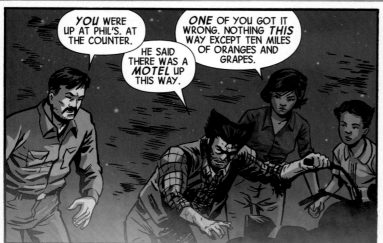

YOU WERE UP AT PHIL'S. AT THE COUNTER.

HE SAID THERE WAS A *MOTEL* UP THIS WAY.

ONE OF YOU GOT IT WRONG. NOTHING *THIS* WAY EXCEPT TEN MILES OF ORANGES AND GRAPES.

THERE'S A COT IN THE *GARAGE* IF YOU WANT IT.

I START BREAKFAST AROUND *SIX,* BUT YOU CAN *SLEEP* AS LATE AS YOU WANT.

ANNA'S GOOD WITH *BIKES...*

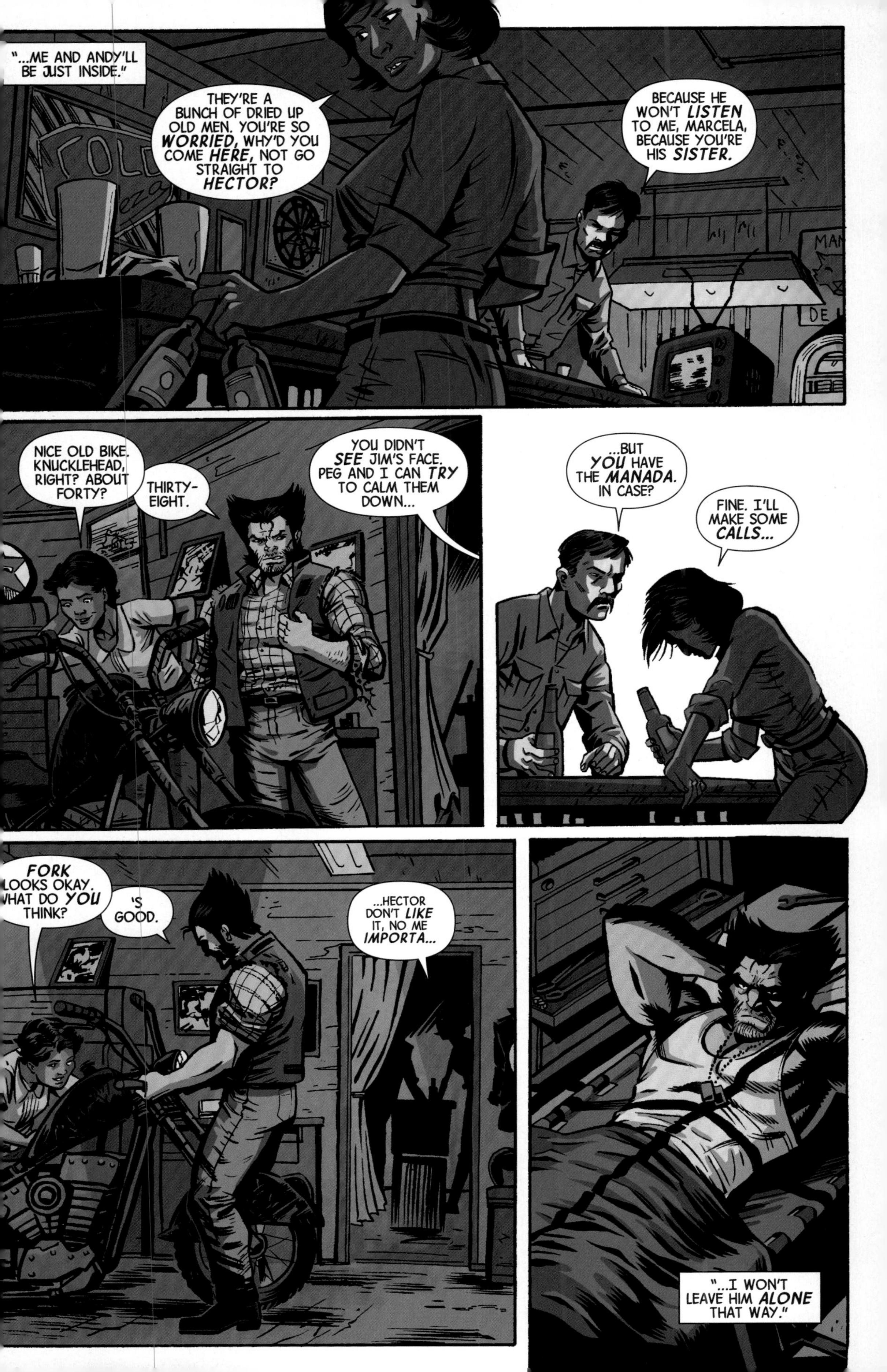
"...ME AND ANDY'LL BE JUST INSIDE."
THEY'RE A BUNCH OF DRIED UP OLD MEN. YOU'RE SO WORRIED, WHY'D YOU COME HERE, NOT GO STRAIGHT TO HECTOR?
BECAUSE HE WON'T LISTEN TO ME, MARCELA, BECAUSE YOU'RE HIS SISTER.
NICE OLD BIKE. KNUCKLEHEAD, RIGHT? ABOUT FORTY?
THIRTY-EIGHT.
YOU DIDN'T SEE JIM'S FACE. PEG AND I CAN TRY TO CALM THEM DOWN...
...BUT YOU HAVE THE MANADA. IN CASE?
FINE. I'LL MAKE SOME CALLS...
FORK LOOKS OKAY. WHAT DO YOU THINK?
'S GOOD.
...HECTOR DON'T LIKE IT, NO ME IMPORTA...
"...I WON'T LEAVE HIM ALONE THAT WAY."

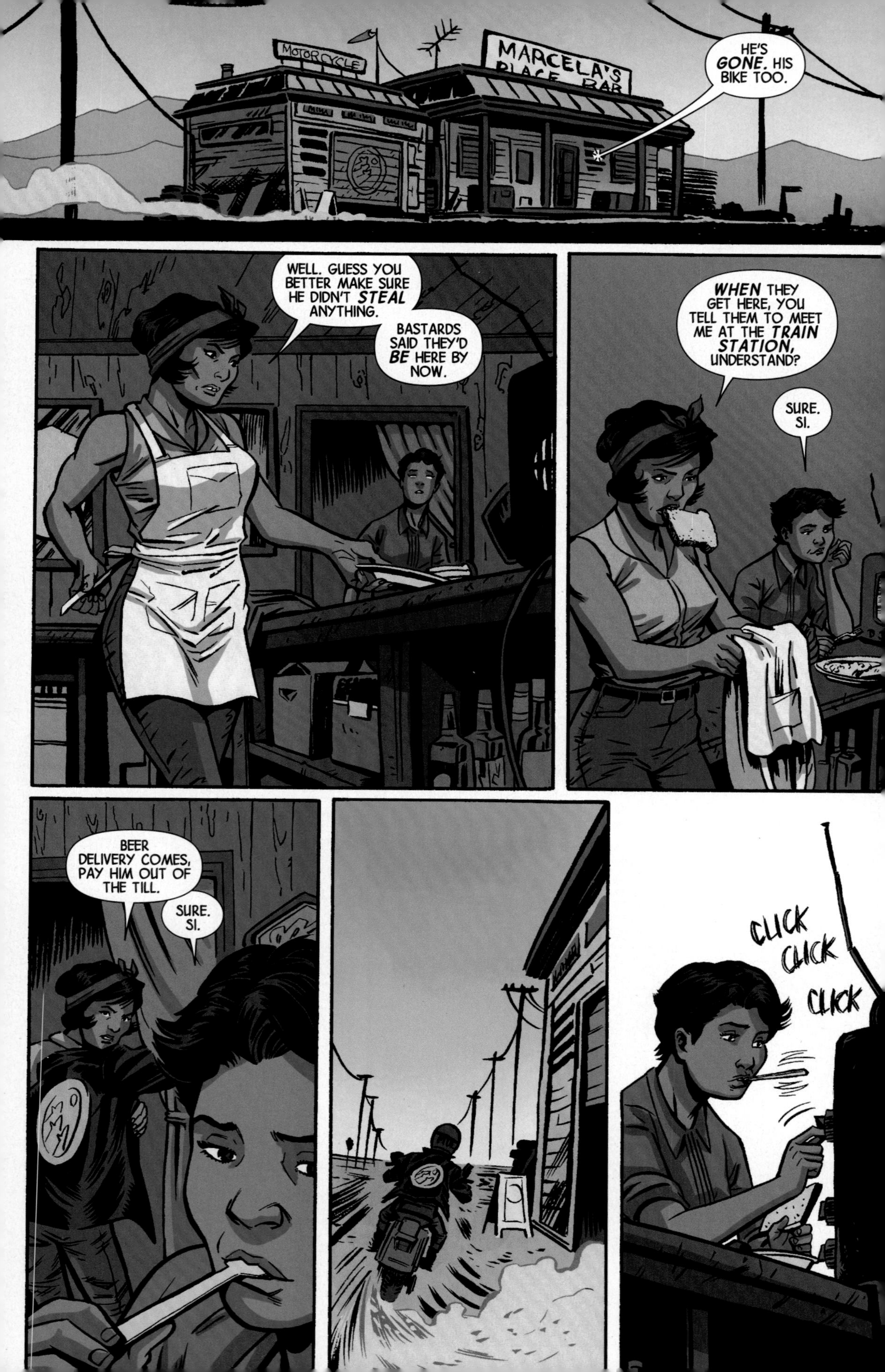
MOTORCYCLE
MARCELA'S PLACE BAR
HE'S GONE. HIS BIKE TOO.
WELL. GUESS YOU BETTER MAKE SURE HE DIDN'T STEAL ANYTHING.
BASTARDS SAID THEY'D BE HERE BY NOW.
WHEN THEY GET HERE, YOU TELL THEM TO MEET ME AT THE TRAIN STATION, UNDERSTAND?
SURE. SI.
BEER DELIVERY COMES, PAY HIM OUT OF THE TILL.
SURE. SI.
CLICK
CLICK
CLICK

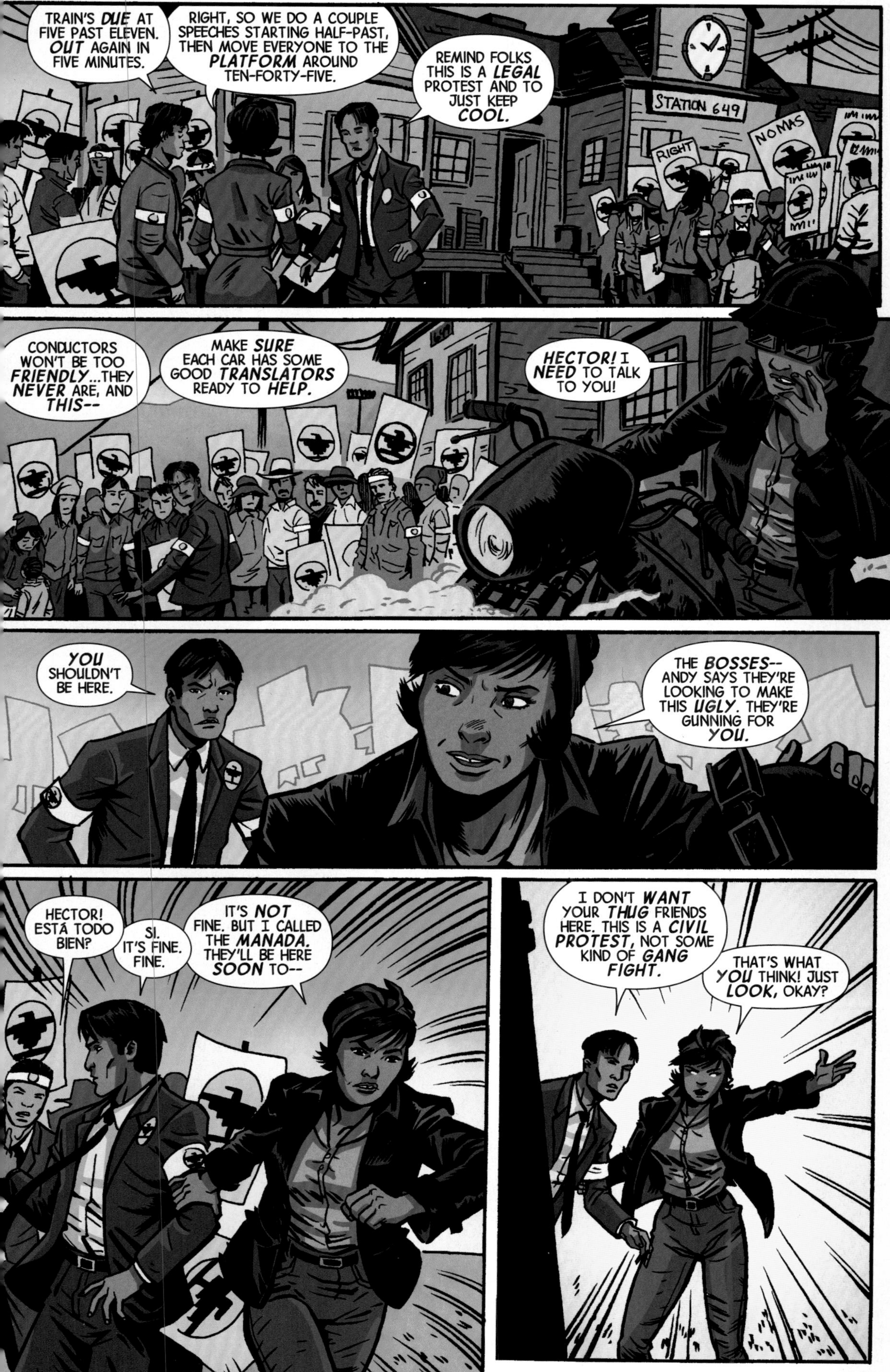
TRAIN'S DUE AT FIVE PAST ELEVEN. OUT AGAIN IN FIVE MINUTES.
RIGHT, SO WE DO A COUPLE SPEECHES STARTING HALF-PAST, THEN MOVE EVERYONE TO THE PLATFORM AROUND TEN-FORTY-FIVE.
REMIND FOLKS THIS IS A LEGAL PROTEST AND TO JUST KEEP COOL.
STATION 649
RIGHT
NO MAS
CONDUCTORS WON'T BE TOO FRIENDLY...THEY NEVER ARE, AND THIS--
MAKE SURE EACH CAR HAS SOME GOOD TRANSLATORS READY TO HELP.
HECTOR! I NEED TO TALK TO YOU!
YOU SHOULDN'T BE HERE.
THE BOSSES-- ANDY SAYS THEY'RE LOOKING TO MAKE THIS UGLY. THEY'RE GUNNING FOR YOU.
HECTOR! ESTÁ TODO BIEN?
SI. IT'S FINE. FINE.
IT'S NOT FINE. BUT I CALLED THE MANADA. THEY'LL BE HERE SOON TO--
I DON'T WANT YOUR THUG FRIENDS HERE. THIS IS A CIVIL PROTEST, NOT SOME KIND OF GANG FIGHT.
THAT'S WHAT YOU THINK! JUST LOOK, OKAY?

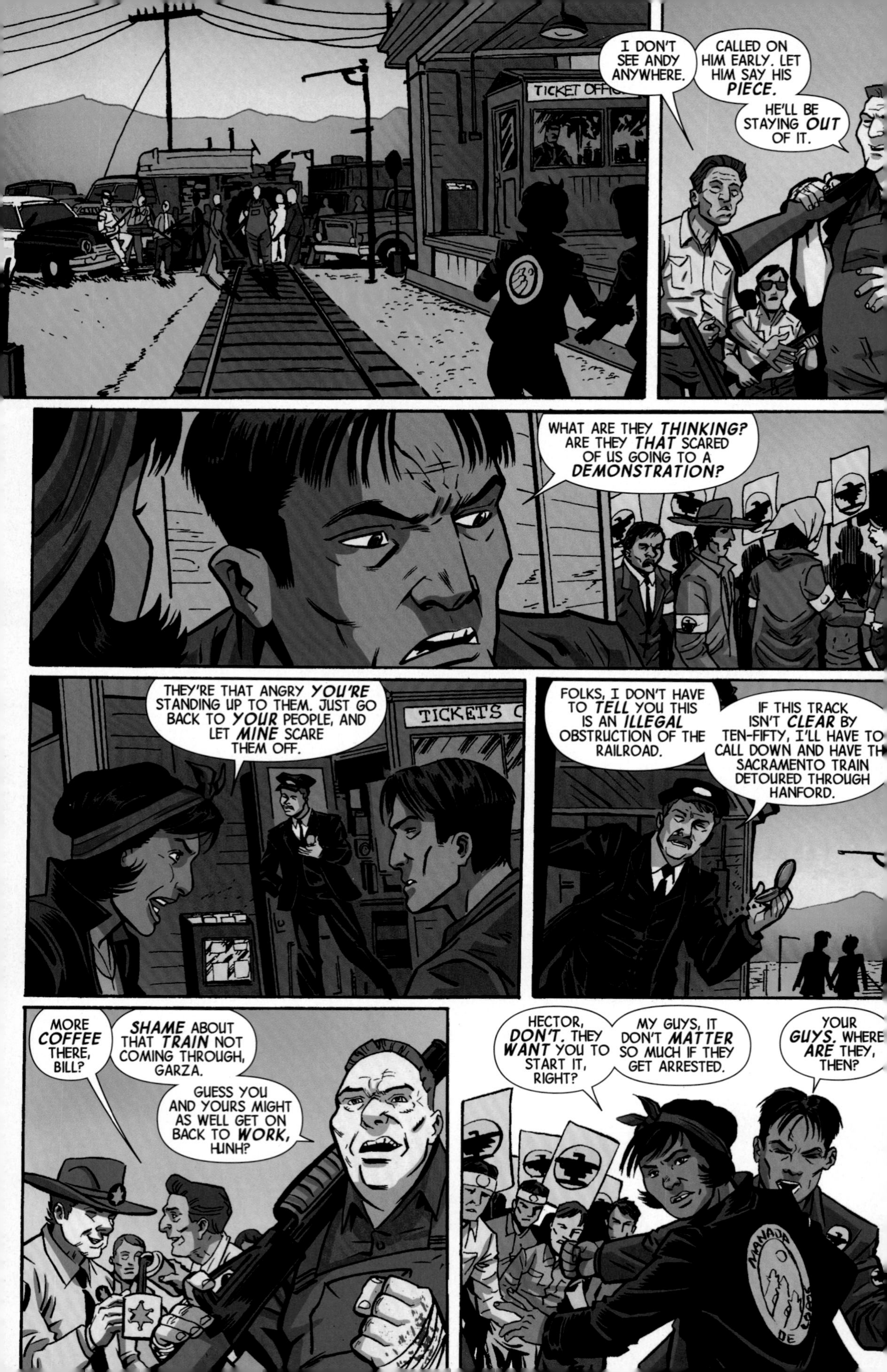
TICKET OFFICE
I DON'T SEE ANDY ANYWHERE.
CALLED ON HIM EARLY. LET HIM SAY HIS *PIECE.*
HE'LL BE STAYING *OUT* OF IT.
WHAT ARE THEY *THINKING?* ARE THEY *THAT* SCARED OF US GOING TO A *DEMONSTRATION?*
THEY'RE THAT ANGRY *YOU'RE* STANDING UP TO THEM. JUST GO BACK TO *YOUR* PEOPLE, AND LET *MINE* SCARE THEM OFF.
TICKETS
FOLKS, I DON'T HAVE TO *TELL* YOU THIS IS AN *ILLEGAL* OBSTRUCTION OF THE RAILROAD.
IF THIS TRACK ISN'T *CLEAR* BY TEN-FIFTY, I'LL HAVE TO CALL DOWN AND HAVE TH SACRAMENTO TRAIN DETOURED THROUGH HANFORD.
MORE *COFFEE* THERE, BILL?
SHAME ABOUT THAT *TRAIN* NOT COMING THROUGH, GARZA.
GUESS YOU AND YOURS MIGHT AS WELL GET ON BACK TO *WORK,* HUNH?
HECTOR, *DON'T.* THEY *WANT* YOU TO START IT, RIGHT?
MY GUYS, IT DON'T *MATTER* SO MUCH IF THEY GET ARRESTED.
YOUR *GUYS.* WHERE *ARE* THEY, THEN?
MANADA
DE

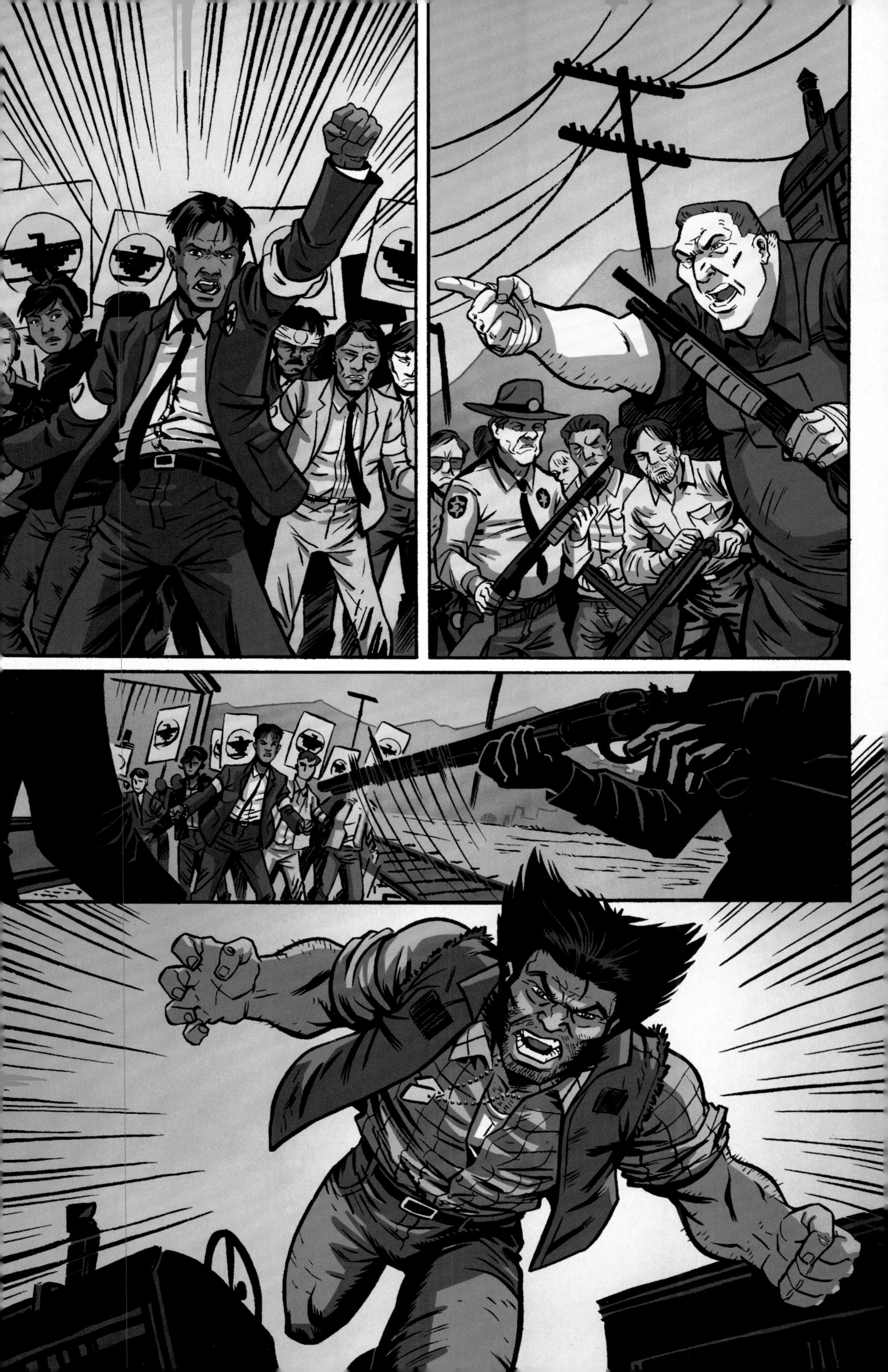

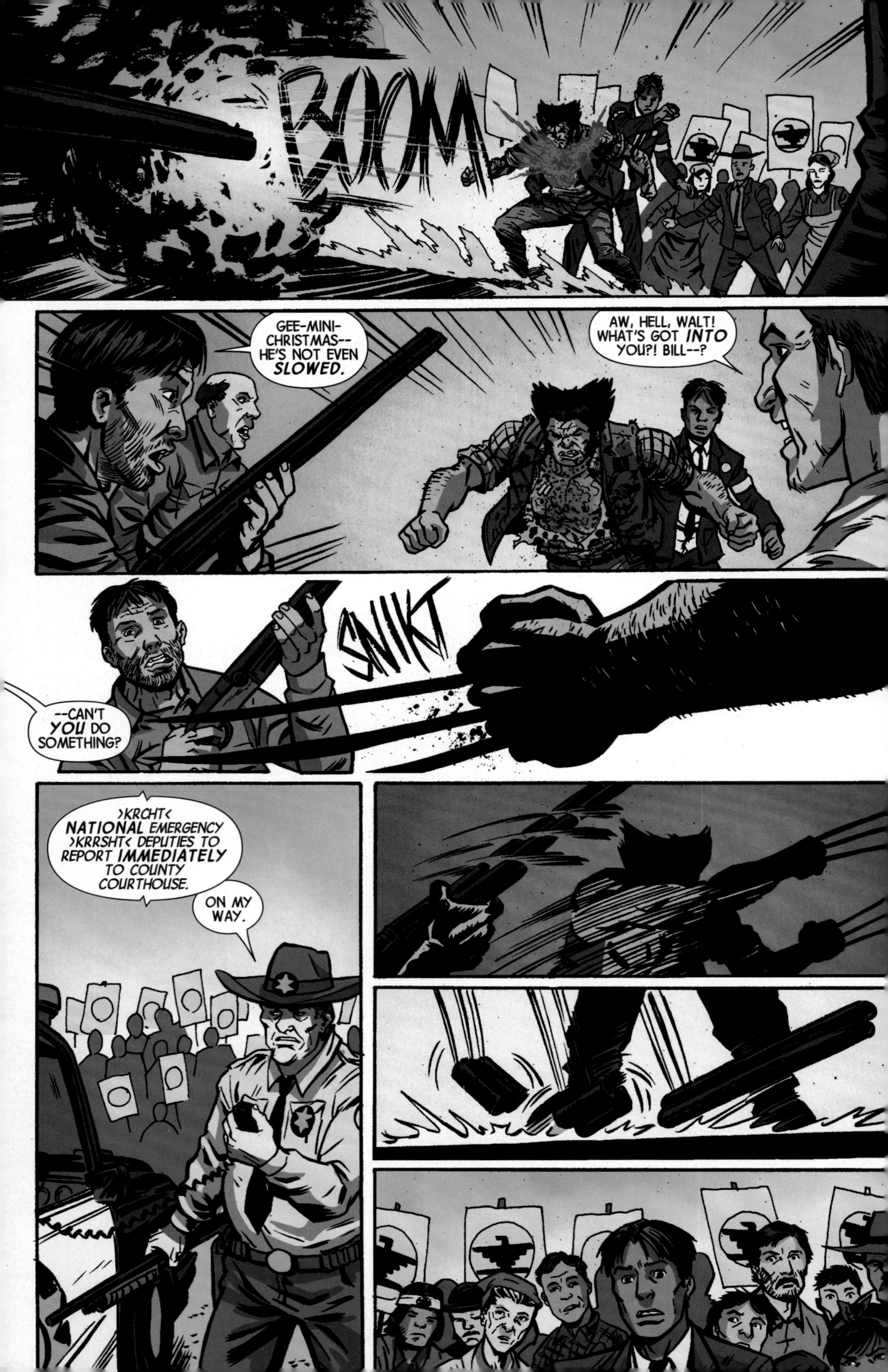
BOOM
GEE-MINI-CHRISTMAS-- HE'S NOT EVEN SLOWED.
AW, HELL, WALT! WHAT'S GOT INTO YOU?! BILL--?
SNIKT
--CAN'T YOU DO SOMETHING?
>KRCHT< NATIONAL EMERGENCY >KRRSHT< DEPUTIES TO REPORT IMMEDIATELY TO COUNTY COURTHOUSE.
ON MY WAY.

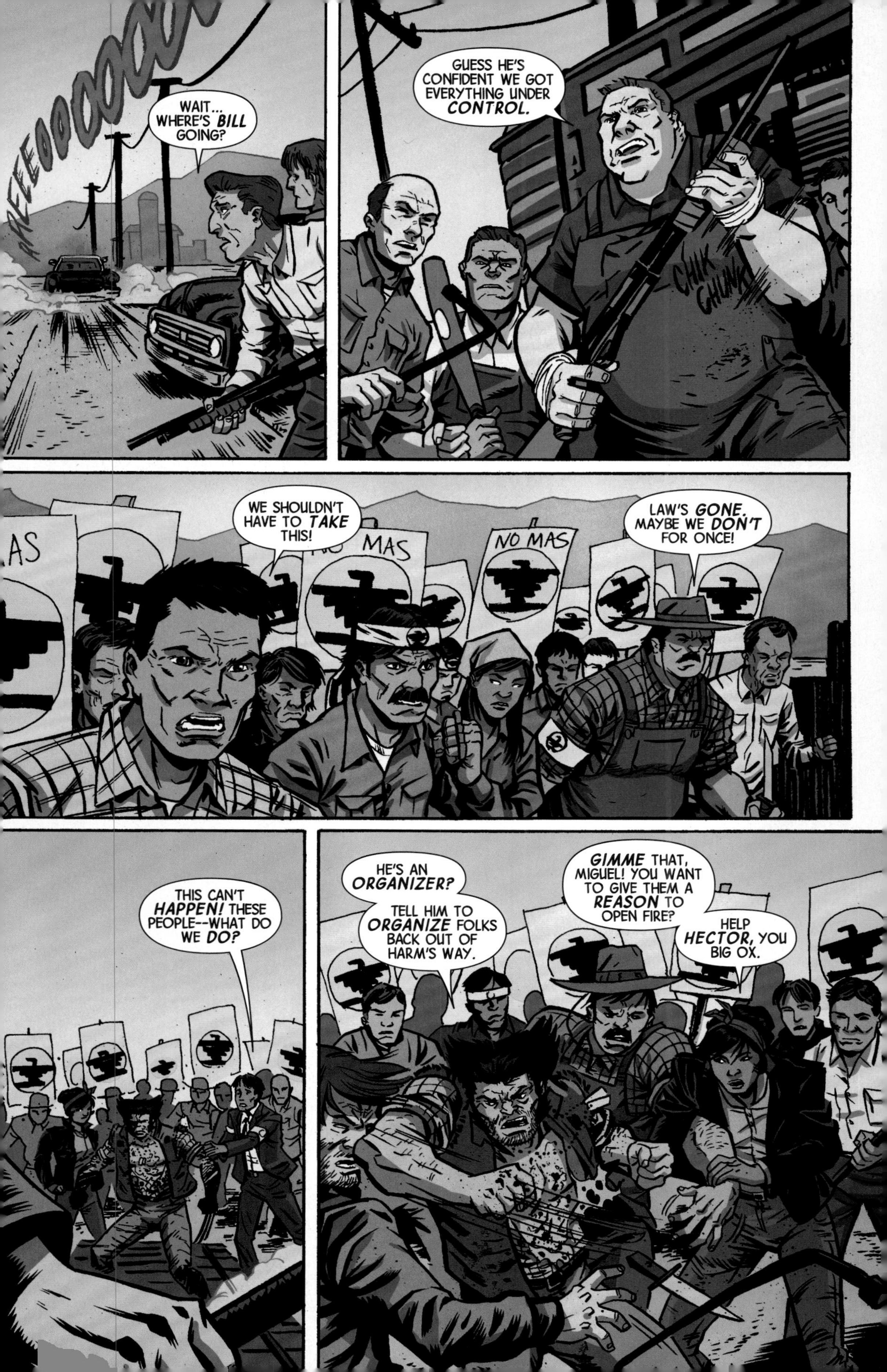
WHEEEOOOOOOO
WAIT... WHERE'S BILL GOING?
GUESS HE'S CONFIDENT WE GOT EVERYTHING UNDER CONTROL.
CHIK CHUNK
WE SHOULDN'T HAVE TO TAKE THIS!
LAW'S GONE. MAYBE WE DON'T FOR ONCE!
NO MAS
THIS CAN'T HAPPEN! THESE PEOPLE--WHAT DO WE DO?
HE'S AN ORGANIZER?
TELL HIM TO ORGANIZE FOLKS BACK OUT OF HARM'S WAY.
GIMME THAT, MIGUEL! YOU WANT TO GIVE THEM A REASON TO OPEN FIRE?
HELP HECTOR, YOU BIG OX.

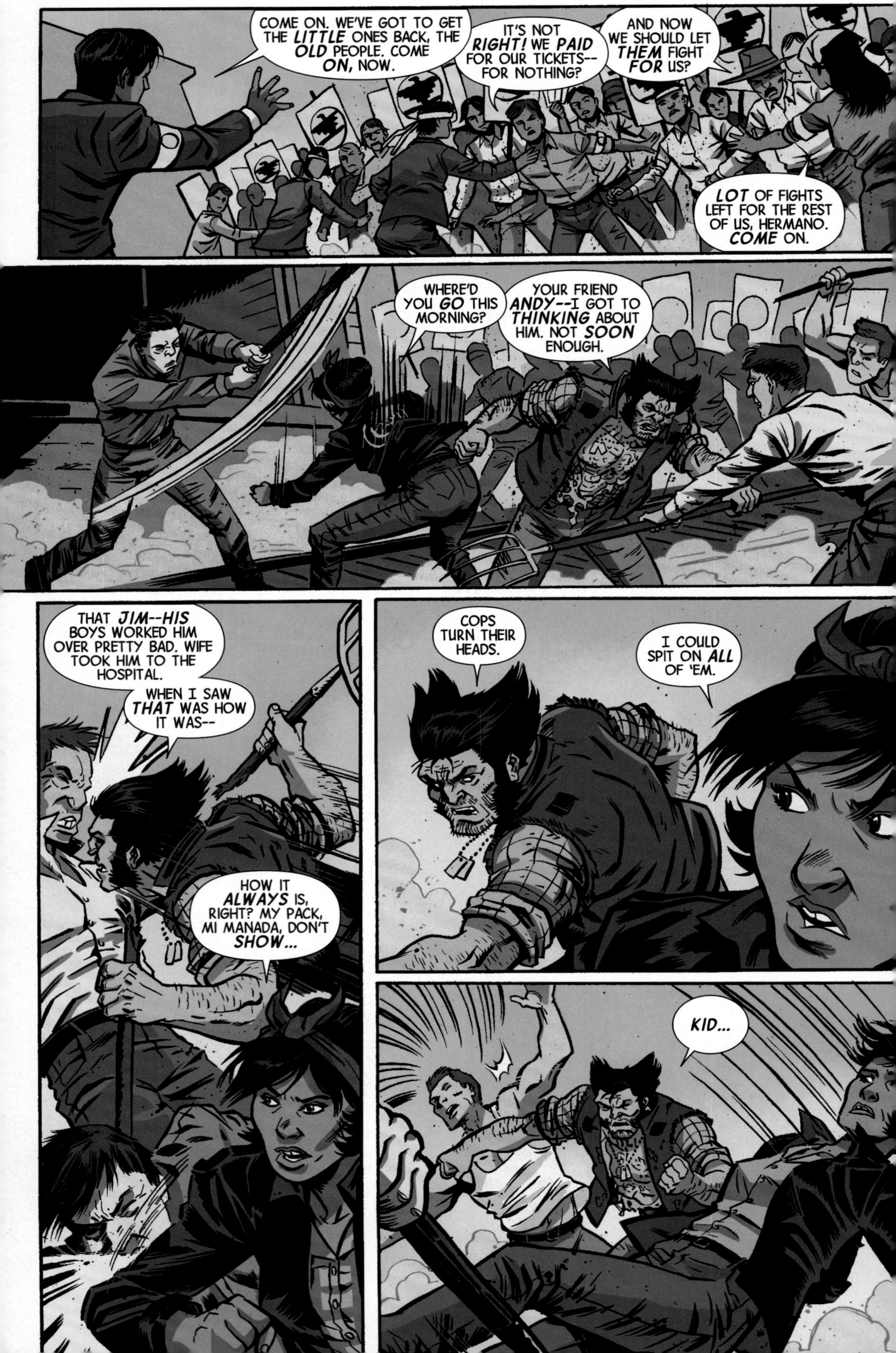
COME ON. WE'VE GOT TO GET THE LITTLE ONES BACK, THE OLD PEOPLE. COME ON, NOW.
IT'S NOT RIGHT! WE PAID FOR OUR TICKETS-- FOR NOTHING?
AND NOW WE SHOULD LET THEM FIGHT FOR US?
LOT OF FIGHTS LEFT FOR THE REST OF US, HERMANO. COME ON.
WHERE'D YOU GO THIS MORNING?
YOUR FRIEND ANDY--I GOT TO THINKING ABOUT HIM. NOT SOON ENOUGH.
THAT JIM--HIS BOYS WORKED HIM OVER PRETTY BAD. WIFE TOOK HIM TO THE HOSPITAL.
WHEN I SAW THAT WAS HOW IT WAS--
HOW IT ALWAYS IS, RIGHT? MY PACK, MI MANADA, DON'T SHOW...
COPS TURN THEIR HEADS.
I COULD SPIT ON ALL OF 'EM.
KID...

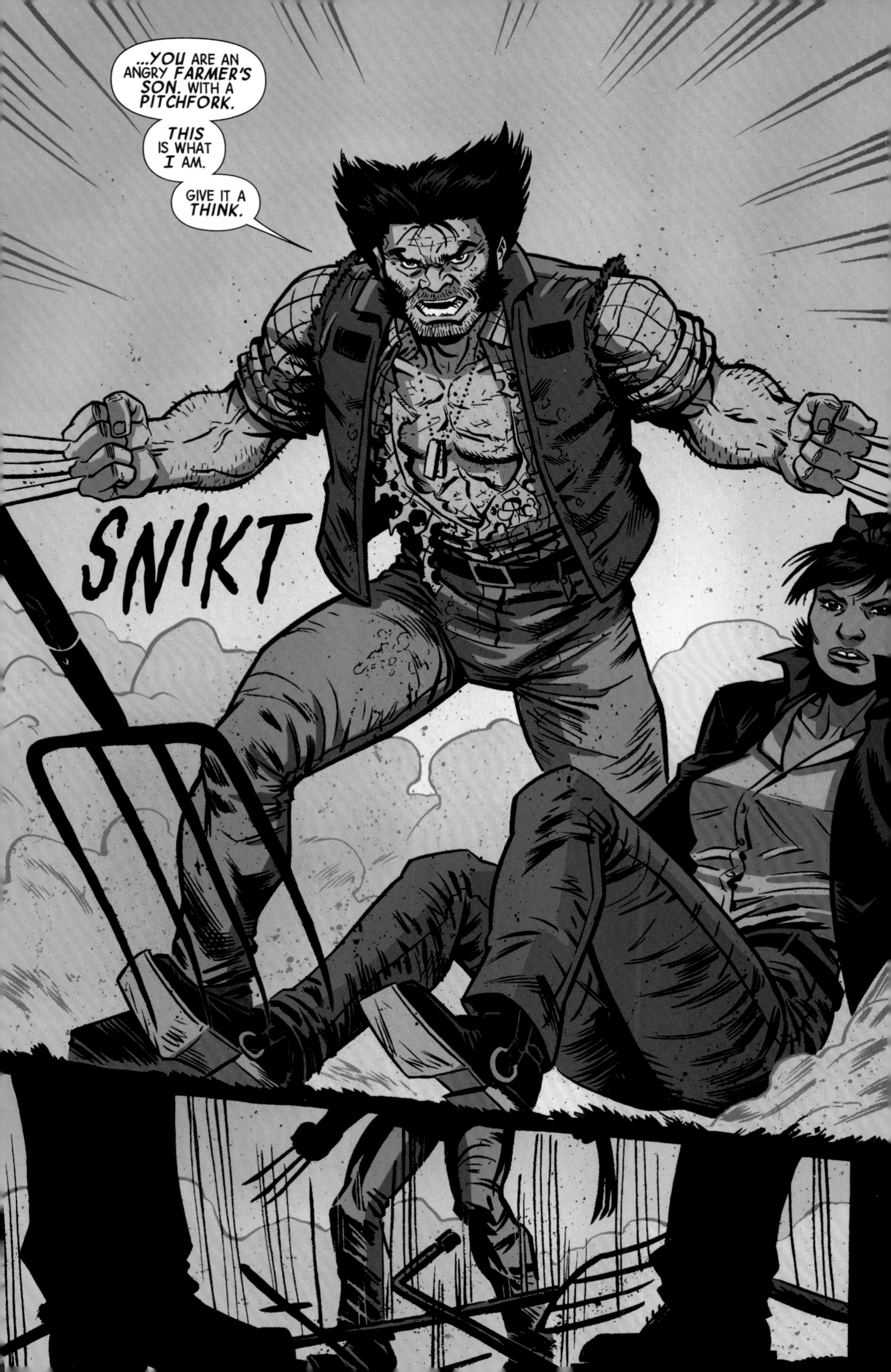
...YOU ARE AN ANGRY FARMER'S SON, WITH A PITCHFORK.
THIS IS WHAT I AM.
GIVE IT A THINK.
SNIKT

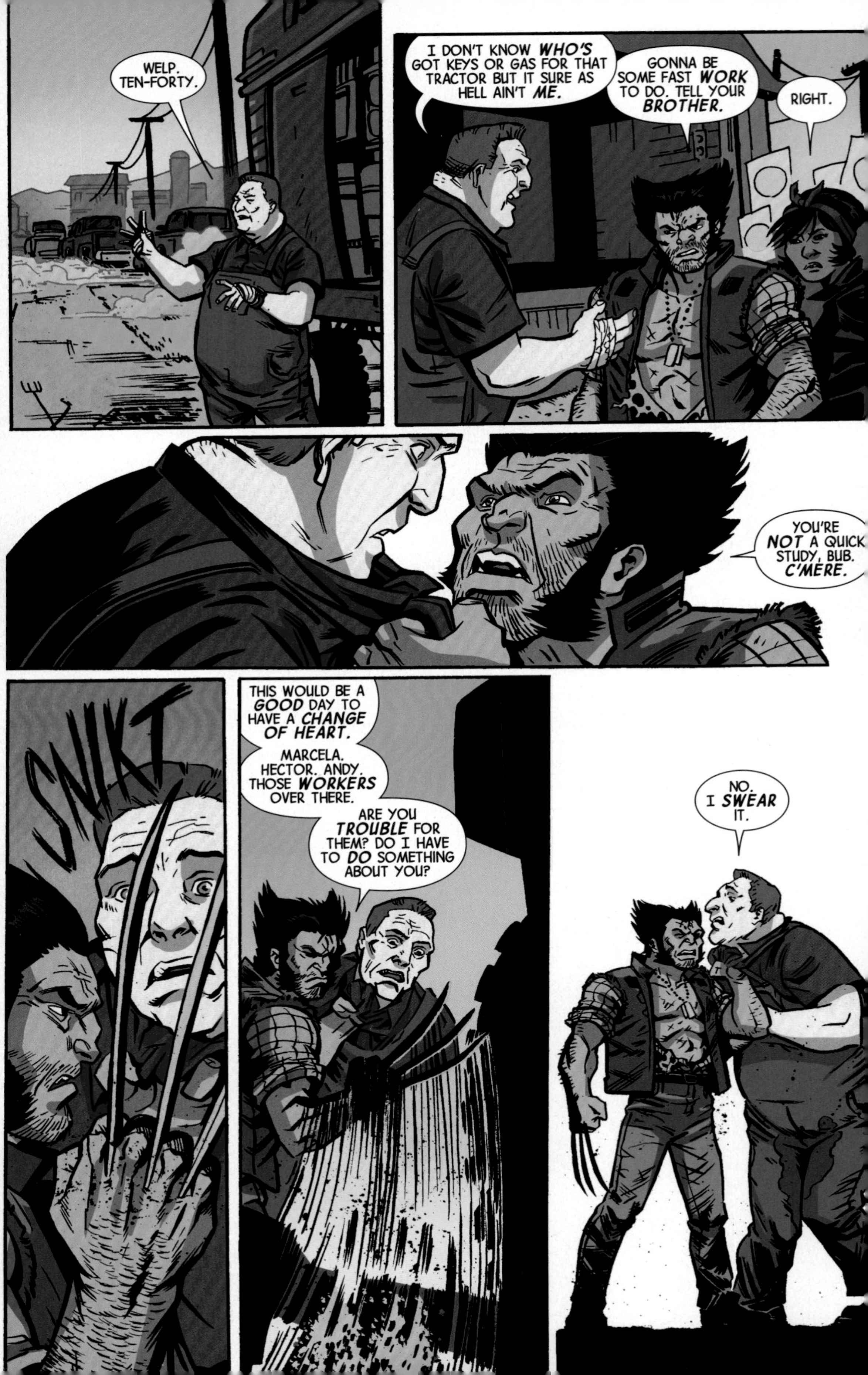
WELP. TEN-FORTY.
I DON'T KNOW WHO'S GOT KEYS OR GAS FOR THAT TRACTOR BUT IT SURE AS HELL AIN'T ME.
GONNA BE SOME FAST WORK TO DO. TELL YOUR BROTHER.
RIGHT.
YOU'RE NOT A QUICK STUDY, BUB. C'MERE.
SNIKT
THIS WOULD BE A GOOD DAY TO HAVE A CHANGE OF HEART.
MARCELA. HECTOR. ANDY. THOSE WORKERS OVER THERE.
ARE YOU TROUBLE FOR THEM? DO I HAVE TO DO SOMETHING ABOUT YOU?
NO. I SWEAR IT.

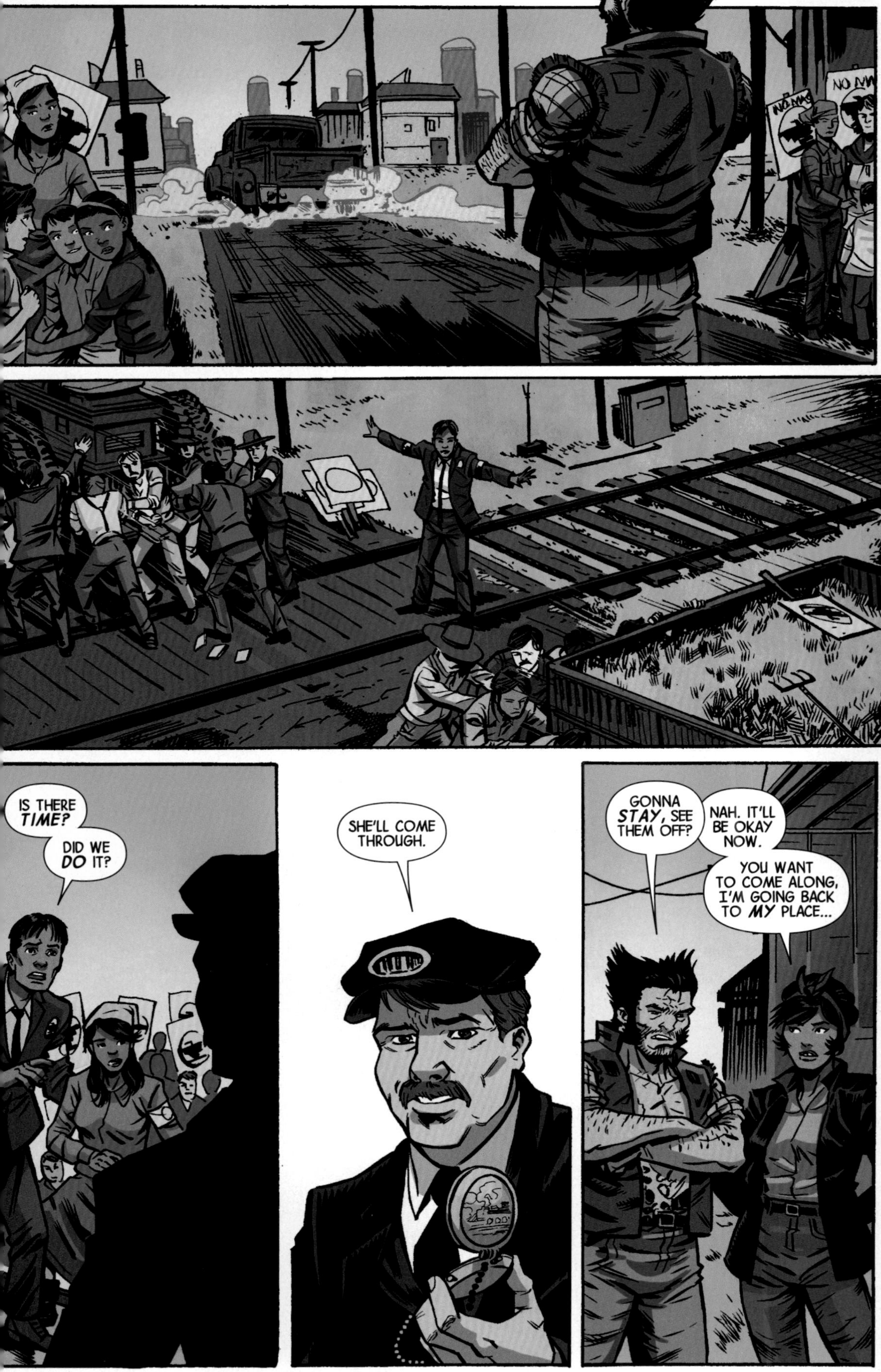
IS THERE TIME?
DID WE DO IT?
SHE'LL COME THROUGH.
GONNA STAY, SEE THEM OFF?
NAH. IT'LL BE OKAY NOW.
YOU WANT TO COME ALONG, I'M GOING BACK TO MY PLACE...

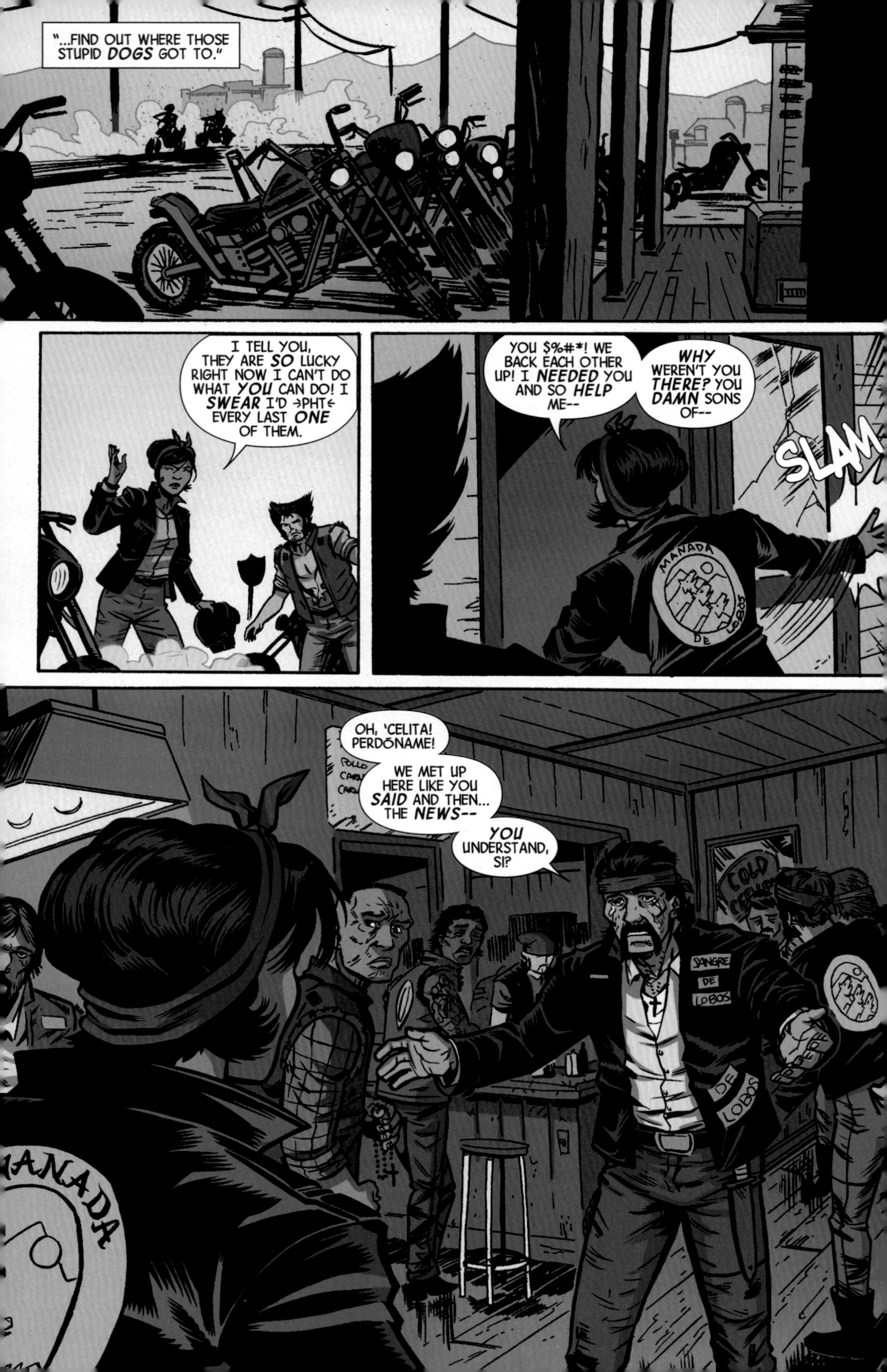
"...FIND OUT WHERE THOSE STUPID DOGS GOT TO."
I TELL YOU, THEY ARE SO LUCKY RIGHT NOW I CAN'T DO WHAT YOU CAN DO! I SWEAR I'D →PHT← EVERY LAST ONE OF THEM.
YOU $%#*! WE BACK EACH OTHER UP! I NEEDED YOU AND SO HELP ME--
WHY WEREN'T YOU THERE? YOU DAMN SONS OF--
SLAM
MANADA DE LOBOS
OH, 'CELITA! PERDÓNAME!
WE MET UP HERE LIKE YOU SAID AND THEN... THE NEWS--
YOU UNDERSTAND, SI?
SANGRE DE LOBOS
DE LOBOS
MANADA

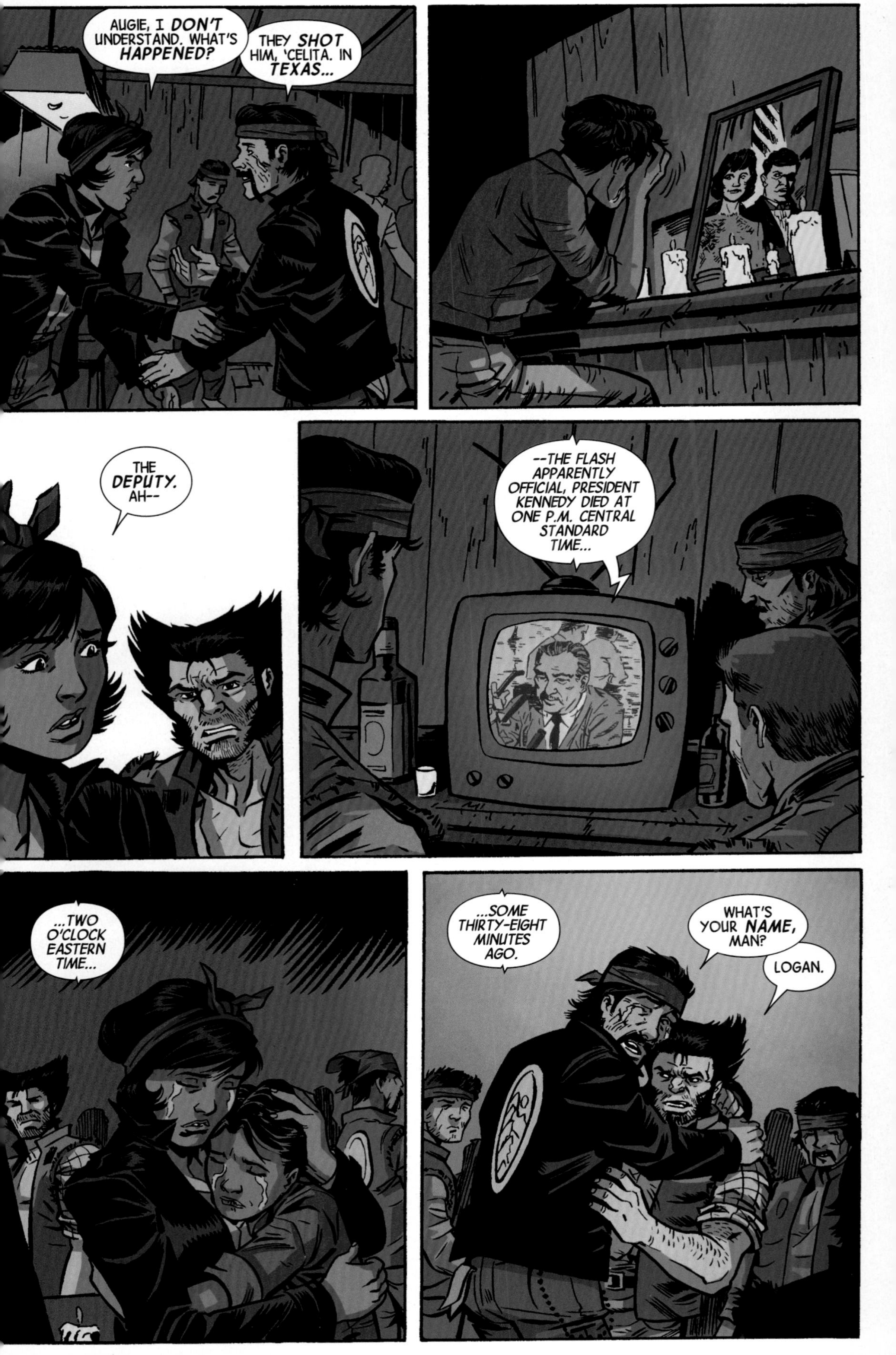
AUGIE, I DON'T UNDERSTAND. WHAT'S HAPPENED?
THEY SHOT HIM, 'CELITA. IN TEXAS...
THE DEPUTY. AH--
--THE FLASH APPARENTLY OFFICIAL, PRESIDENT KENNEDY DIED AT ONE P.M. CENTRAL STANDARD TIME...
...TWO O'CLOCK EASTERN TIME...
...SOME THIRTY-EIGHT MINUTES AGO.
WHAT'S YOUR NAME, MAN?
LOGAN.

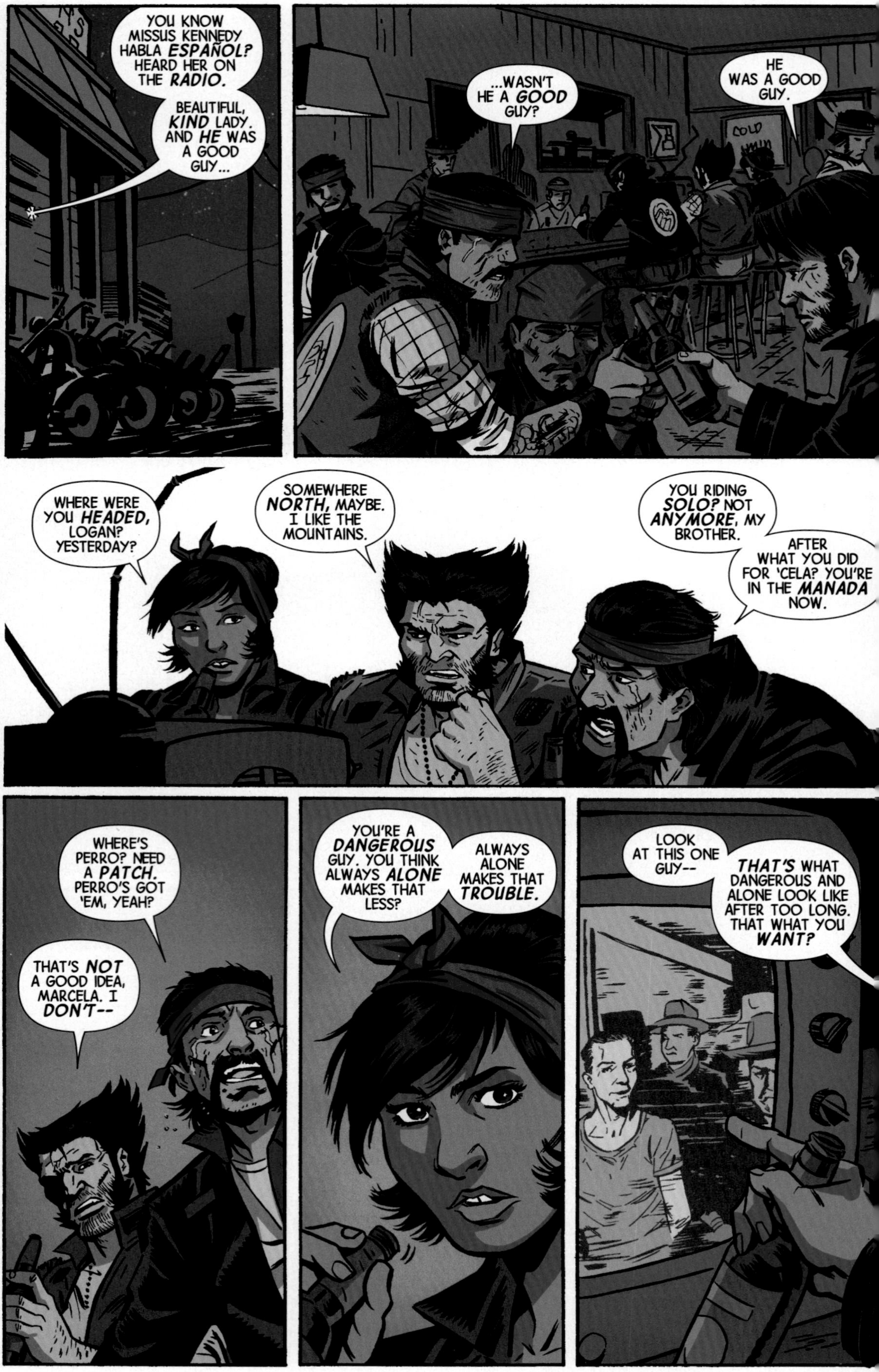
YOU KNOW MISSUS KENNEDY HABLA ESPAÑOL? HEARD HER ON THE RADIO.
BEAUTIFUL, KIND LADY. AND HE WAS A GOOD GUY...
...WASN'T HE A GOOD GUY?
HE WAS A GOOD GUY.
COLD
WHERE WERE YOU HEADED, LOGAN? YESTERDAY?
SOMEWHERE NORTH, MAYBE. I LIKE THE MOUNTAINS.
YOU RIDING SOLO? NOT ANYMORE, MY BROTHER.
AFTER WHAT YOU DID FOR 'CELA? YOU'RE IN THE MANADA NOW.
WHERE'S PERRO? NEED A PATCH. PERRO'S GOT 'EM, YEAH?
THAT'S NOT A GOOD IDEA, MARCELA. I DON'T--
YOU'RE A DANGEROUS GUY. YOU THINK ALWAYS ALONE MAKES THAT LESS?
ALWAYS ALONE MAKES THAT TROUBLE.
LOOK AT THIS ONE GUY--
THAT'S WHAT DANGEROUS AND ALONE LOOK LIKE AFTER TOO LONG. THAT WHAT YOU WANT?

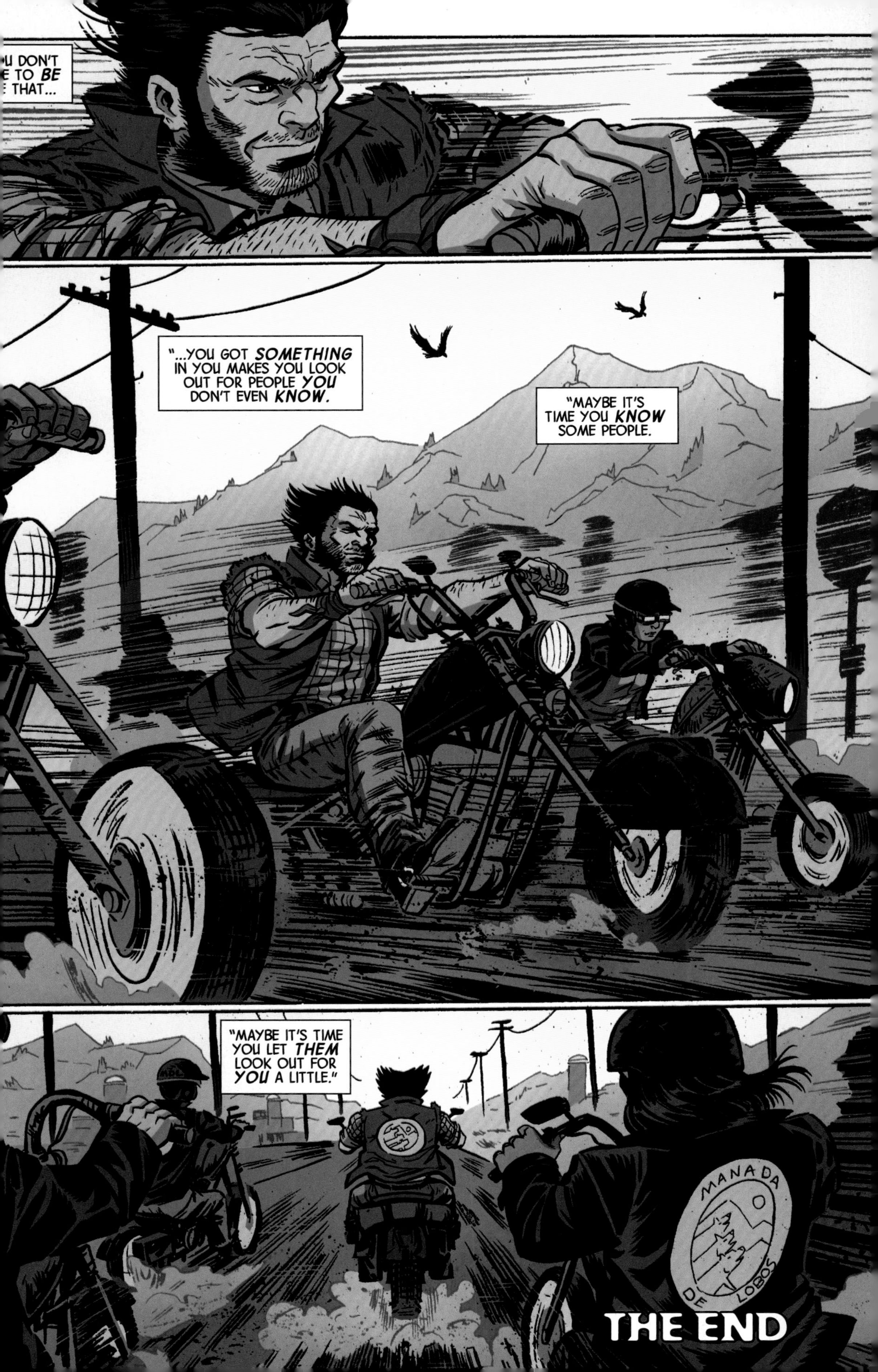
...U DON'T
E TO BE
E THAT...
"...YOU GOT SOMETHING IN YOU MAKES YOU LOOK OUT FOR PEOPLE YOU DON'T EVEN KNOW.
"MAYBE IT'S TIME YOU KNOW SOME PEOPLE.
"MAYBE IT'S TIME YOU LET THEM LOOK OUT FOR YOU A LITTLE."
MANADA DE LOBOS
THE END

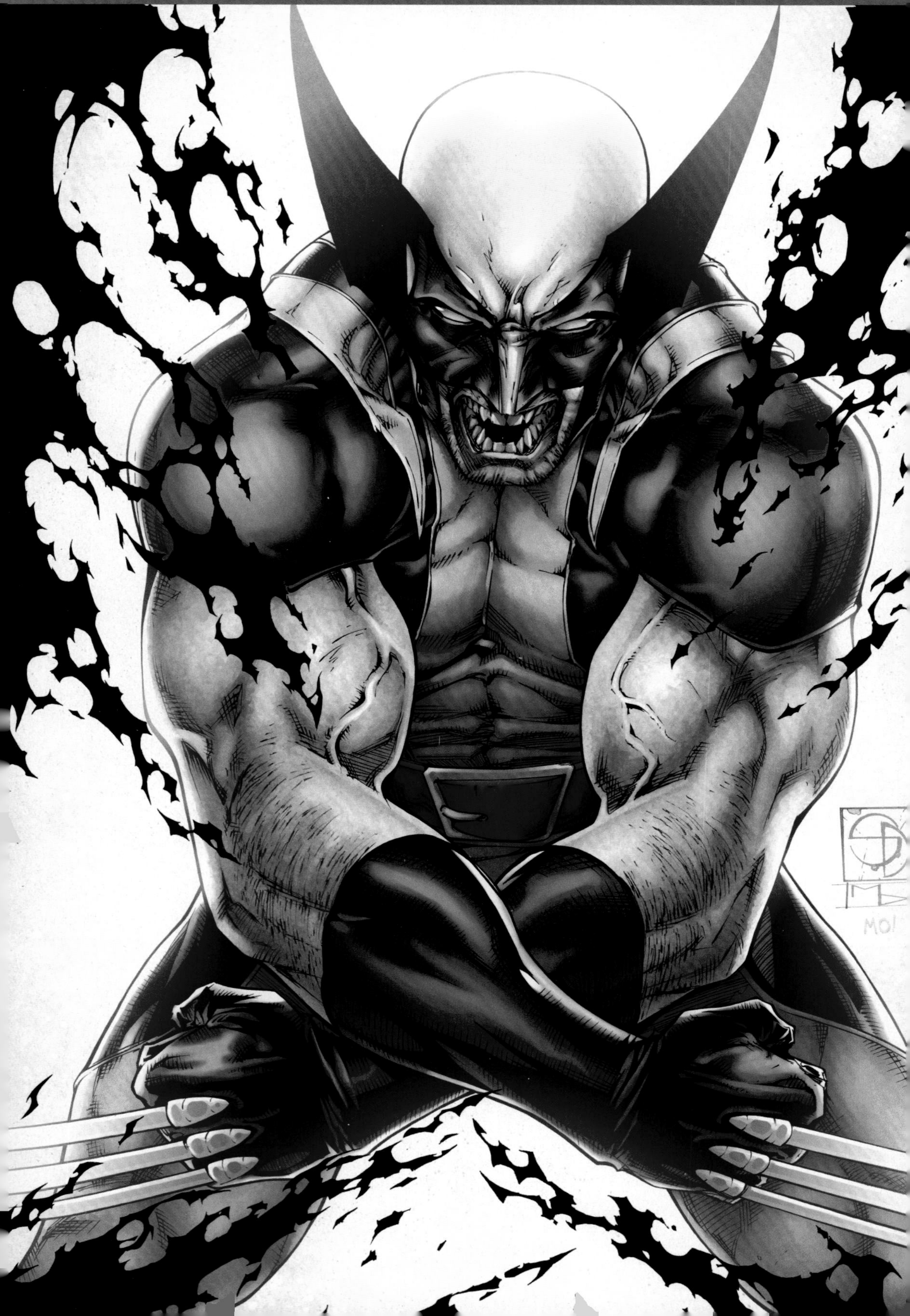

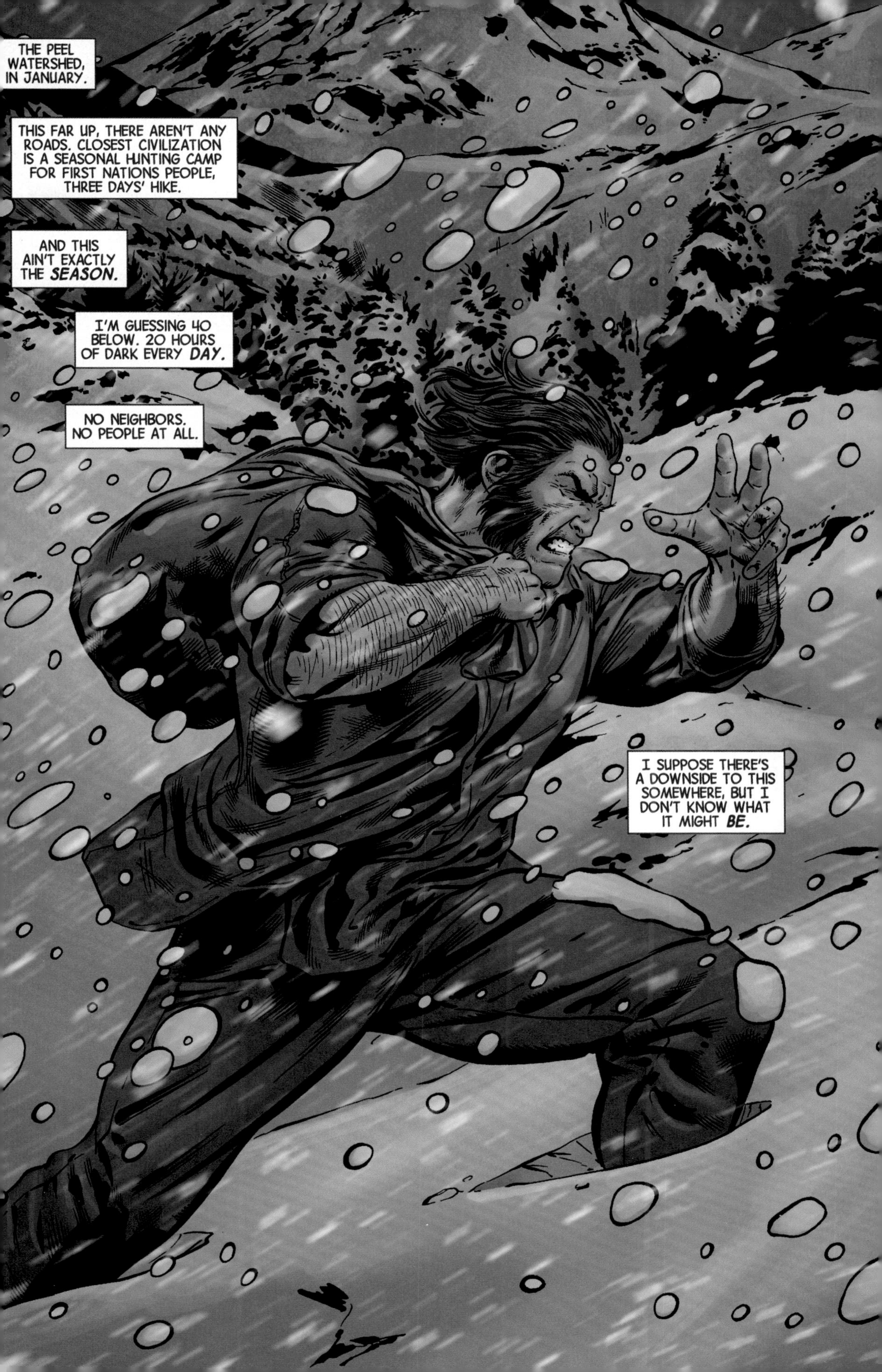
THE PEEL WATERSHED, IN JANUARY.
THIS FAR UP, THERE AREN'T ANY ROADS. CLOSEST CIVILIZATION IS A SEASONAL HUNTING CAMP FOR FIRST NATIONS PEOPLE, THREE DAYS' HIKE.
AND THIS AIN'T EXACTLY THE *SEASON.*
I'M GUESSING 40 BELOW. 20 HOURS OF DARK EVERY *DAY.*
NO NEIGHBORS. NO PEOPLE AT ALL.
I SUPPOSE THERE'S A DOWNSIDE TO THIS SOMEWHERE, BUT I DON'T KNOW WHAT IT MIGHT *BE.*

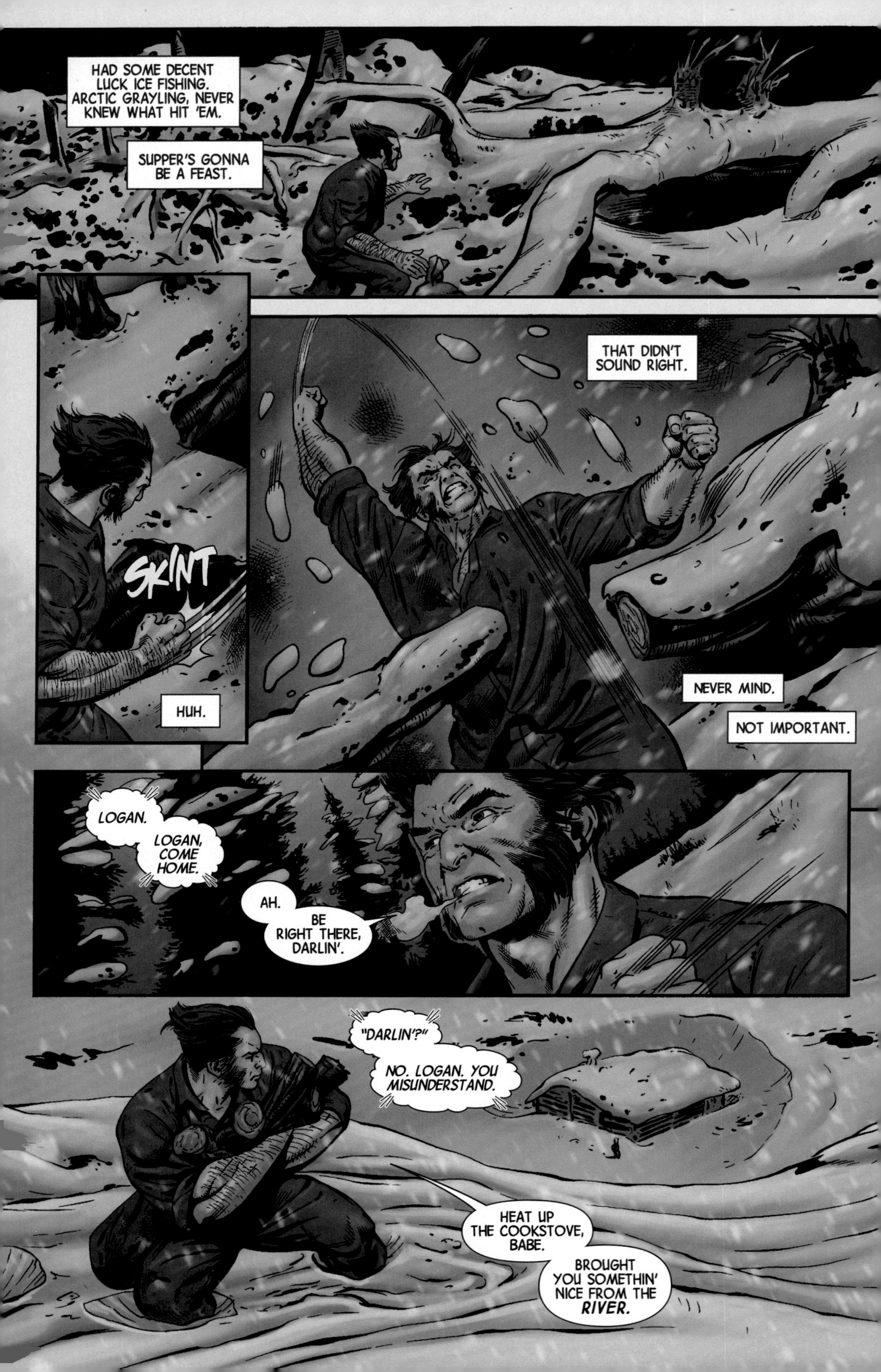
HAD SOME DECENT LUCK ICE FISHING. ARCTIC GRAYLING, NEVER KNEW WHAT HIT 'EM.
SUPPER'S GONNA BE A FEAST.
SKINT
HUH.
THAT DIDN'T SOUND RIGHT.
NEVER MIND.
NOT IMPORTANT.
LOGAN.
LOGAN, COME HOME.
AH.
BE RIGHT THERE, DARLIN'.
"DARLIN'?"
NO. LOGAN. YOU MISUNDERSTAND.
HEAT UP THE COOKSTOVE, BABE.
BROUGHT YOU SOMETHIN' NICE FROM THE RIVER.

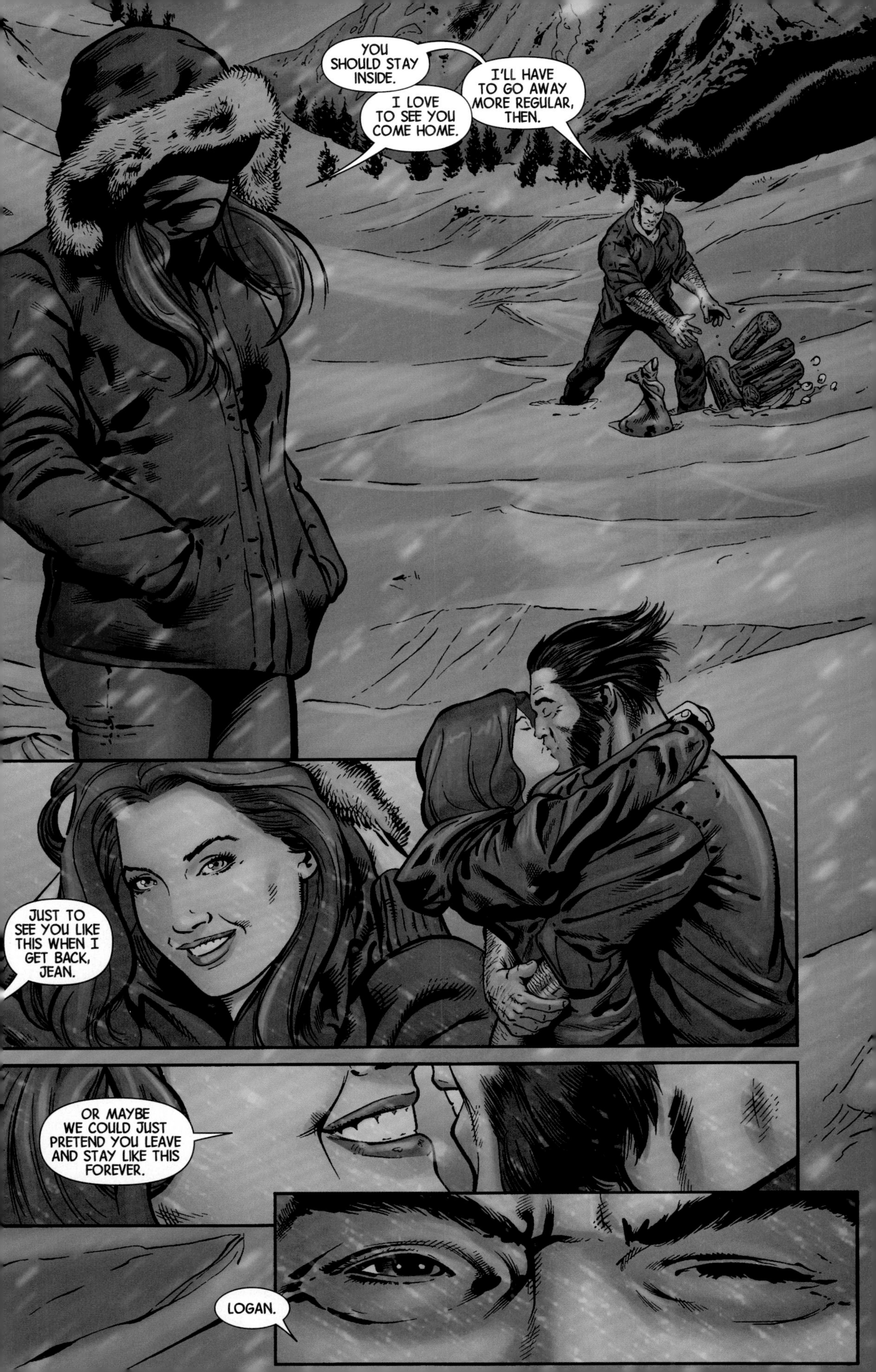
YOU SHOULD STAY INSIDE.
I LOVE TO SEE YOU COME HOME.
I'LL HAVE TO GO AWAY MORE REGULAR, THEN.
JUST TO SEE YOU LIKE THIS WHEN I GET BACK, JEAN.
OR MAYBE WE COULD JUST PRETEND YOU LEAVE AND STAY LIKE THIS FOREVER.
LOGAN.

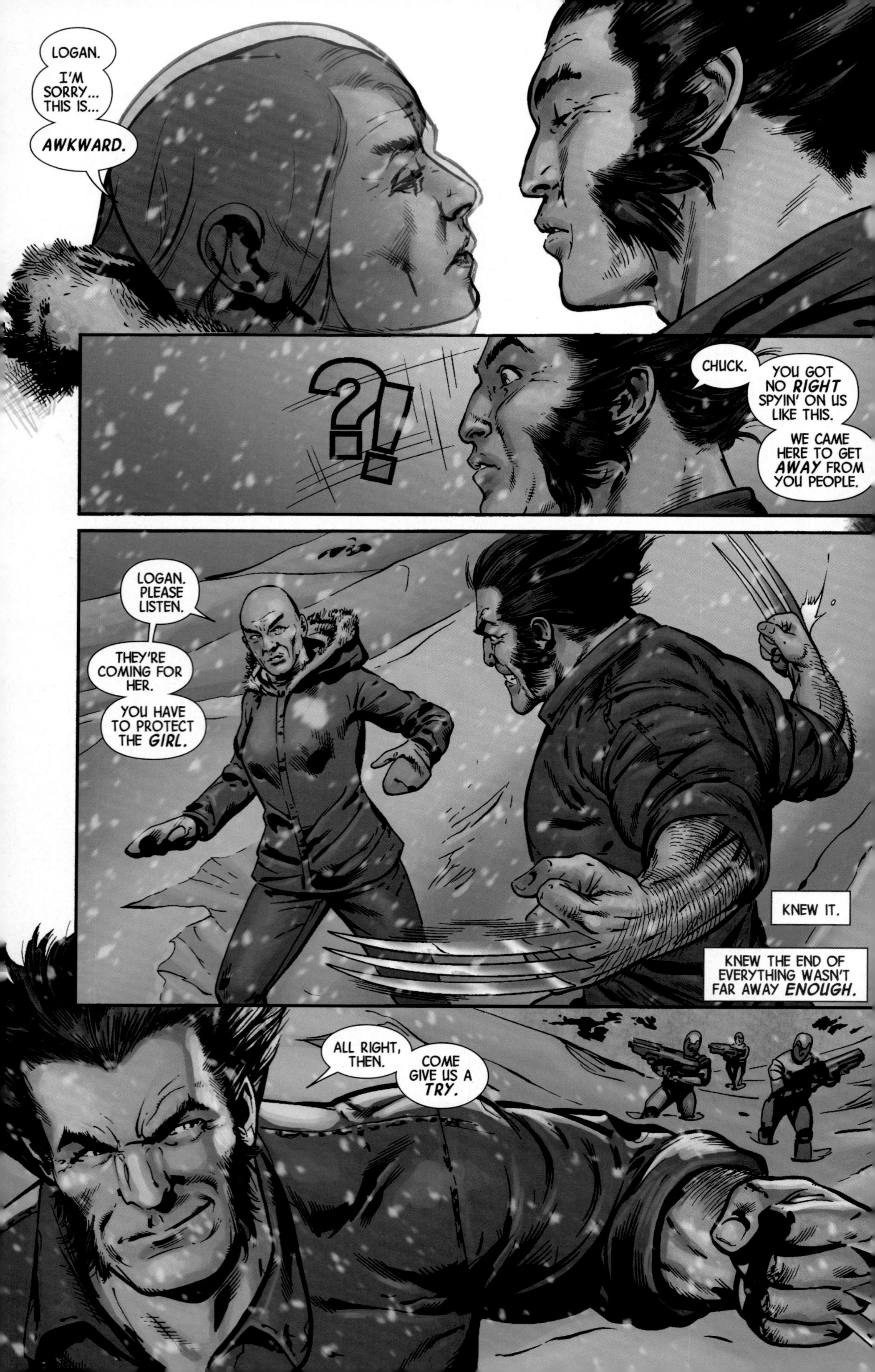
LOGAN.
I'M SORRY... THIS IS...
AWKWARD.
?!
CHUCK.
YOU GOT NO RIGHT SPYIN' ON US LIKE THIS.
WE CAME HERE TO GET AWAY FROM YOU PEOPLE.
LOGAN. PLEASE LISTEN.
THEY'RE COMING FOR HER.
YOU HAVE TO PROTECT THE GIRL.
KNEW IT.
KNEW THE END OF EVERYTHING WASN'T FAR AWAY ENOUGH.
ALL RIGHT, THEN.
COME GIVE US A TRY.

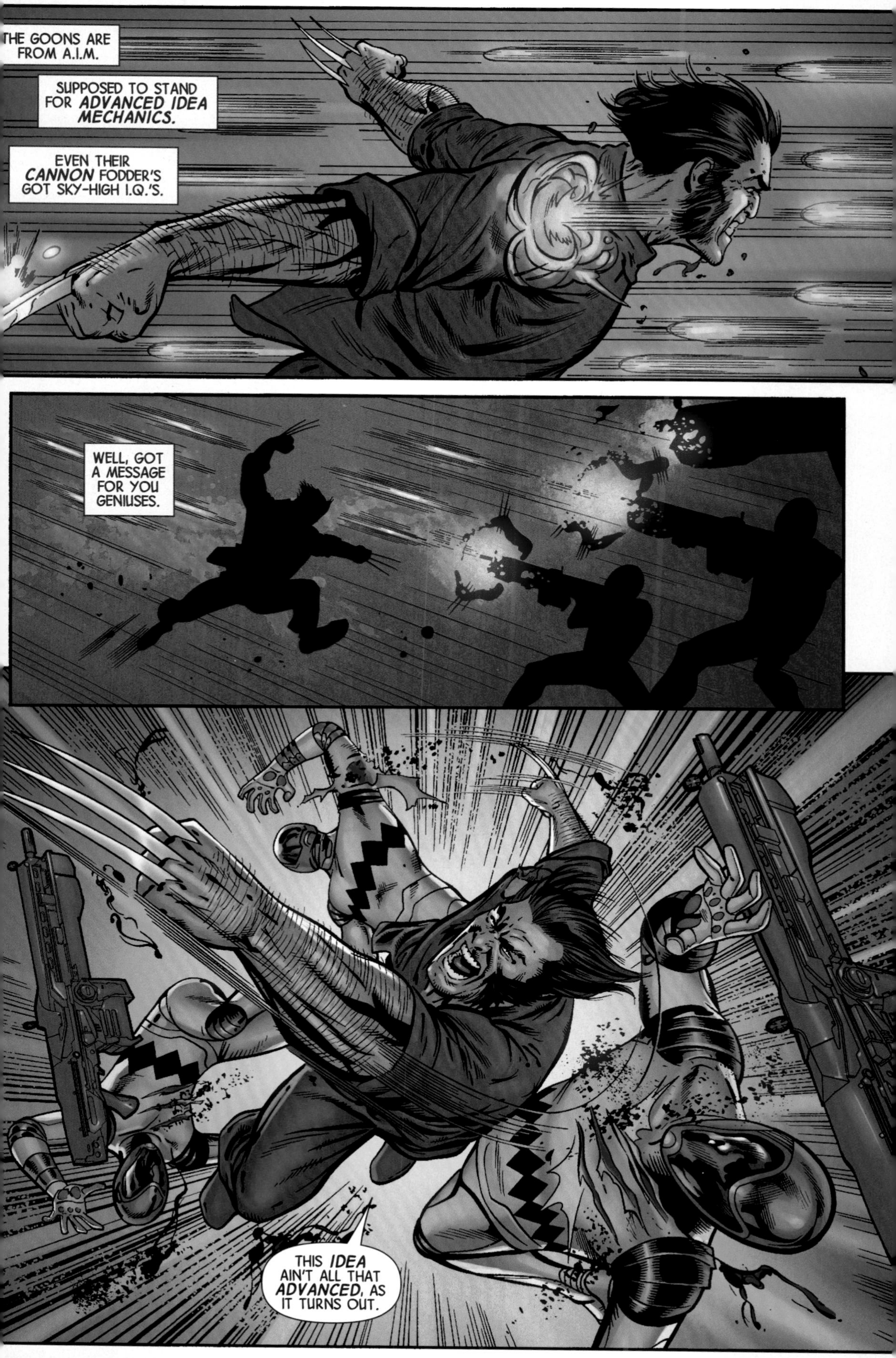

THE GOONS ARE FROM A.I.M.
SUPPOSED TO STAND FOR ADVANCED IDEA MECHANICS.
EVEN THEIR CANNON FODDER'S GOT SKY-HIGH I.Q.'S.
WELL, GOT A MESSAGE FOR YOU GENIUSES.
THIS IDEA AIN'T ALL THAT ADVANCED, AS IT TURNS OUT.

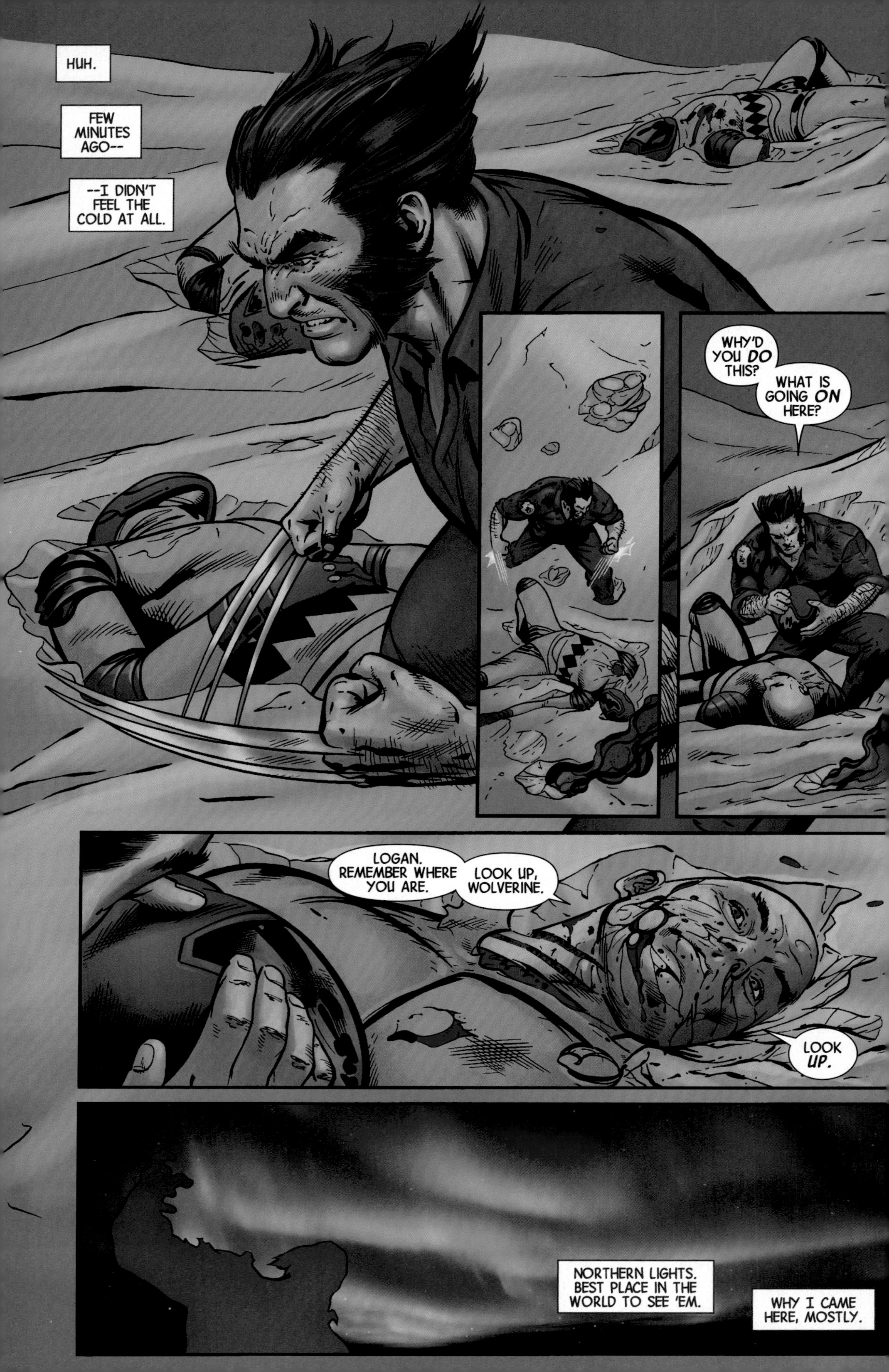
HUH.
FEW MINUTES AGO--
--I DIDN'T FEEL THE COLD AT ALL.
WHY'D YOU DO THIS?
WHAT IS GOING ON HERE?
LOGAN. REMEMBER WHERE YOU ARE.
LOOK UP, WOLVERINE.
LOOK UP.
NORTHERN LIGHTS. BEST PLACE IN THE WORLD TO SEE 'EM.
WHY I CAME HERE, MOSTLY.

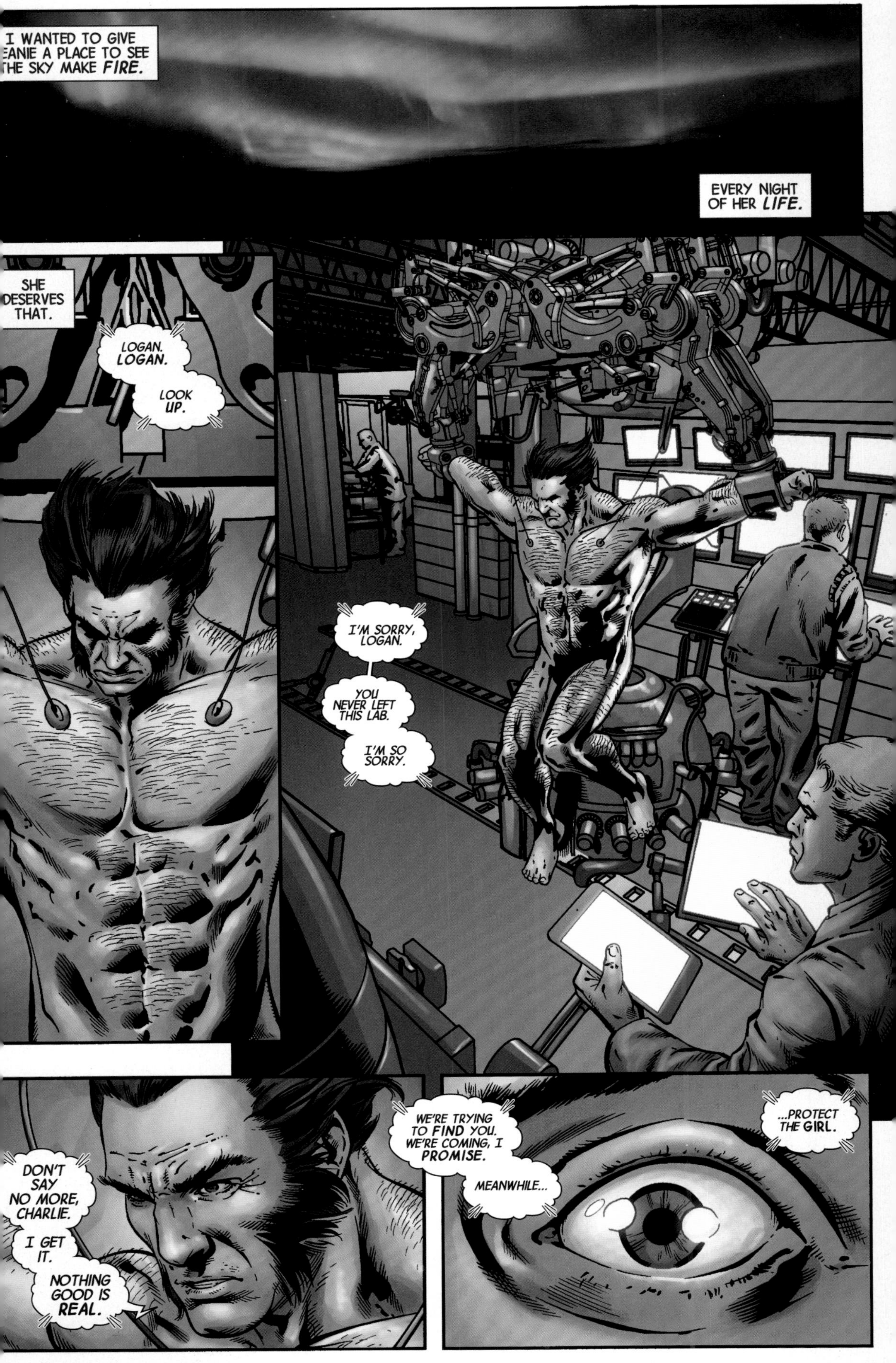
I WANTED TO GIVE
EANIE A PLACE TO SEE
THE SKY MAKE FIRE.
EVERY NIGHT OF HER LIFE.
SHE DESERVES THAT.
LOGAN. LOGAN.
LOOK UP.
I'M SORRY, LOGAN.
YOU NEVER LEFT THIS LAB.
I'M SO SORRY.
DON'T SAY NO MORE, CHARLIE.
I GET IT.
NOTHING GOOD IS REAL.
WE'RE TRYING TO FIND YOU. WE'RE COMING, I PROMISE.
MEANWHILE...
...PROTECT THE GIRL.

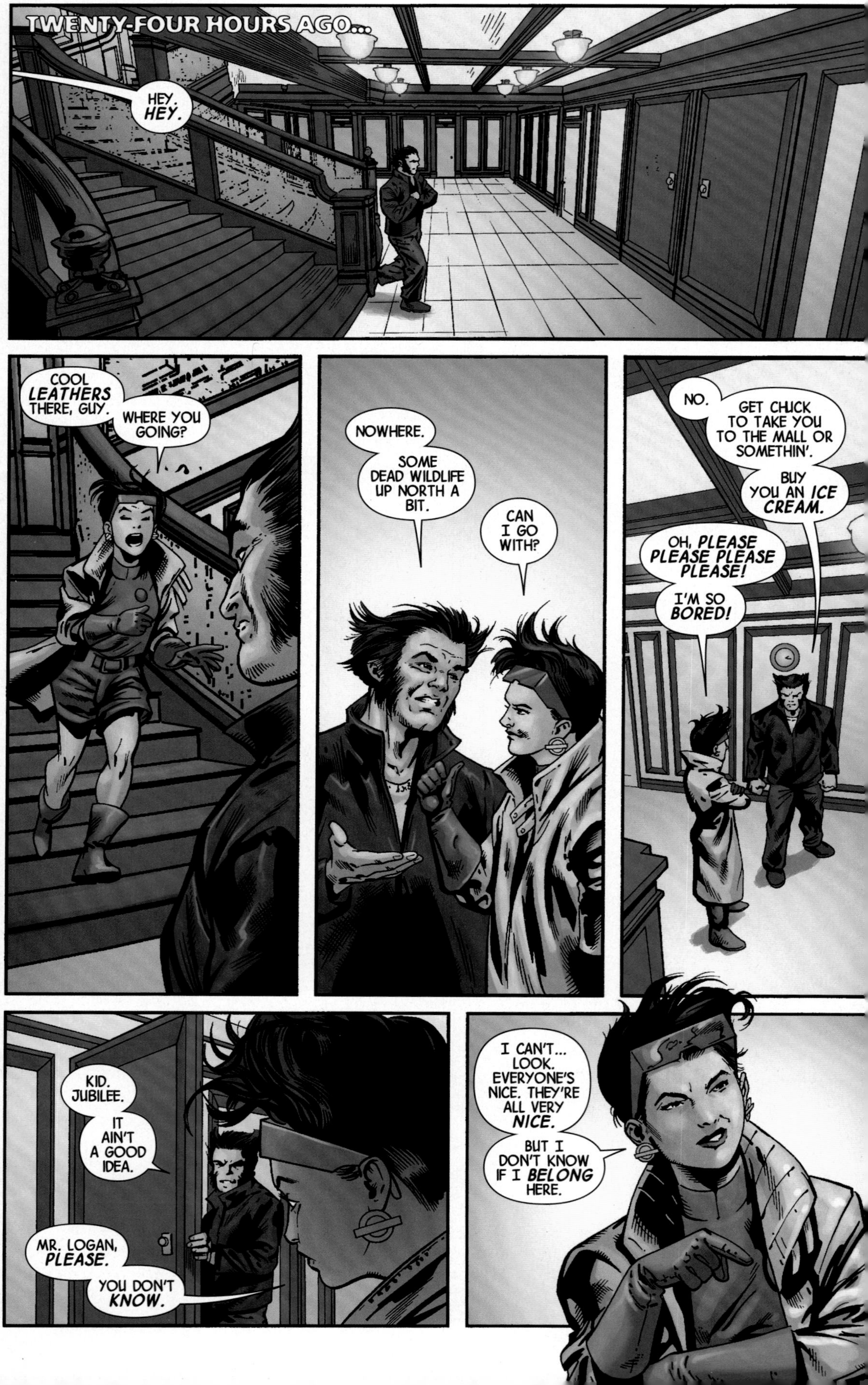

TWENTY-FOUR HOURS AGO...
HEY. HEY.
COOL LEATHERS THERE, GUY.
WHERE YOU GOING?
NOWHERE.
SOME DEAD WILDLIFE UP NORTH A BIT.
CAN I GO WITH?
NO.
GET CHUCK TO TAKE YOU TO THE MALL OR SOMETHIN'.
BUY YOU AN ICE CREAM.
OH, PLEASE PLEASE PLEASE PLEASE!
I'M SO BORED!
KID. JUBILEE.
IT AIN'T A GOOD IDEA.
MR. LOGAN, PLEASE.
YOU DON'T KNOW.
I CAN'T... LOOK. EVERYONE'S NICE. THEY'RE ALL VERY NICE.
BUT I DON'T KNOW IF I BELONG HERE.

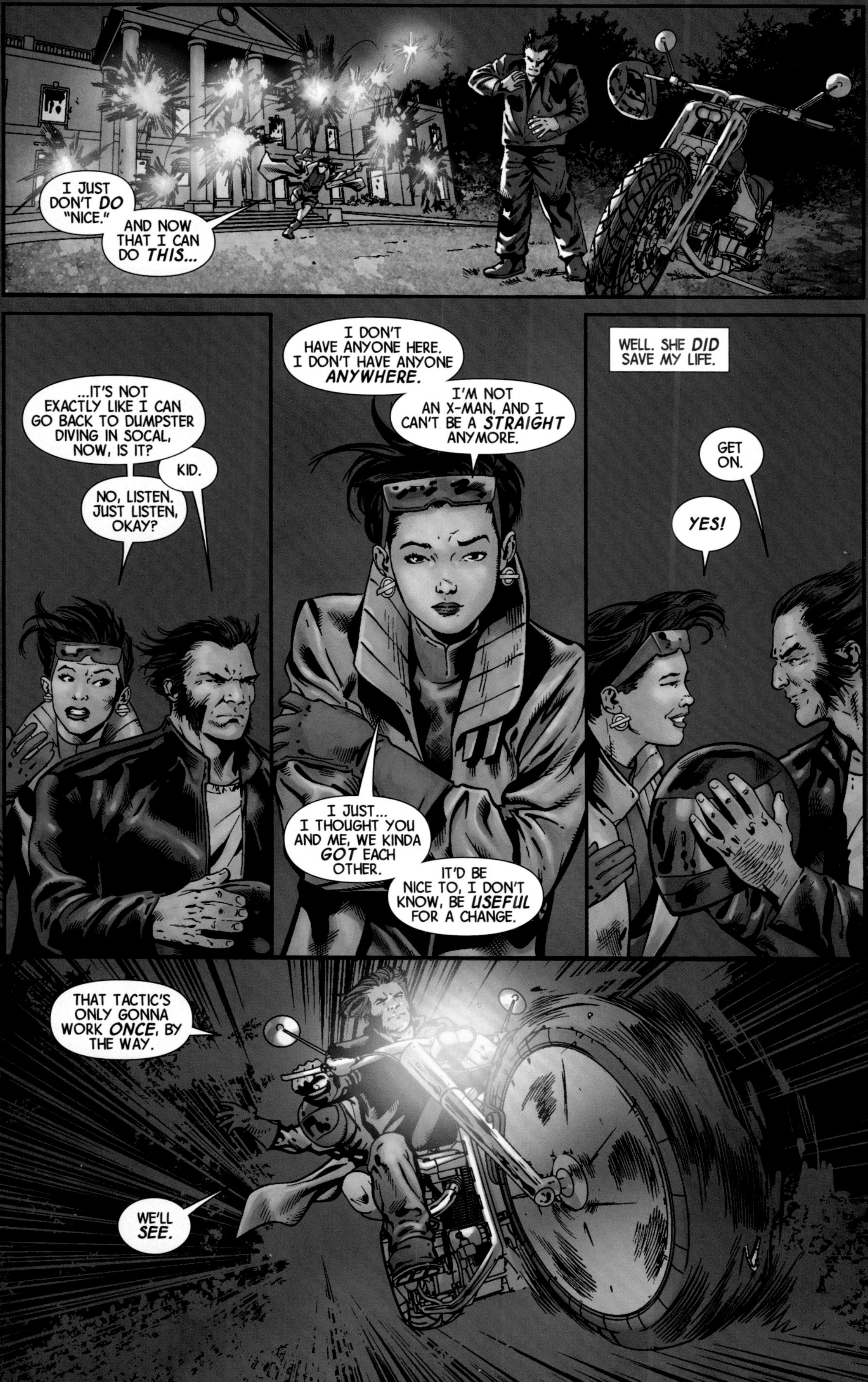
I JUST DON'T *DO* "NICE."
AND NOW THAT I CAN DO *THIS...*
...IT'S NOT EXACTLY LIKE I CAN GO BACK TO DUMPSTER DIVING IN SOCAL, NOW, IS IT?
KID.
NO, LISTEN. JUST LISTEN, OKAY?
I DON'T HAVE ANYONE HERE. I DON'T HAVE ANYONE *ANYWHERE.*
I'M NOT AN X-MAN, AND I CAN'T BE A *STRAIGHT* ANYMORE.
I JUST... I THOUGHT YOU AND ME, WE KINDA *GOT* EACH OTHER.
IT'D BE NICE TO, I DON'T KNOW, BE *USEFUL* FOR A CHANGE.
WELL. SHE *DID* SAVE MY LIFE.
GET ON.
YES!
THAT TACTIC'S ONLY GONNA WORK *ONCE*, BY THE WAY.
WE'LL *SEE.*

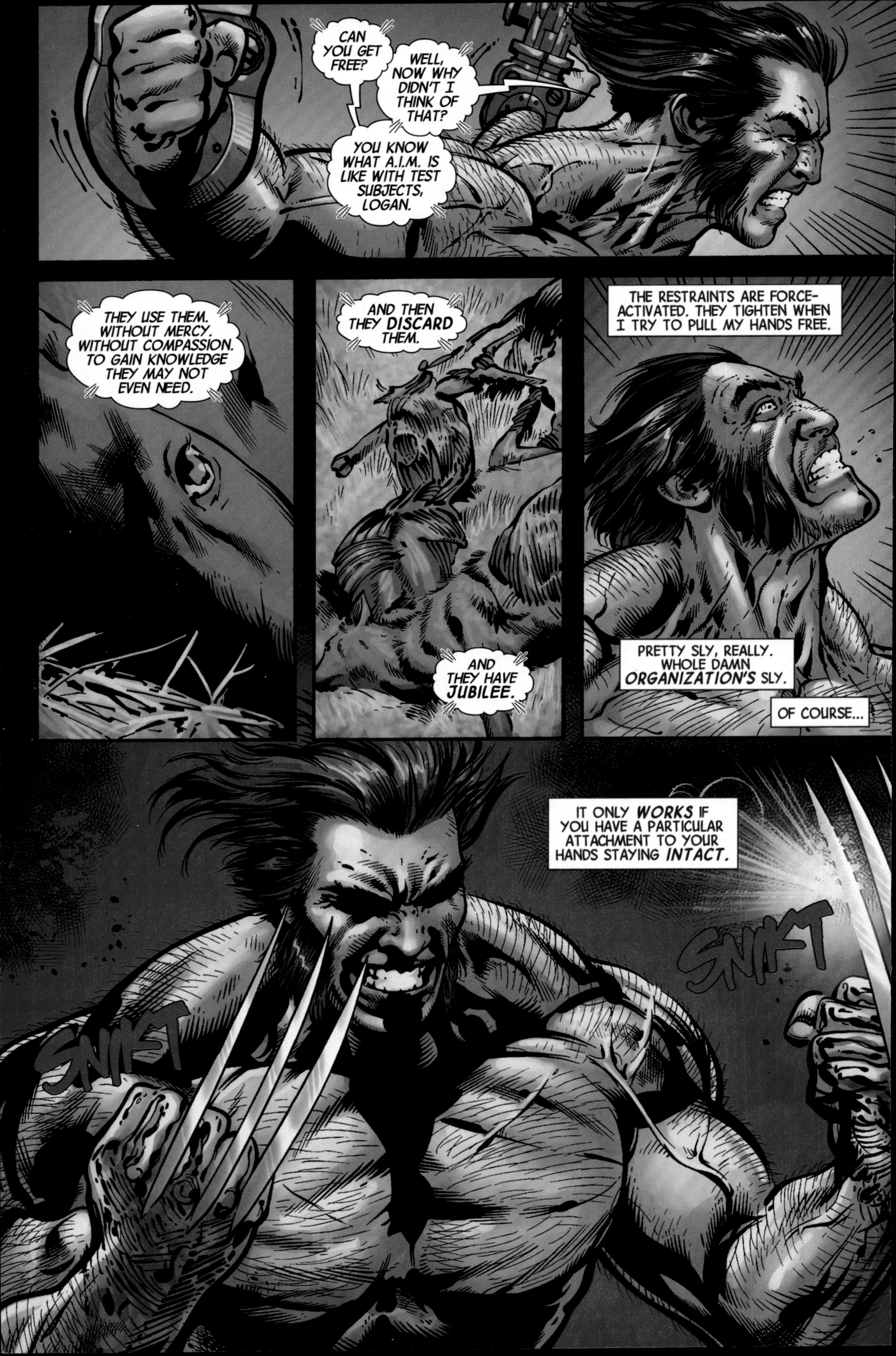
CAN YOU GET FREE?
WELL, NOW WHY DIDN'T I THINK OF THAT?
YOU KNOW WHAT A.I.M. IS LIKE WITH TEST SUBJECTS, LOGAN.
THEY USE THEM. WITHOUT MERCY. WITHOUT COMPASSION. TO GAIN KNOWLEDGE THEY MAY NOT EVEN NEED.
AND THEN THEY DISCARD THEM.
AND THEY HAVE JUBILEE.
THE RESTRAINTS ARE FORCE-ACTIVATED. THEY TIGHTEN WHEN I TRY TO PULL MY HANDS FREE.
PRETTY SLY, REALLY. WHOLE DAMN ORGANIZATION'S SLY.
OF COURSE...
IT ONLY WORKS IF YOU HAVE A PARTICULAR ATTACHMENT TO YOUR HANDS STAYING INTACT.
SNIKT
SNIKT

READINGS ARE OFF THE SCALE. THE VIRAL REPLICATION IS *EXTRAORDINARY.*

IT'S HIS HEALING FACTOR. *RAINBOW'S* TRYING TO OVERCOME IT.

YES. I'LL BE HONEST, I THOUGHT HE'D BE MORE OF A CHALLENGE.

I ALWAYS 'ARD HE WAS *SAVAGE.*

NO, HE'S GONE ALL CIVILIZED NOW, INTEL SAYS.

THREATEN A KID OR A WOMAN, HE GOES SOFT LIKE BUTTERMILK.

TAME AS A *KITTEN.*

MEOW.

GUHNG!

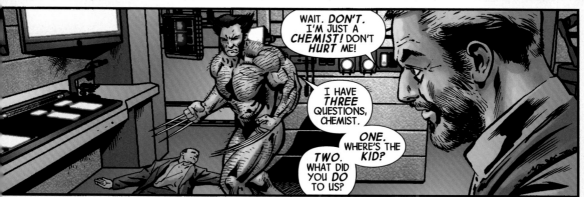

WAIT. *DON'T.* I'M JUST A *CHEMIST!* DON'T *HURT* ME!

I HAVE *THREE* QUESTIONS, CHEMIST.

ONE. WHERE'S THE *KID?*

TWO. WHAT DID YOU *DO* TO US?

AND *WHERE* THE HELL ARE MY *DAMN* PANTS?

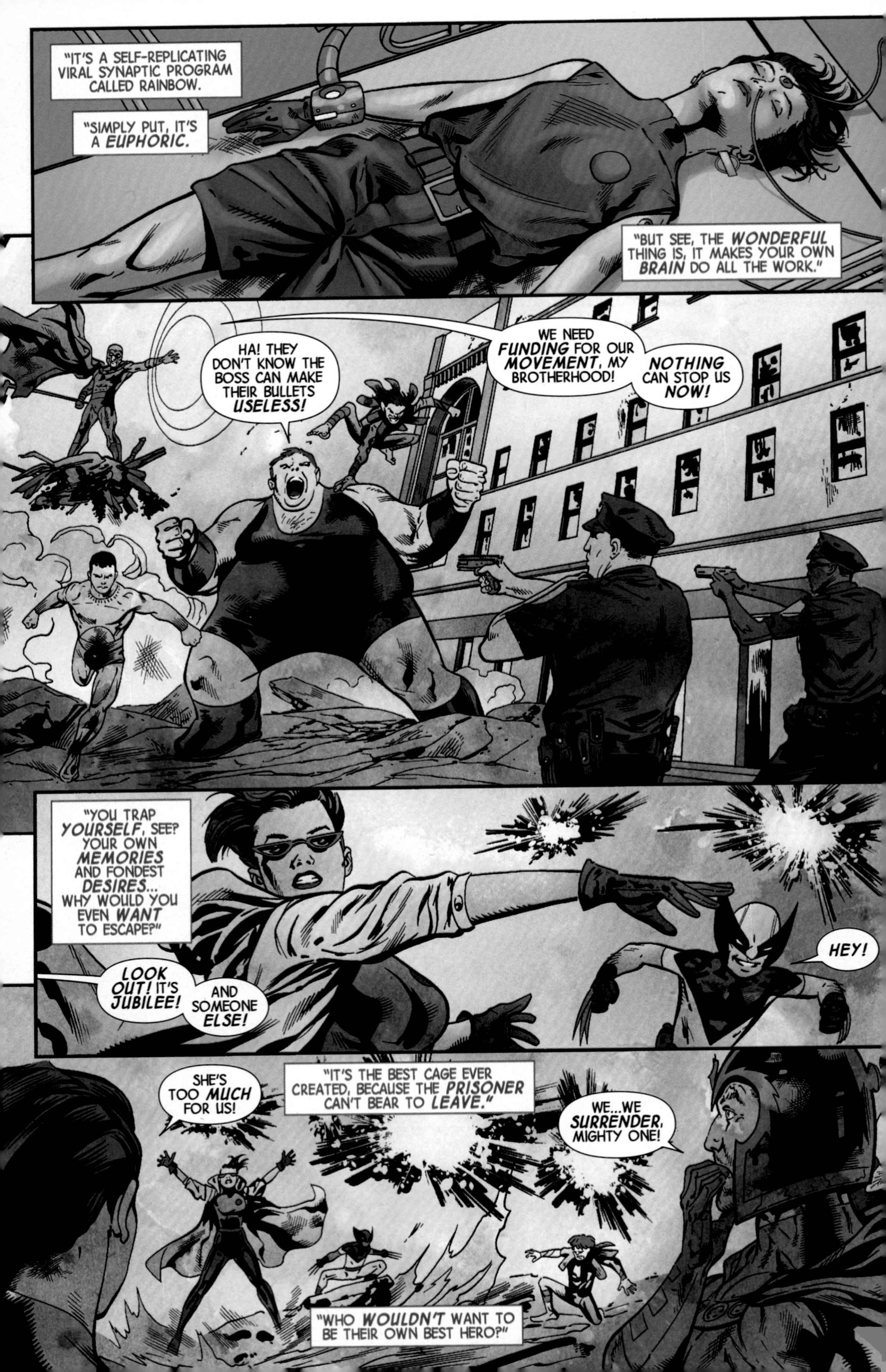
"IT'S A SELF-REPLICATING VIRAL SYNAPTIC PROGRAM CALLED RAINBOW.
"SIMPLY PUT, IT'S A EUPHORIC.
"BUT SEE, THE WONDERFUL THING IS, IT MAKES YOUR OWN BRAIN DO ALL THE WORK."
HA! THEY DON'T KNOW THE BOSS CAN MAKE THEIR BULLETS USELESS!
WE NEED FUNDING FOR OUR MOVEMENT, MY BROTHERHOOD!
NOTHING CAN STOP US NOW!
"YOU TRAP YOURSELF, SEE? YOUR OWN MEMORIES AND FONDEST DESIRES... WHY WOULD YOU EVEN WANT TO ESCAPE?"
LOOK OUT! IT'S JUBILEE!
AND SOMEONE ELSE!
HEY!
SHE'S TOO MUCH FOR US!
"IT'S THE BEST CAGE EVER CREATED, BECAUSE THE PRISONER CAN'T BEAR TO LEAVE."
WE...WE SURRENDER, MIGHTY ONE!
"WHO WOULDN'T WANT TO BE THEIR OWN BEST HERO?"

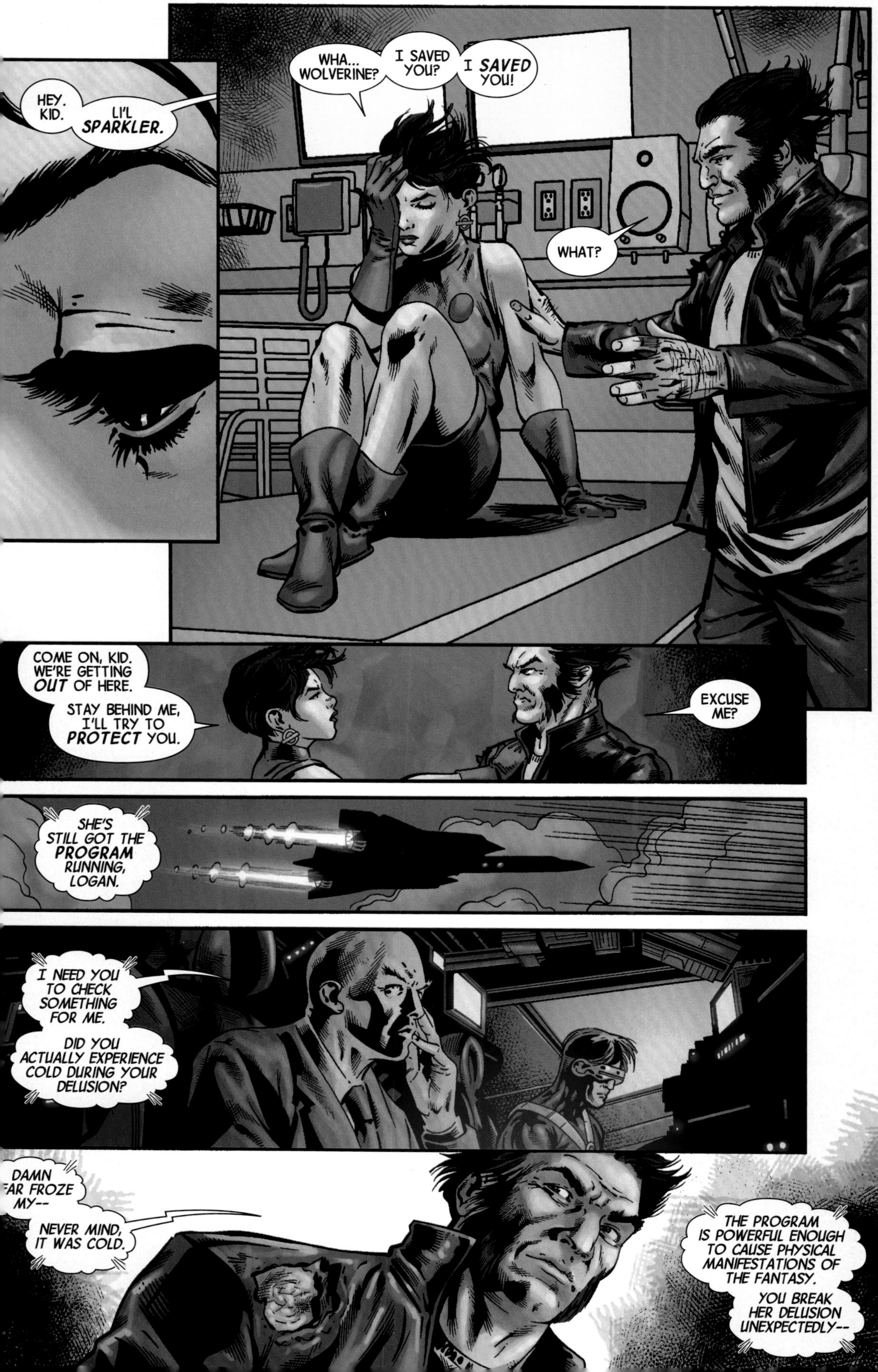
HEY. KID.
LI'L SPARKLER.
WHA... WOLVERINE?
I SAVED YOU?
I SAVED YOU!
WHAT?
COME ON, KID. WE'RE GETTING OUT OF HERE.
STAY BEHIND ME, I'LL TRY TO PROTECT YOU.
EXCUSE ME?
SHE'S STILL GOT THE PROGRAM RUNNING, LOGAN.
I NEED YOU TO CHECK SOMETHING FOR ME.
DID YOU ACTUALLY EXPERIENCE COLD DURING YOUR DELUSION?
DAMN FAR FROZE MY--
NEVER MIND, IT WAS COLD.
THE PROGRAM IS POWERFUL ENOUGH TO CAUSE PHYSICAL MANIFESTATIONS OF THE FANTASY.
YOU BREAK HER DELUSION UNEXPECTEDLY--

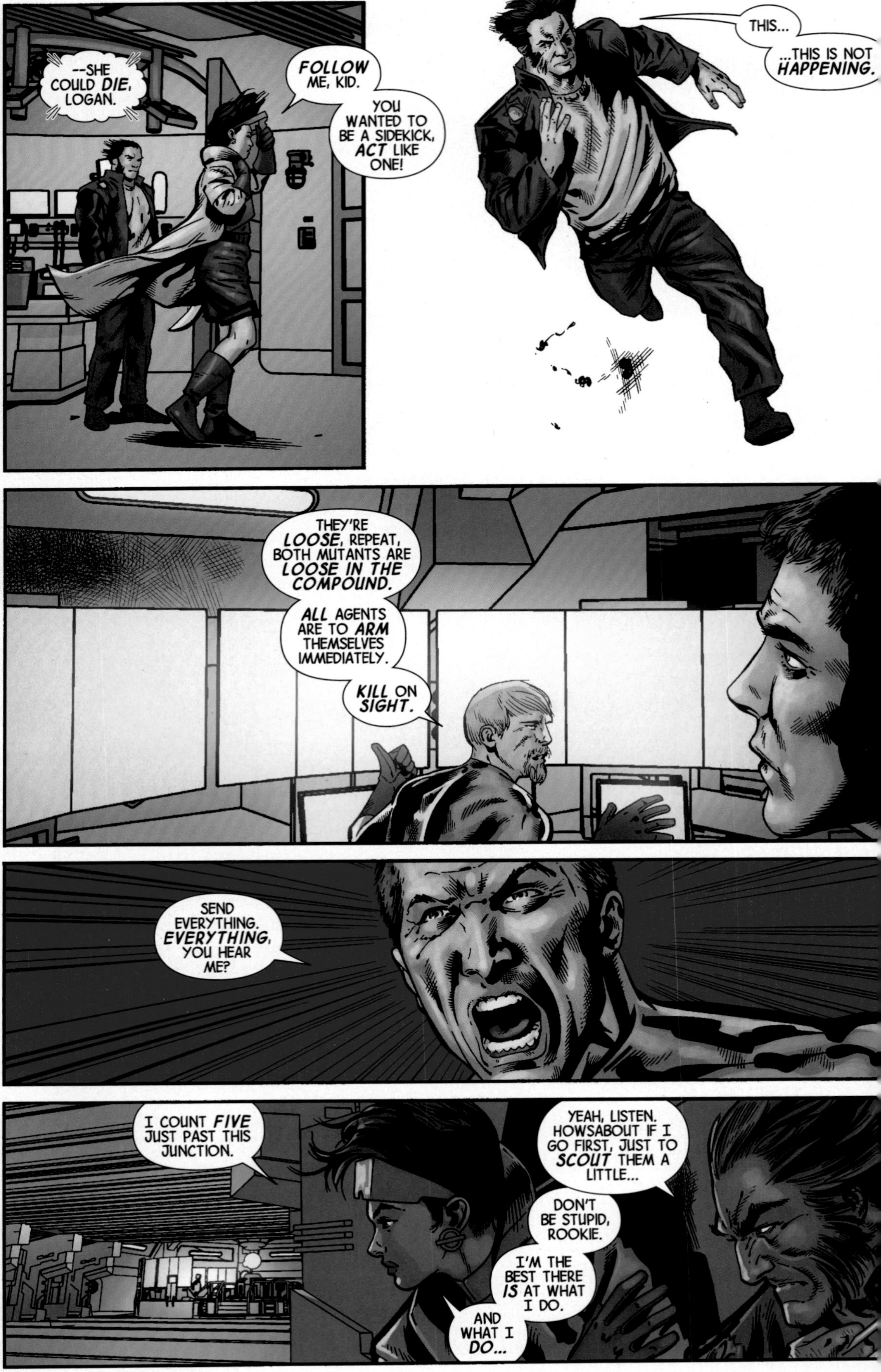
--SHE COULD DIE, LOGAN.
FOLLOW ME, KID.
YOU WANTED TO BE A SIDEKICK, ACT LIKE ONE!
THIS...
...THIS IS NOT HAPPENING.
THEY'RE LOOSE, REPEAT, BOTH MUTANTS ARE LOOSE IN THE COMPOUND.
ALL AGENTS ARE TO ARM THEMSELVES IMMEDIATELY.
KILL ON SIGHT.
SEND EVERYTHING. EVERYTHING, YOU HEAR ME?
I COUNT FIVE JUST PAST THIS JUNCTION.
YEAH, LISTEN. HOWSABOUT IF I GO FIRST, JUST TO SCOUT THEM A LITTLE...
DON'T BE STUPID, ROOKIE.
I'M THE BEST THERE IS AT WHAT I DO.
AND WHAT I DO...

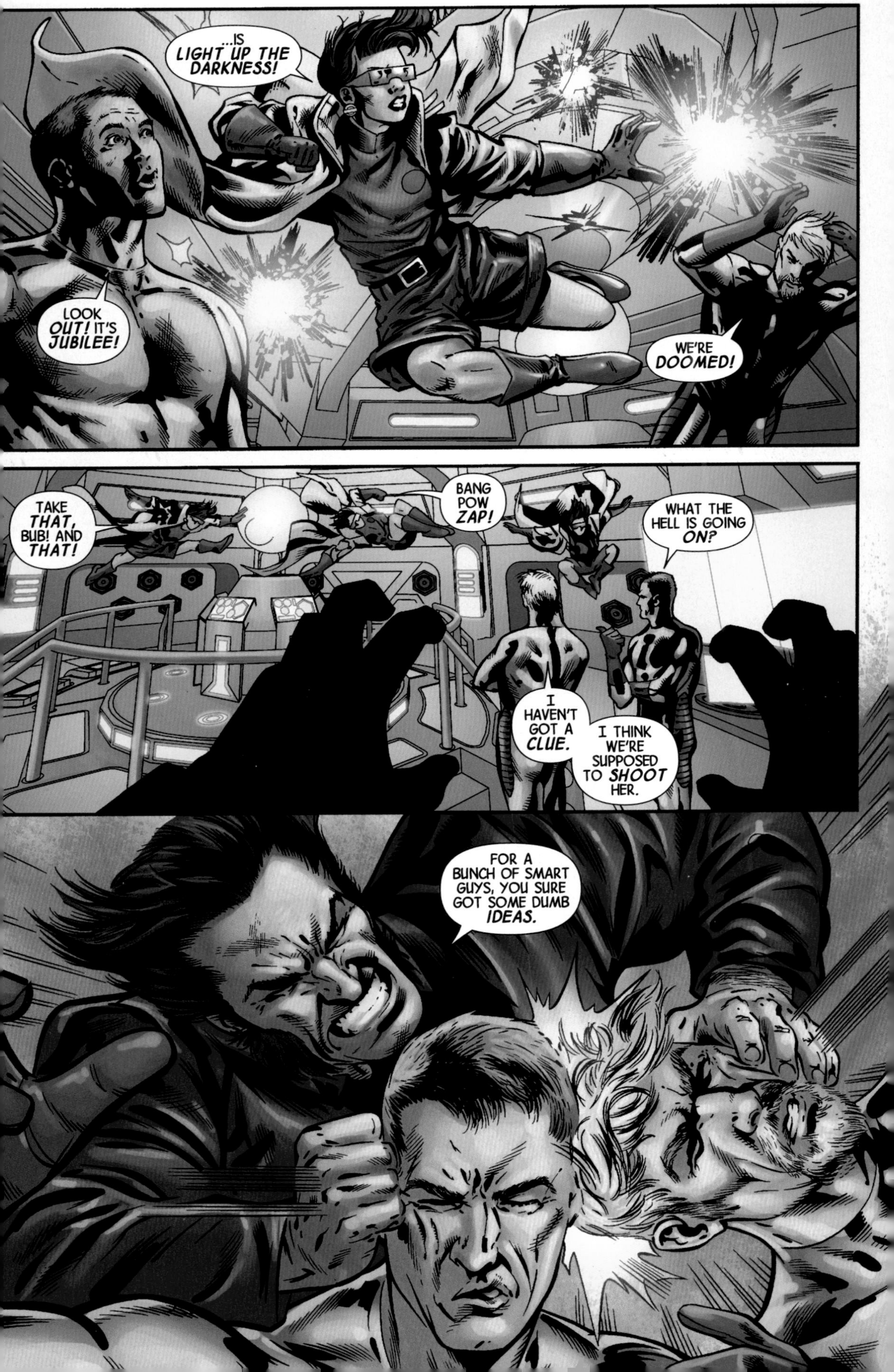
...IS LIGHT UP THE DARKNESS!
LOOK OUT! IT'S JUBILEE!
WE'RE DOOMED!
TAKE THAT, BUB! AND THAT!
BANG POW ZAP!
WHAT THE HELL IS GOING ON?
I HAVEN'T GOT A CLUE.
I THINK WE'RE SUPPOSED TO SHOOT HER.
FOR A BUNCH OF SMART GUYS, YOU SURE GOT SOME DUMB IDEAS.

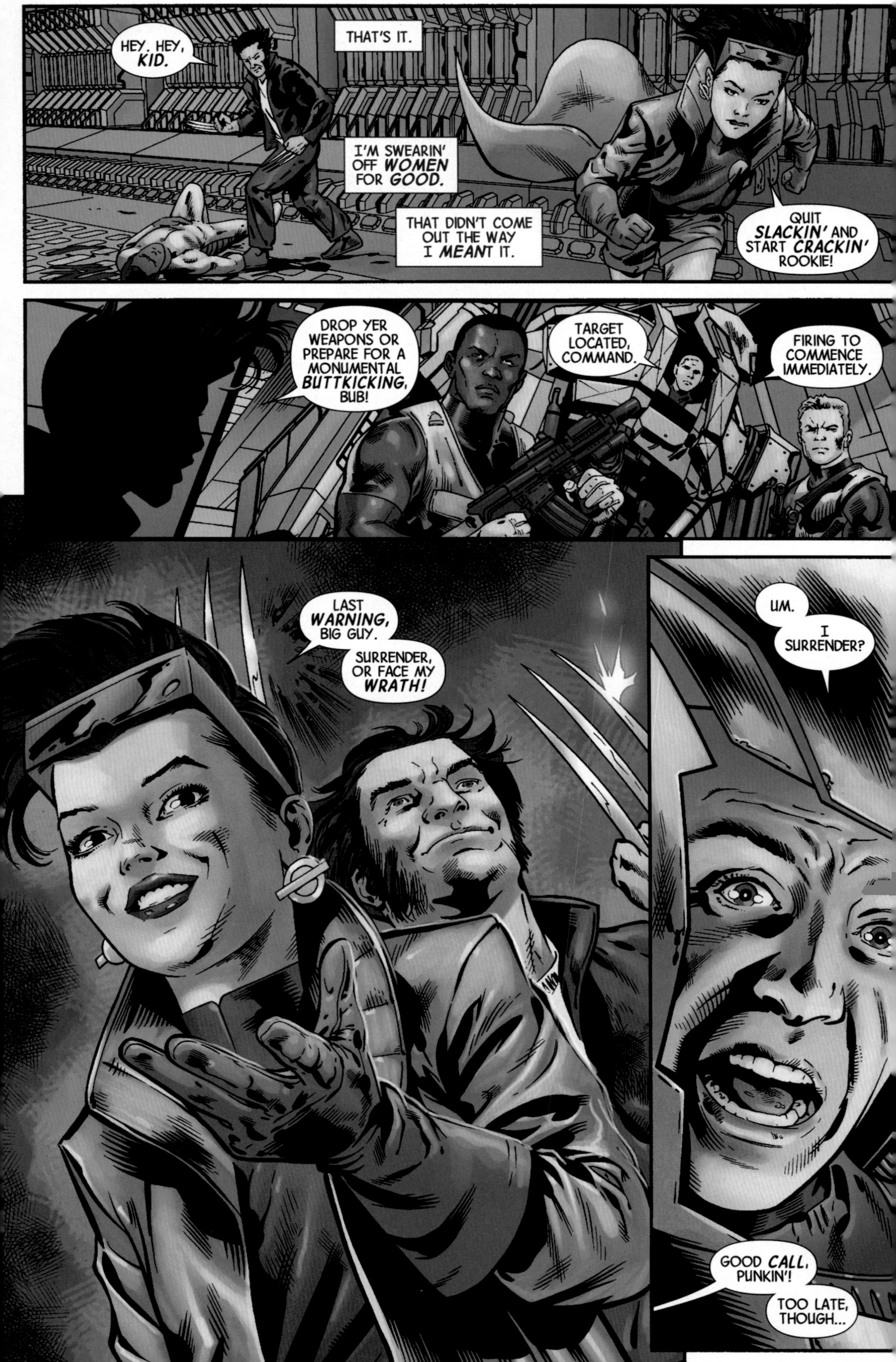
HEY. HEY, KID.
THAT'S IT.
I'M SWEARIN' OFF WOMEN FOR GOOD.
THAT DIDN'T COME OUT THE WAY I MEANT IT.
QUIT SLACKIN' AND START CRACKIN' ROOKIE!
DROP YER WEAPONS OR PREPARE FOR A MONUMENTAL BUTTKICKING, BUB!
TARGET LOCATED, COMMAND.
FIRING TO COMMENCE IMMEDIATELY.
LAST WARNING, BIG GUY.
SURRENDER, OR FACE MY WRATH!
UM.
I SURRENDER?
GOOD CALL, PUNKIN'!
TOO LATE, THOUGH...

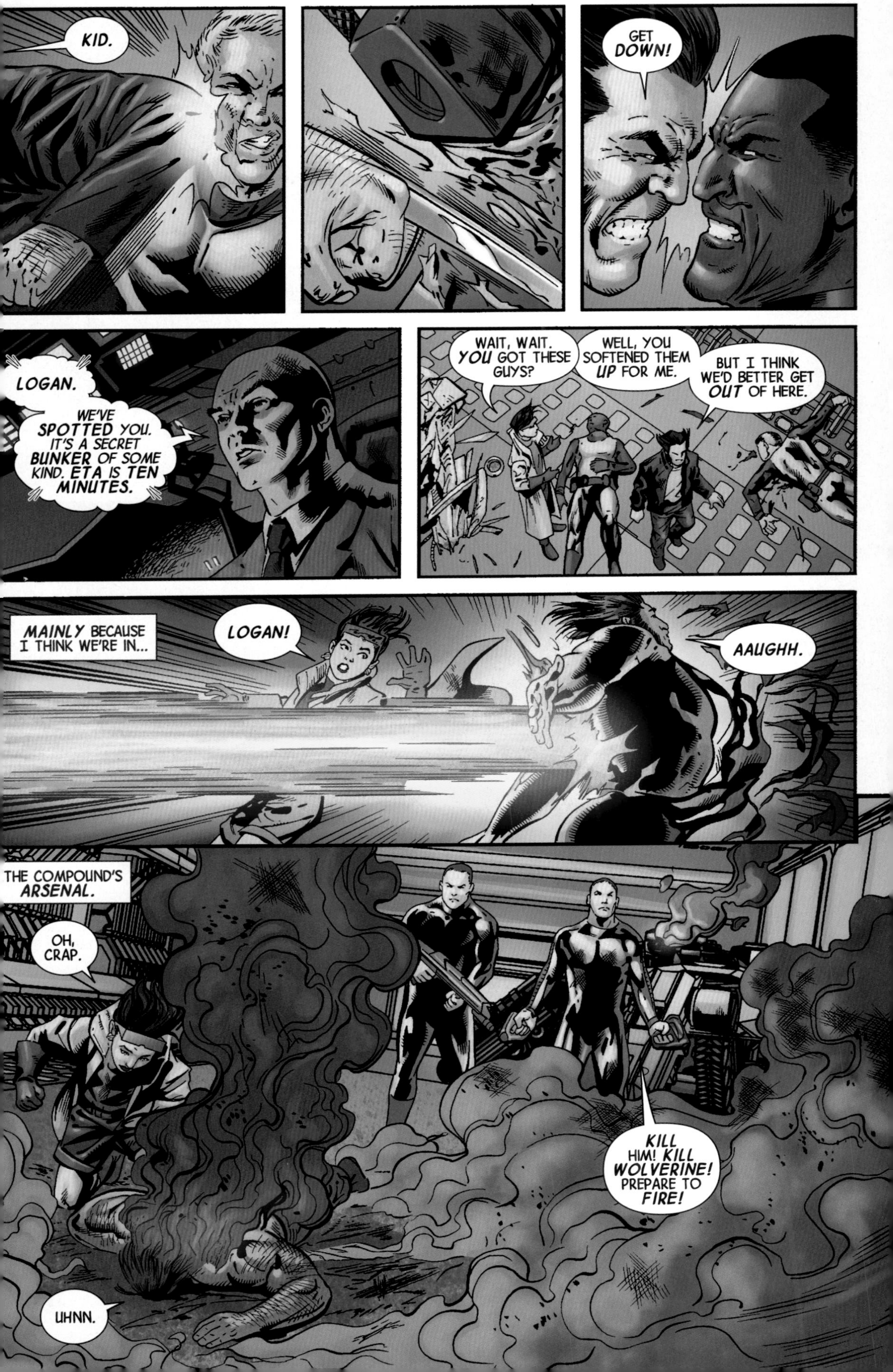
KID.
GET DOWN!
LOGAN.
WE'VE SPOTTED YOU. IT'S A SECRET BUNKER OF SOME KIND. ETA IS TEN MINUTES.
WAIT, WAIT. YOU GOT THESE GUYS?
WELL, YOU SOFTENED THEM UP FOR ME.
BUT I THINK WE'D BETTER GET OUT OF HERE.
MAINLY BECAUSE I THINK WE'RE IN...
LOGAN!
AAUGHH.
THE COMPOUND'S ARSENAL.
OH, CRAP.
KILL HIM! KILL WOLVERINE! PREPARE TO FIRE!
UHNN.

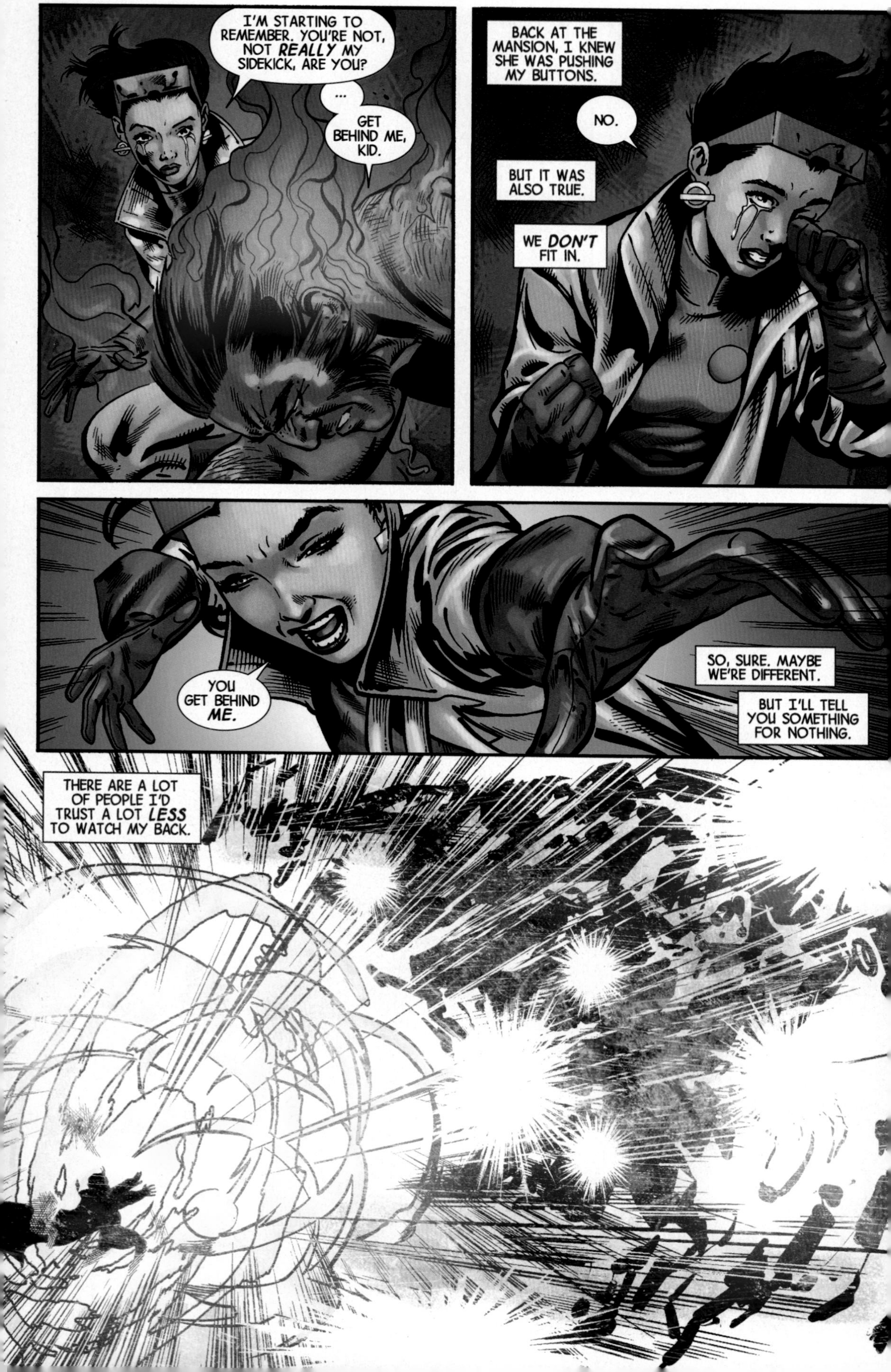
I'M STARTING TO REMEMBER. YOU'RE NOT, NOT *REALLY* MY SIDEKICK, ARE YOU?
...
GET BEHIND ME, KID.
BACK AT THE MANSION, I KNEW SHE WAS PUSHING MY BUTTONS.
NO.
BUT IT WAS ALSO TRUE.
WE *DON'T* FIT IN.
YOU GET BEHIND *ME.*
SO, SURE. MAYBE WE'RE DIFFERENT.
BUT I'LL TELL YOU SOMETHING FOR NOTHING.
THERE ARE A LOT OF PEOPLE I'D TRUST A LOT *LESS* TO WATCH MY BACK.

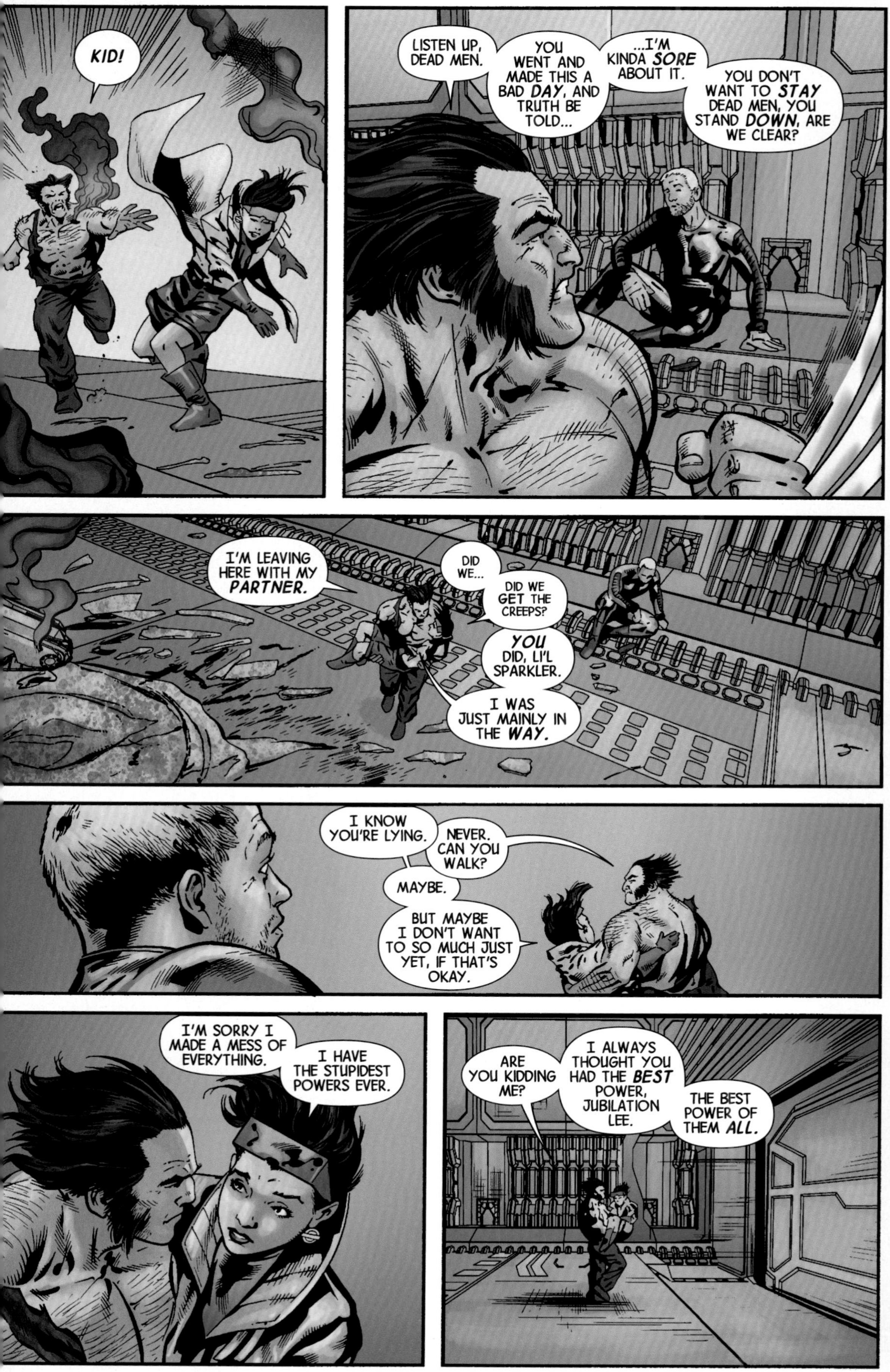
KID!
LISTEN UP, DEAD MEN.
YOU WENT AND MADE THIS A BAD DAY, AND TRUTH BE TOLD...
...I'M KINDA SORE ABOUT IT.
YOU DON'T WANT TO STAY DEAD MEN, YOU STAND DOWN, ARE WE CLEAR?
I'M LEAVING HERE WITH MY PARTNER.
DID WE...
DID WE GET THE CREEPS?
YOU DID, LI'L SPARKLER.
I WAS JUST MAINLY IN THE WAY.
I KNOW YOU'RE LYING.
NEVER. CAN YOU WALK?
MAYBE.
BUT MAYBE I DON'T WANT TO SO MUCH JUST YET, IF THAT'S OKAY.
I'M SORRY I MADE A MESS OF EVERYTHING.
I HAVE THE STUPIDEST POWERS EVER.
ARE YOU KIDDING ME?
I ALWAYS THOUGHT YOU HAD THE BEST POWER, JUBILATION LEE.
THE BEST POWER OF THEM ALL.

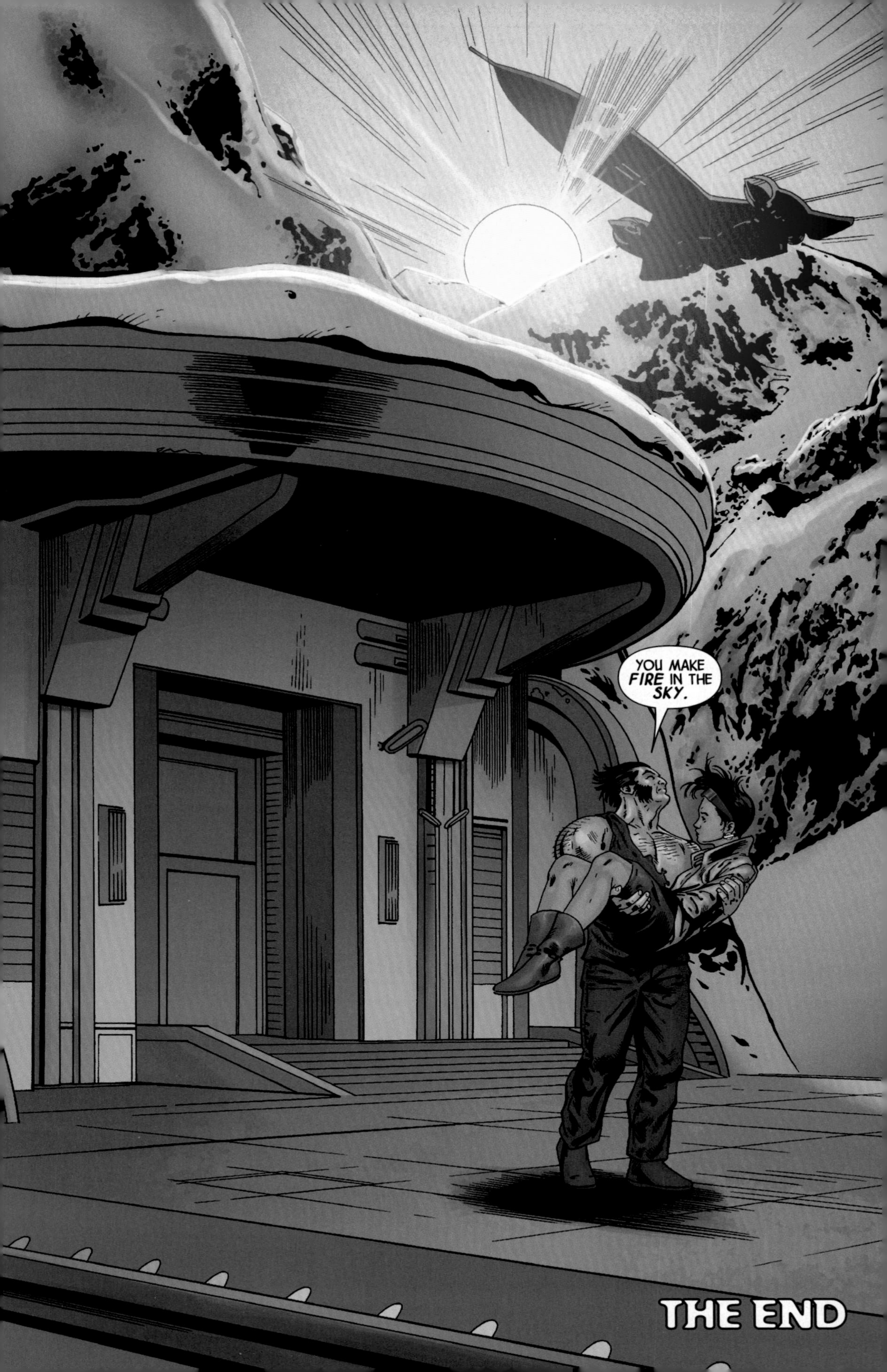
YOU MAKE FIRE IN THE SKY.
THE END

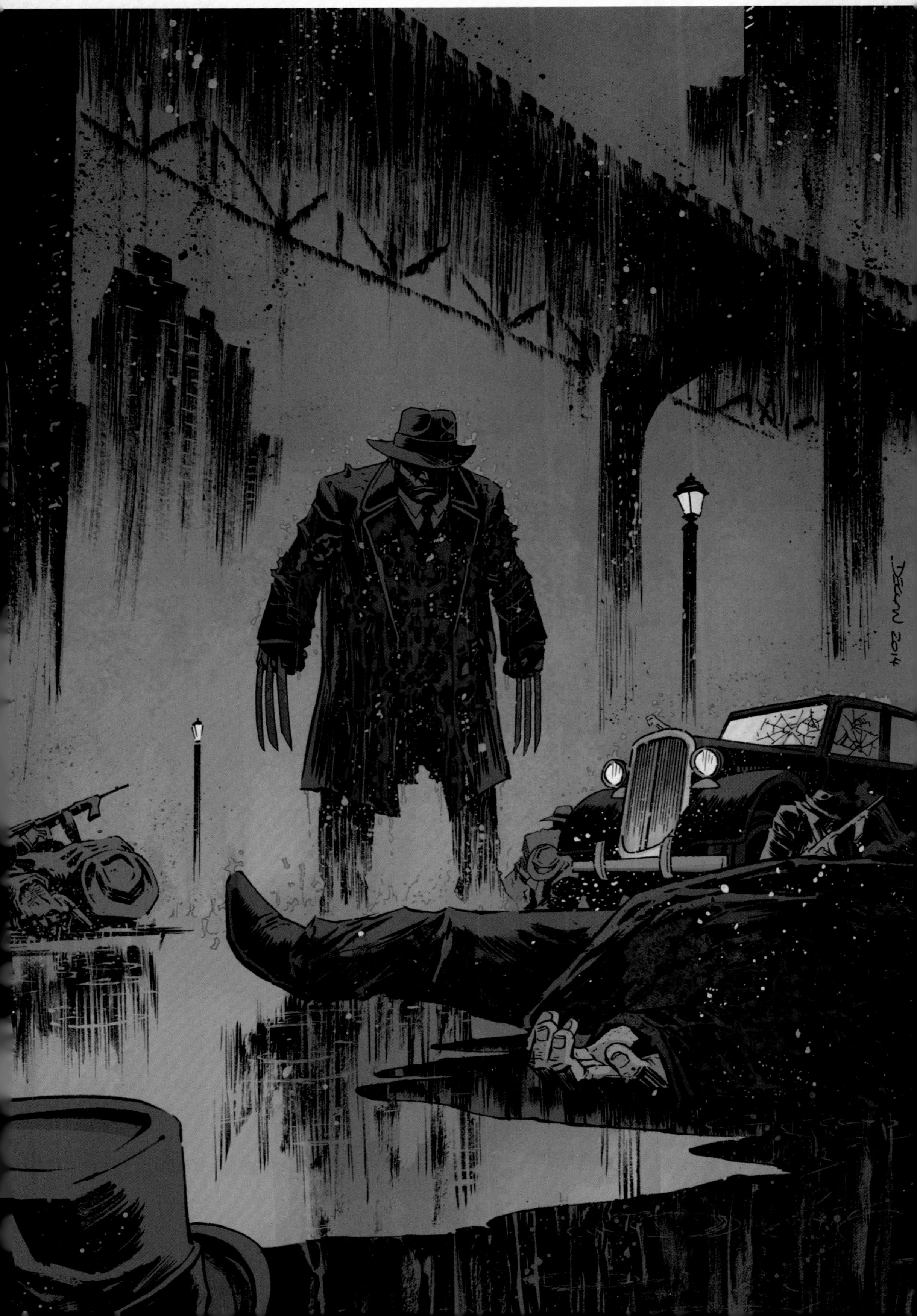

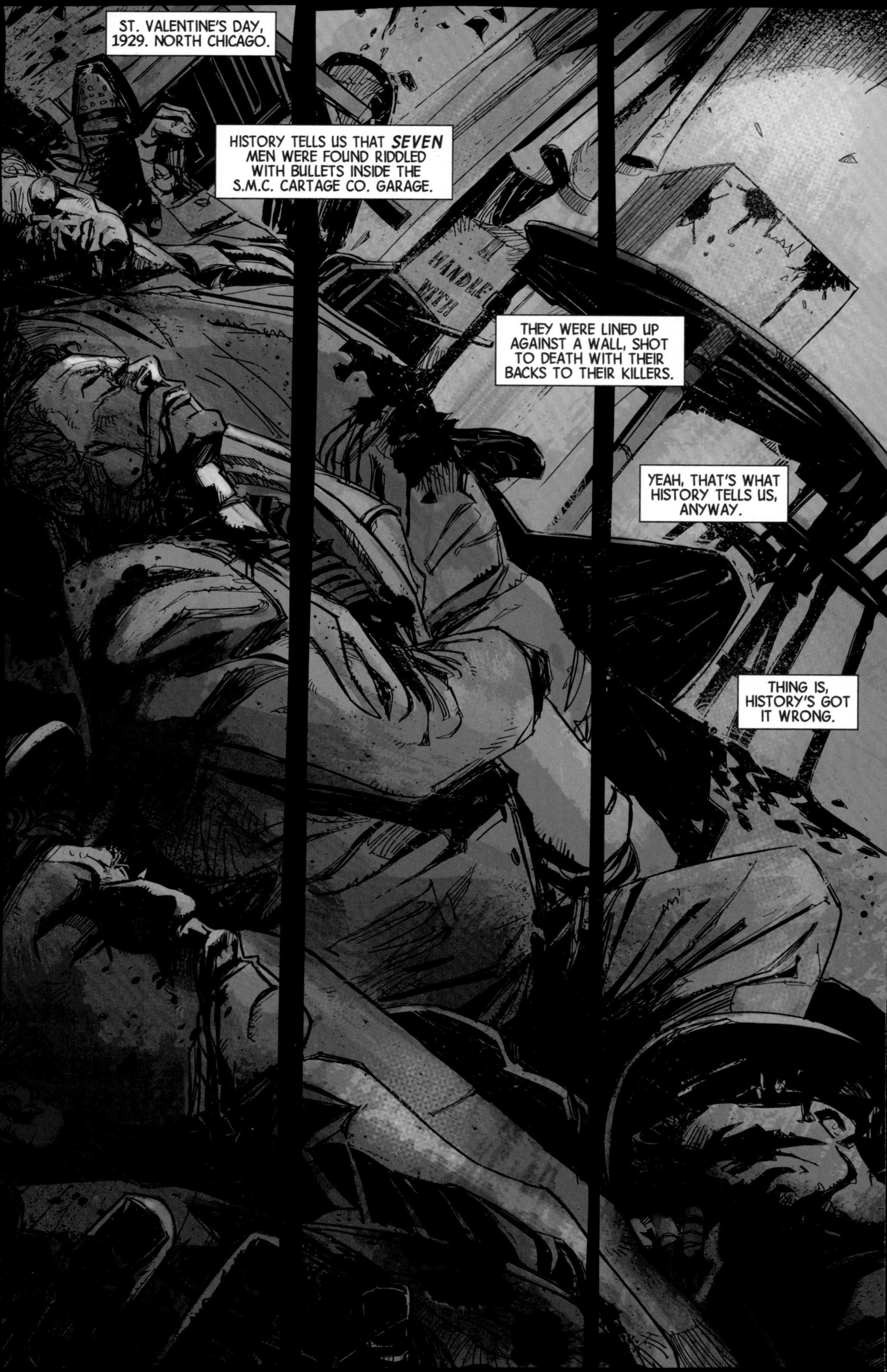
ST. VALENTINE'S DAY, 1929. NORTH CHICAGO.
HISTORY TELLS US THAT SEVEN MEN WERE FOUND RIDDLED WITH BULLETS INSIDE THE S.M.C. CARTAGE CO. GARAGE.
THEY WERE LINED UP AGAINST A WALL, SHOT TO DEATH WITH THEIR BACKS TO THEIR KILLERS.
YEAH, THAT'S WHAT HISTORY TELLS US, ANYWAY.
THING IS, HISTORY'S GOT IT WRONG.

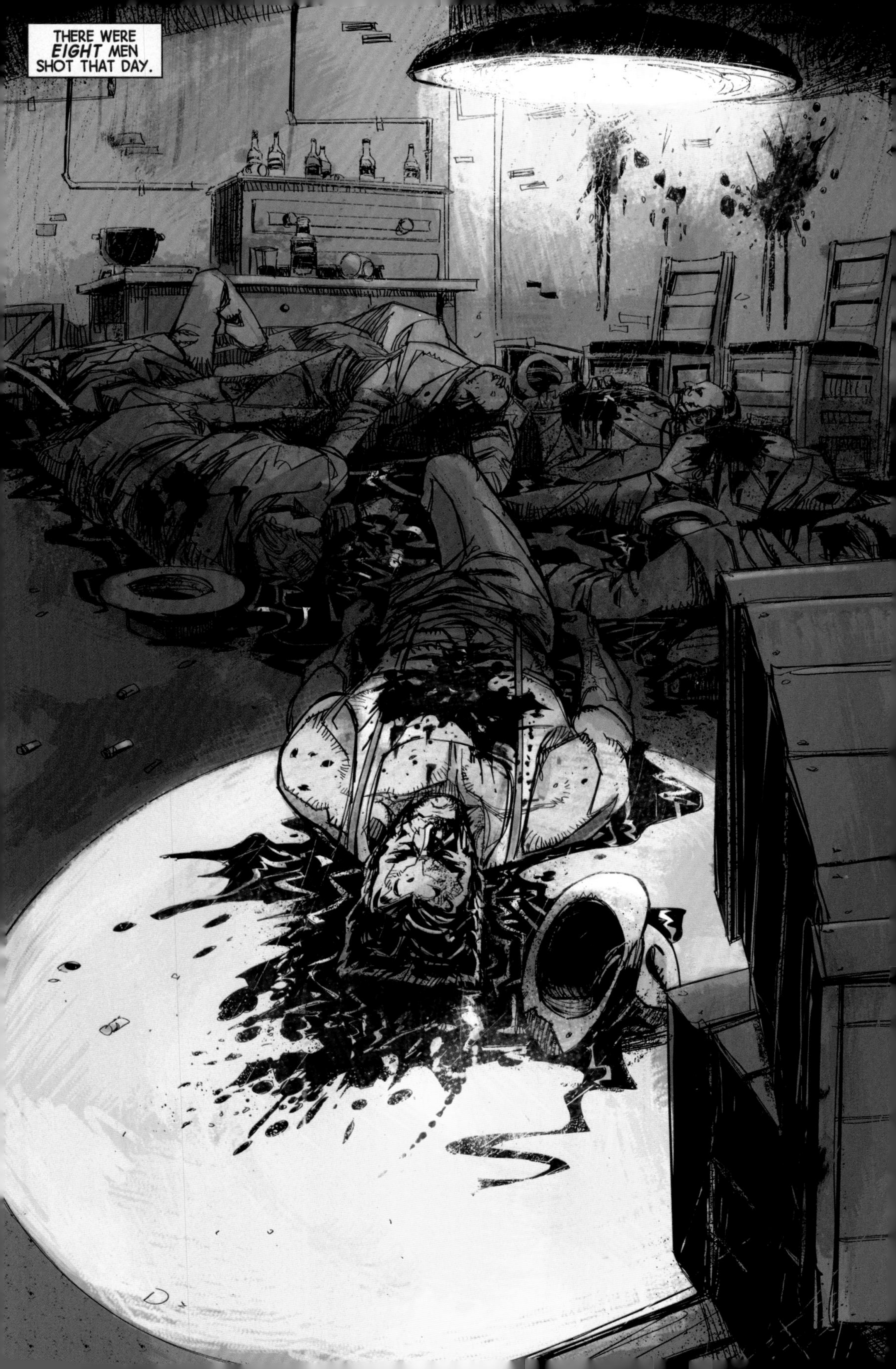
THERE WERE *EIGHT* MEN SHOT THAT DAY.

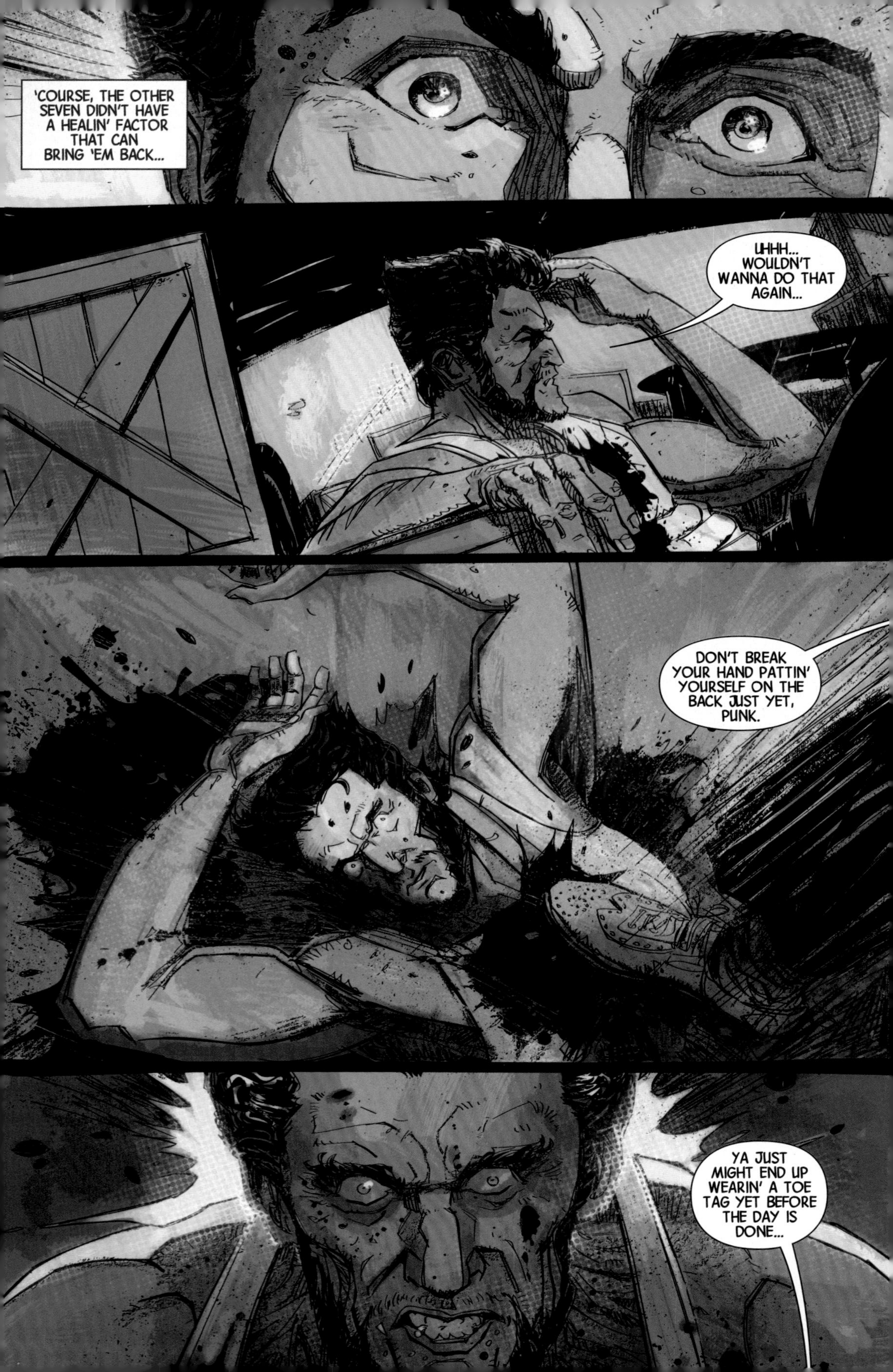
'COURSE, THE OTHER SEVEN DIDN'T HAVE A HEALIN' FACTOR THAT CAN BRING 'EM BACK...
UHHH... WOULDN'T WANNA DO THAT AGAIN...
DON'T BREAK YOUR HAND PATTIN' YOURSELF ON THE BACK JUST YET, PUNK.
YA JUST MIGHT END UP WEARIN' A TOE TAG YET BEFORE THE DAY IS DONE...

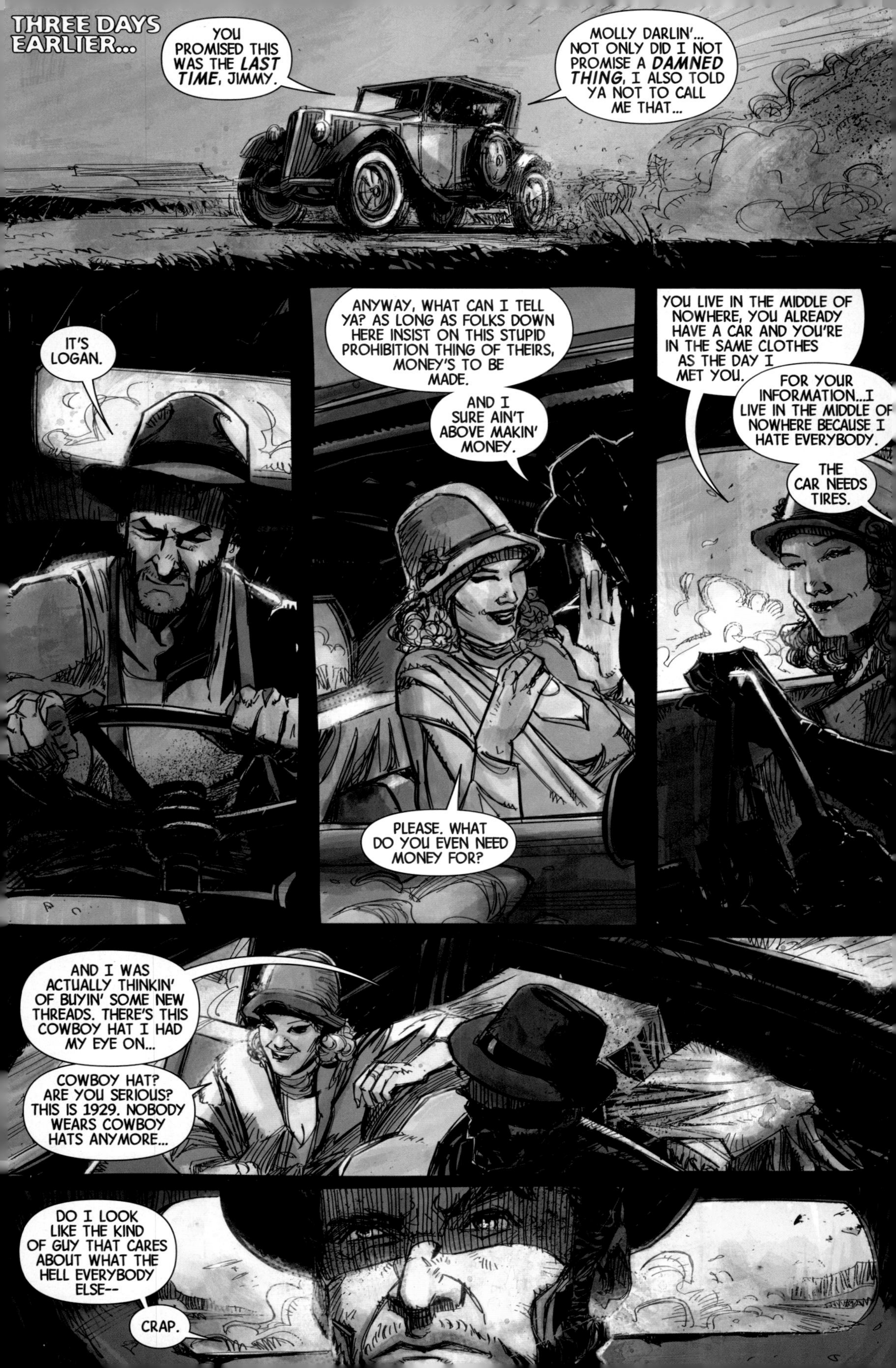
THREE DAYS EARLIER...
YOU PROMISED THIS WAS THE LAST TIME, JIMMY.
MOLLY DARLIN'... NOT ONLY DID I NOT PROMISE A DAMNED THING, I ALSO TOLD YA NOT TO CALL ME THAT...
IT'S LOGAN.
ANYWAY, WHAT CAN I TELL YA? AS LONG AS FOLKS DOWN HERE INSIST ON THIS STUPID PROHIBITION THING OF THEIRS, MONEY'S TO BE MADE.
AND I SURE AIN'T ABOVE MAKIN' MONEY.
PLEASE. WHAT DO YOU EVEN NEED MONEY FOR?
YOU LIVE IN THE MIDDLE OF NOWHERE, YOU ALREADY HAVE A CAR AND YOU'RE IN THE SAME CLOTHES AS THE DAY I MET YOU.
FOR YOUR INFORMATION...I LIVE IN THE MIDDLE OF NOWHERE BECAUSE I HATE EVERYBODY.
THE CAR NEEDS TIRES.
AND I WAS ACTUALLY THINKIN' OF BUYIN' SOME NEW THREADS. THERE'S THIS COWBOY HAT I HAD MY EYE ON...
COWBOY HAT? ARE YOU SERIOUS? THIS IS 1929. NOBODY WEARS COWBOY HATS ANYMORE...
DO I LOOK LIKE THE KIND OF GUY THAT CARES ABOUT WHAT THE HELL EVERYBODY ELSE--
CRAP.

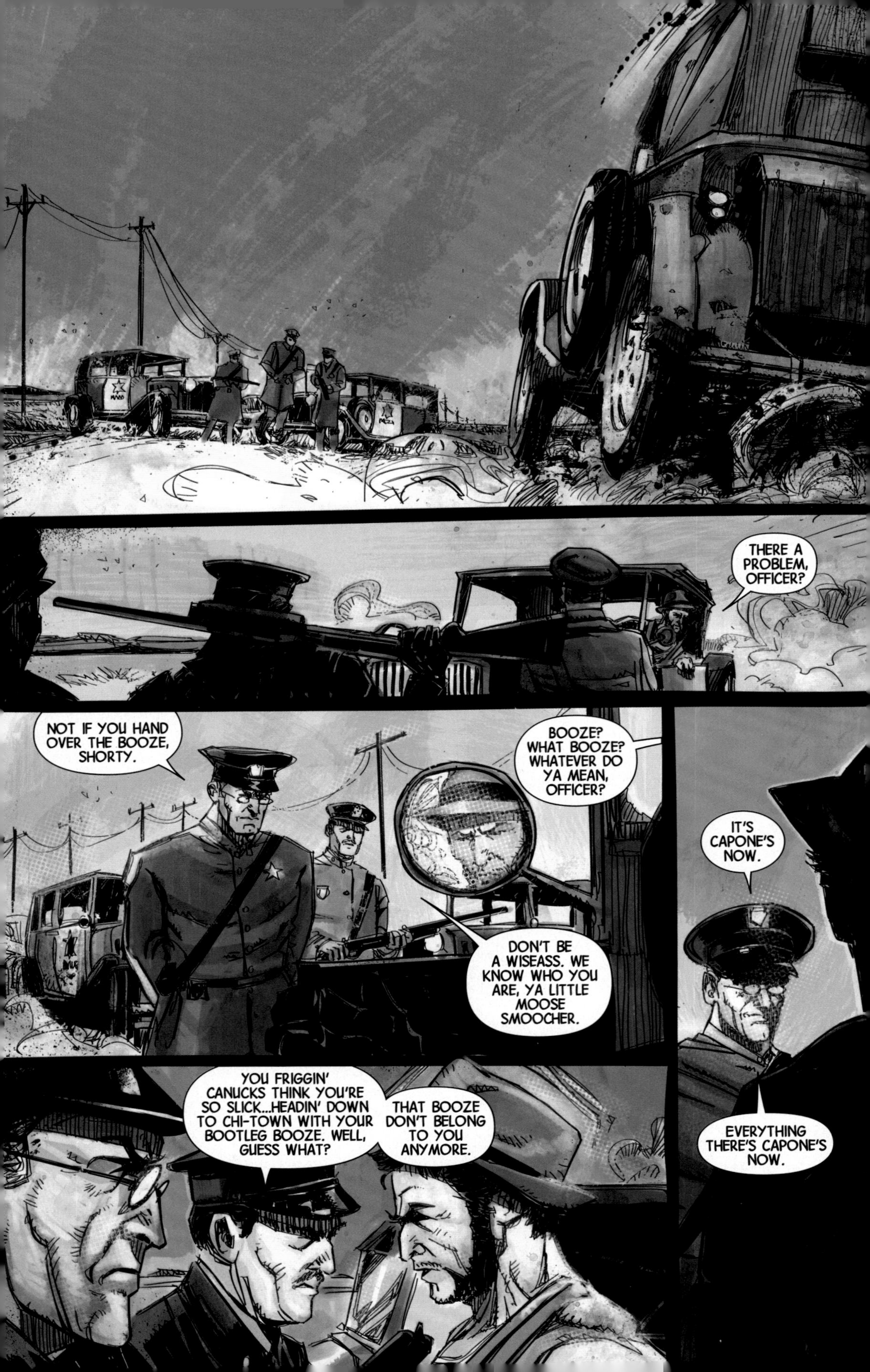
THERE A PROBLEM, OFFICER?
NOT IF YOU HAND OVER THE BOOZE, SHORTY.
BOOZE? WHAT BOOZE? WHATEVER DO YA MEAN, OFFICER?
DON'T BE A WISEASS. WE KNOW WHO YOU ARE, YA LITTLE MOOSE SMOOCHER.
YOU FRIGGIN' CANUCKS THINK YOU'RE SO SLICK...HEADIN' DOWN TO CHI-TOWN WITH YOUR BOOTLEG BOOZE. WELL, GUESS WHAT?
THAT BOOZE DON'T BELONG TO YOU ANYMORE.
IT'S CAPONE'S NOW.
EVERYTHING THERE'S CAPONE'S NOW.

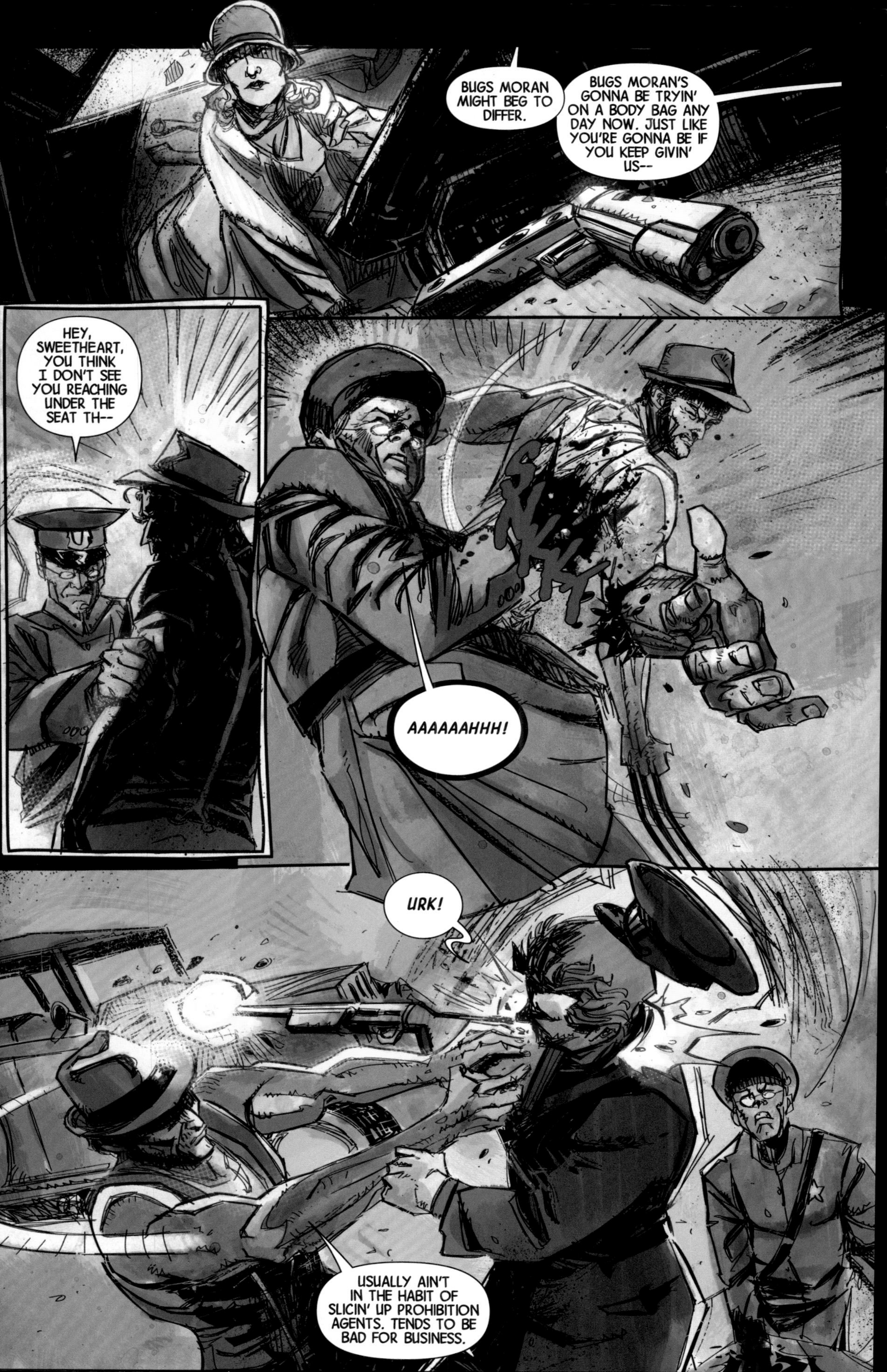
BUGS MORAN MIGHT BEG TO DIFFER.
BUGS MORAN'S GONNA BE TRYIN' ON A BODY BAG ANY DAY NOW. JUST LIKE YOU'RE GONNA BE IF YOU KEEP GIVIN' US--
HEY, SWEETHEART, YOU THINK I DON'T SEE YOU REACHING UNDER THE SEAT TH--
AAAAAAHHH!
URK!
USUALLY AIN'T IN THE HABIT OF SLICIN' UP PROHIBITION AGENTS. TENDS TO BE BAD FOR BUSINESS.

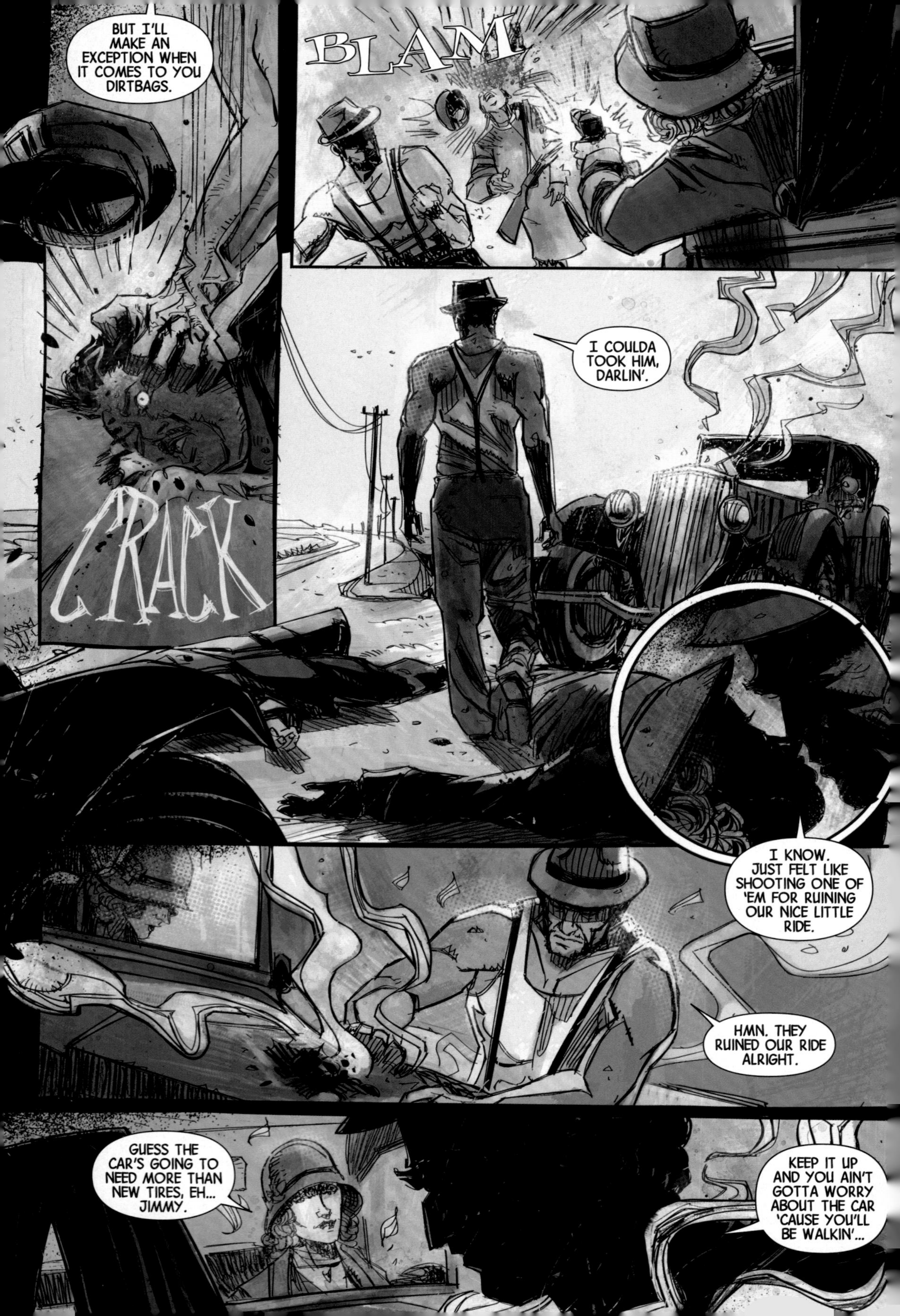
BUT I'LL MAKE AN EXCEPTION WHEN IT COMES TO YOU DIRTBAGS.
BLAM
CRACK
I COULDA TOOK HIM, DARLIN'.
I KNOW. JUST FELT LIKE SHOOTING ONE OF 'EM FOR RUINING OUR NICE LITTLE RIDE.
HMN. THEY RUINED OUR RIDE ALRIGHT.
GUESS THE CAR'S GOING TO NEED MORE THAN NEW TIRES, EH... JIMMY.
KEEP IT UP AND YOU AIN'T GOTTA WORRY ABOUT THE CAR 'CAUSE YOU'LL BE WALKIN'...

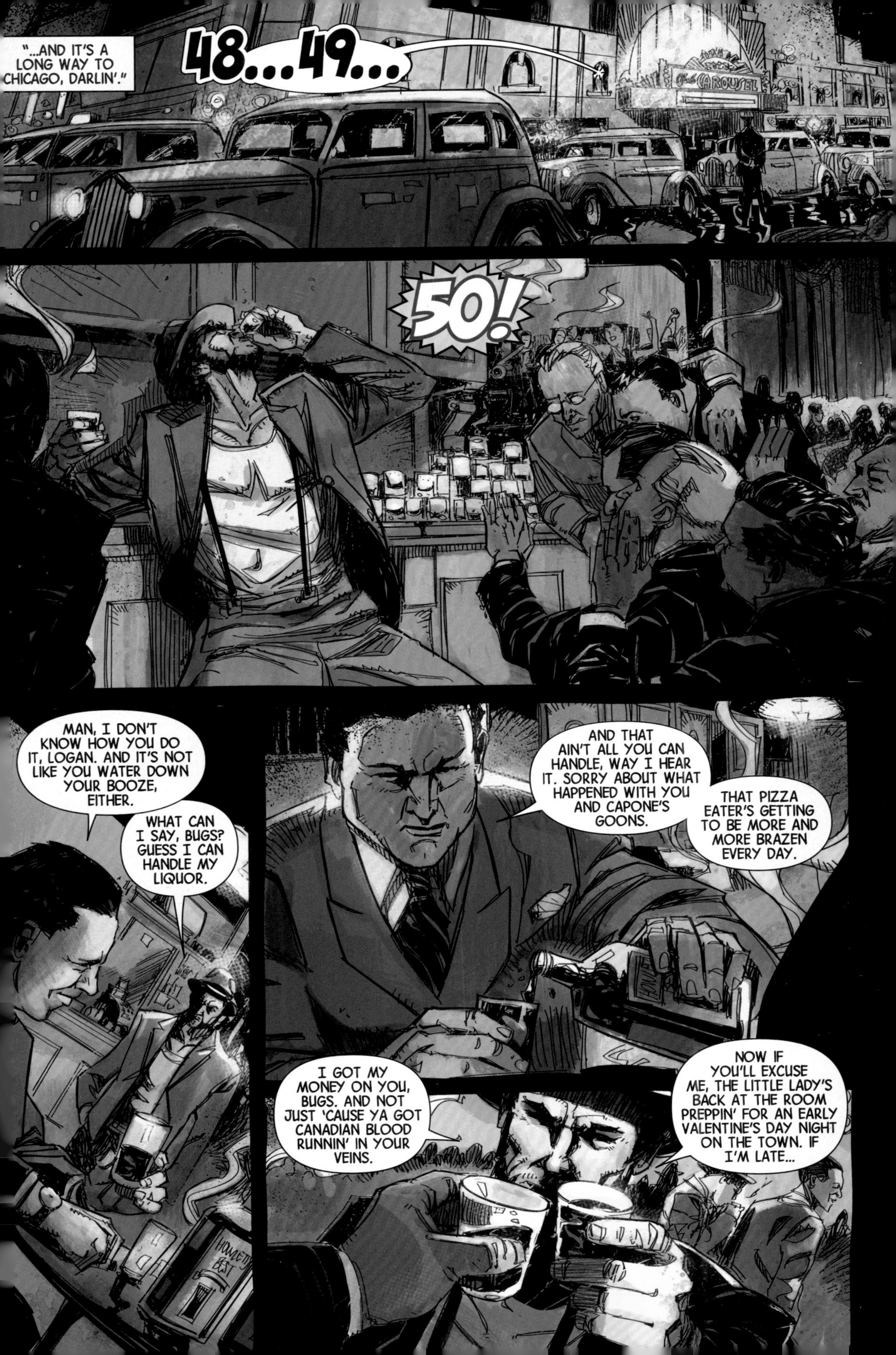
"...AND IT'S A LONG WAY TO CHICAGO, DARLIN'."
48...49...
Club CAROUSEL
50!
MAN, I DON'T KNOW HOW YOU DO IT, LOGAN. AND IT'S NOT LIKE YOU WATER DOWN YOUR BOOZE, EITHER.
WHAT CAN I SAY, BUGS? GUESS I CAN HANDLE MY LIQUOR.
AND THAT AIN'T ALL YOU CAN HANDLE, WAY I HEAR IT. SORRY ABOUT WHAT HAPPENED WITH YOU AND CAPONE'S GOONS.
THAT PIZZA EATER'S GETTING TO BE MORE AND MORE BRAZEN EVERY DAY.
I GOT MY MONEY ON YOU, BUGS. AND NOT JUST 'CAUSE YA GOT CANADIAN BLOOD RUNNIN' IN YOUR VEINS.
NOW IF YOU'LL EXCUSE ME, THE LITTLE LADY'S BACK AT THE ROOM PREPPIN' FOR AN EARLY VALENTINE'S DAY NIGHT ON THE TOWN. IF I'M LATE...

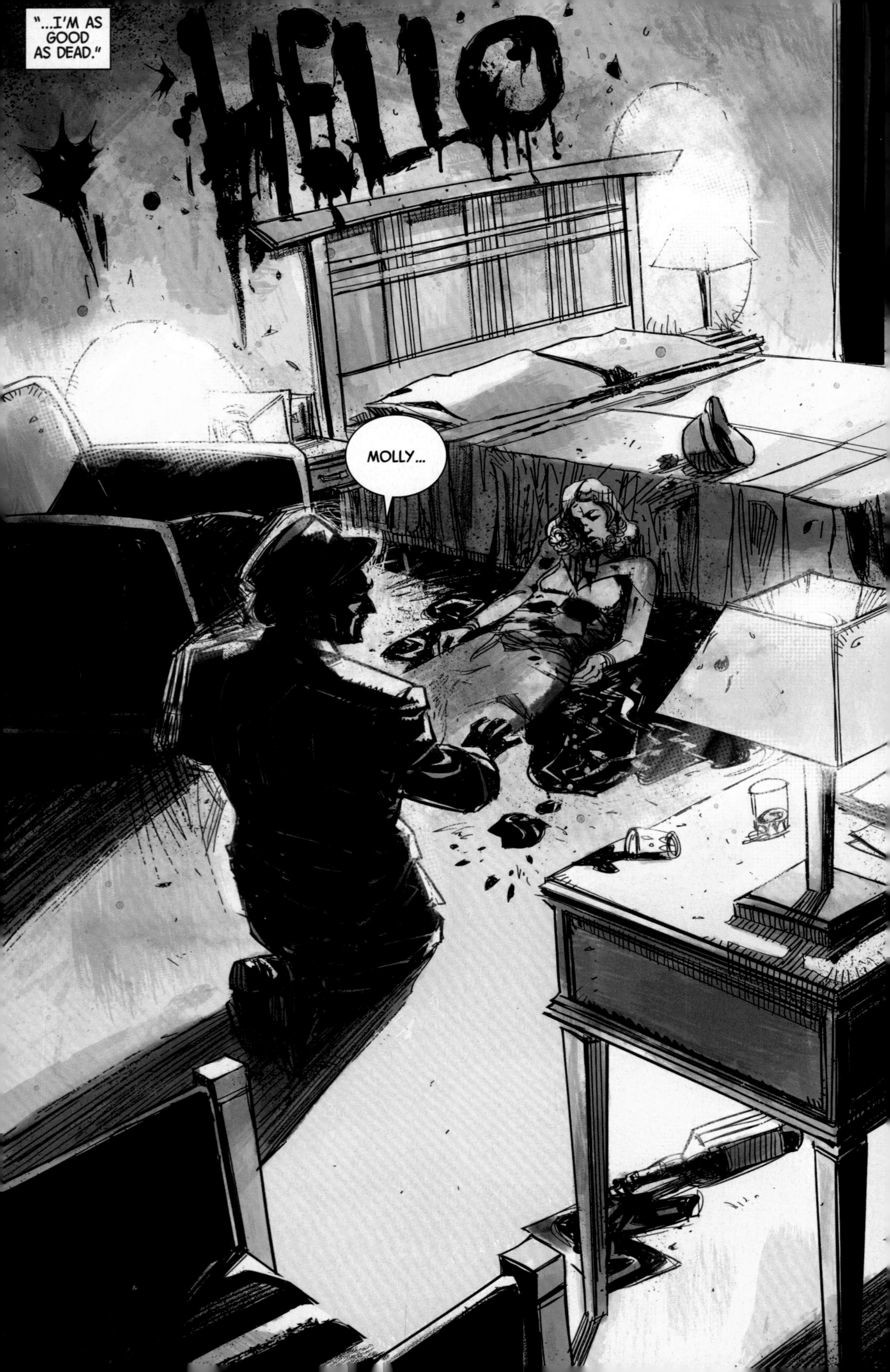
"...I'M AS GOOD AS DEAD."
HELLO
MOLLY...

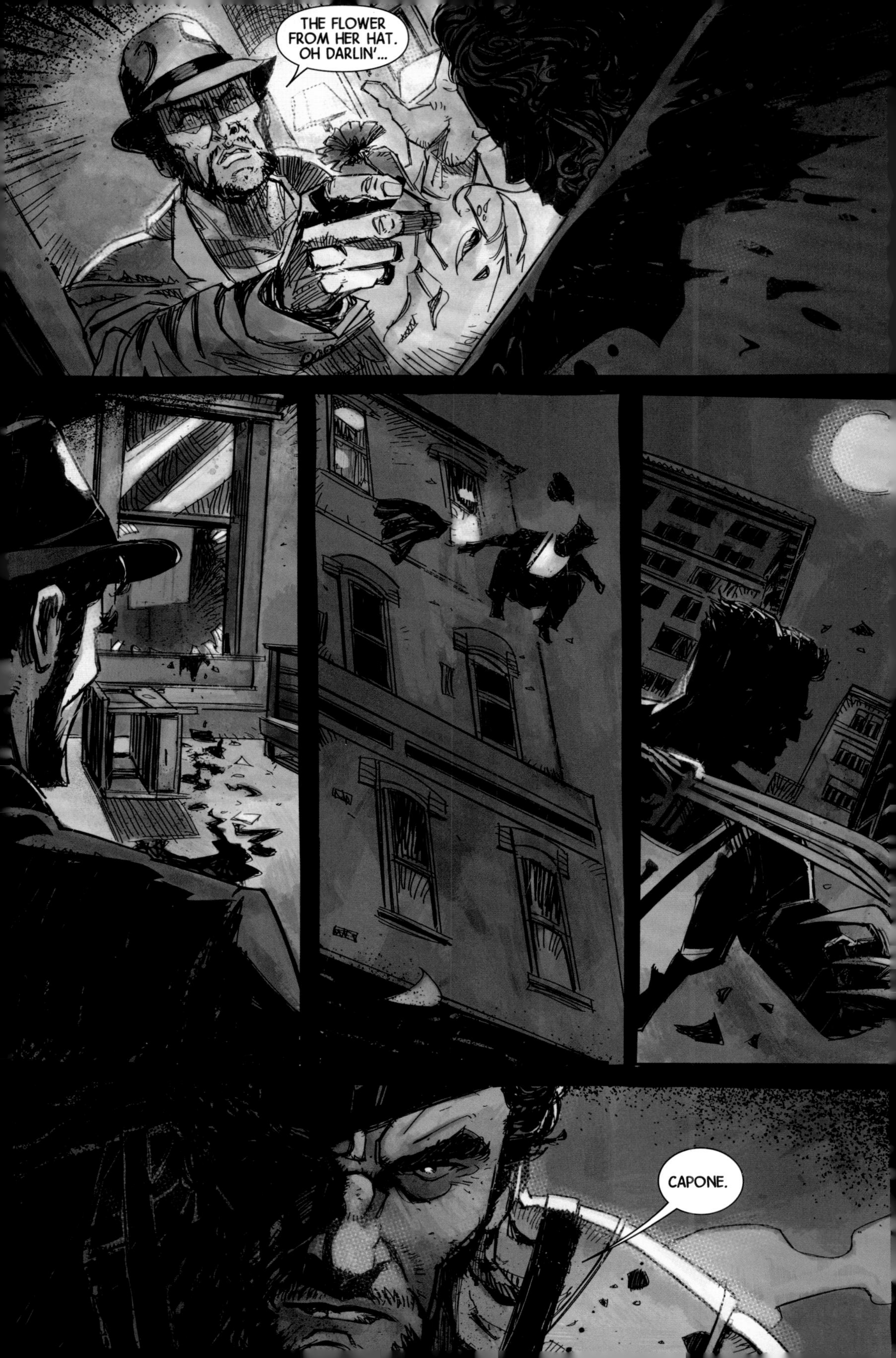
THE FLOWER FROM HER HAT. OH DARLIN'...
CAPONE.

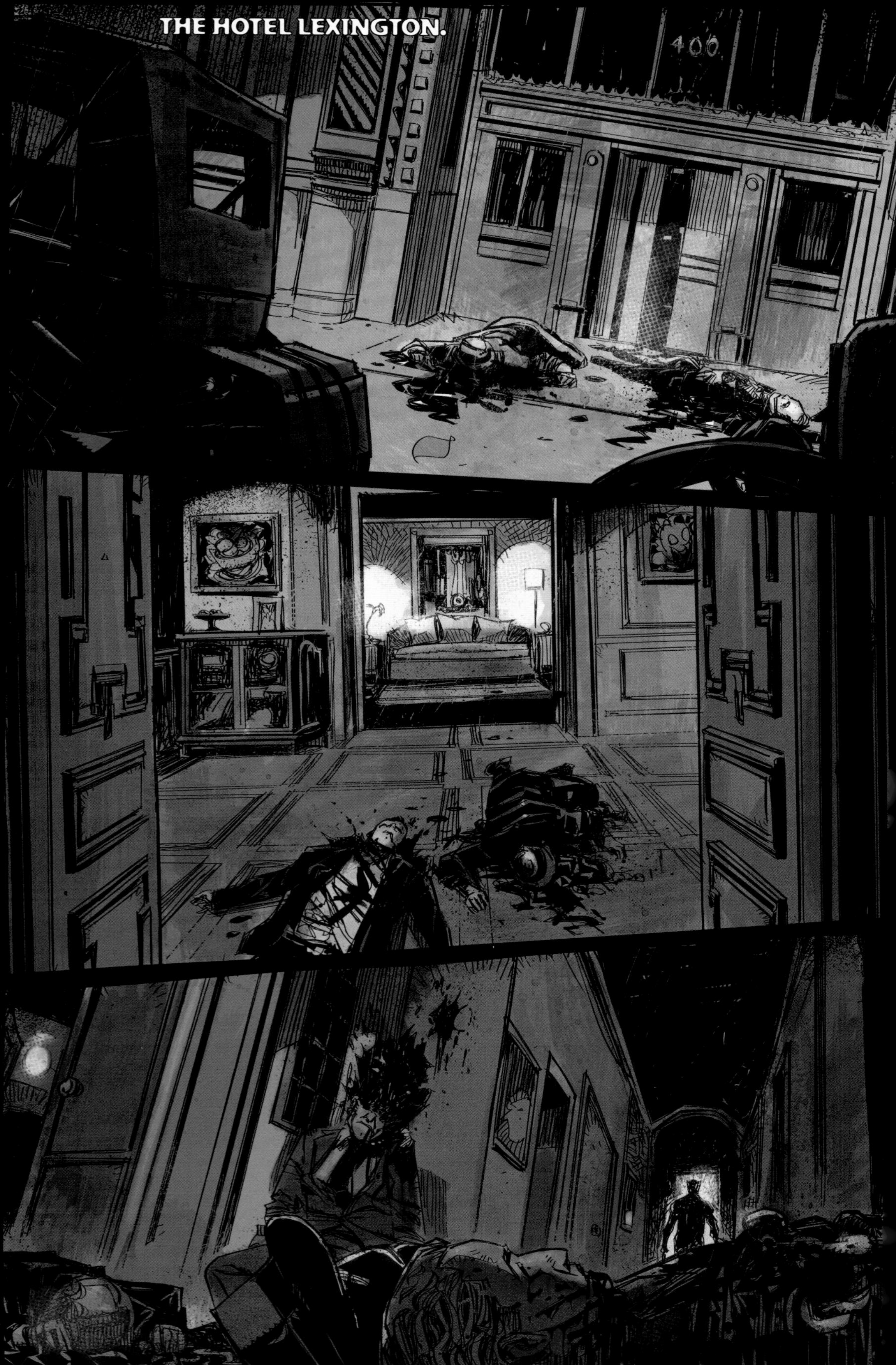
THE HOTEL LEXINGTON.
400

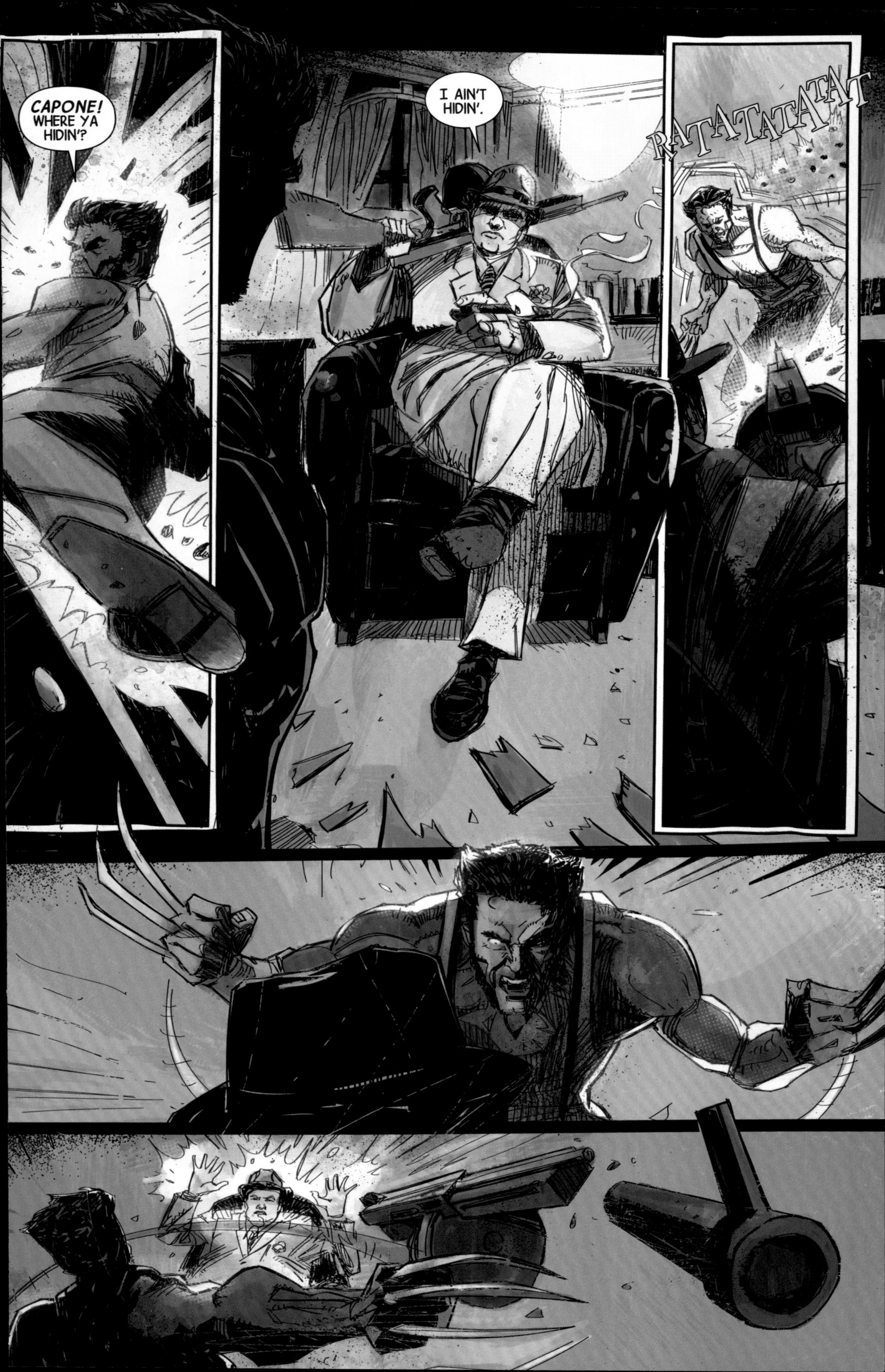
CAPONE! WHERE YA HIDIN'?
I AIN'T HIDIN'.
RATATATATAT

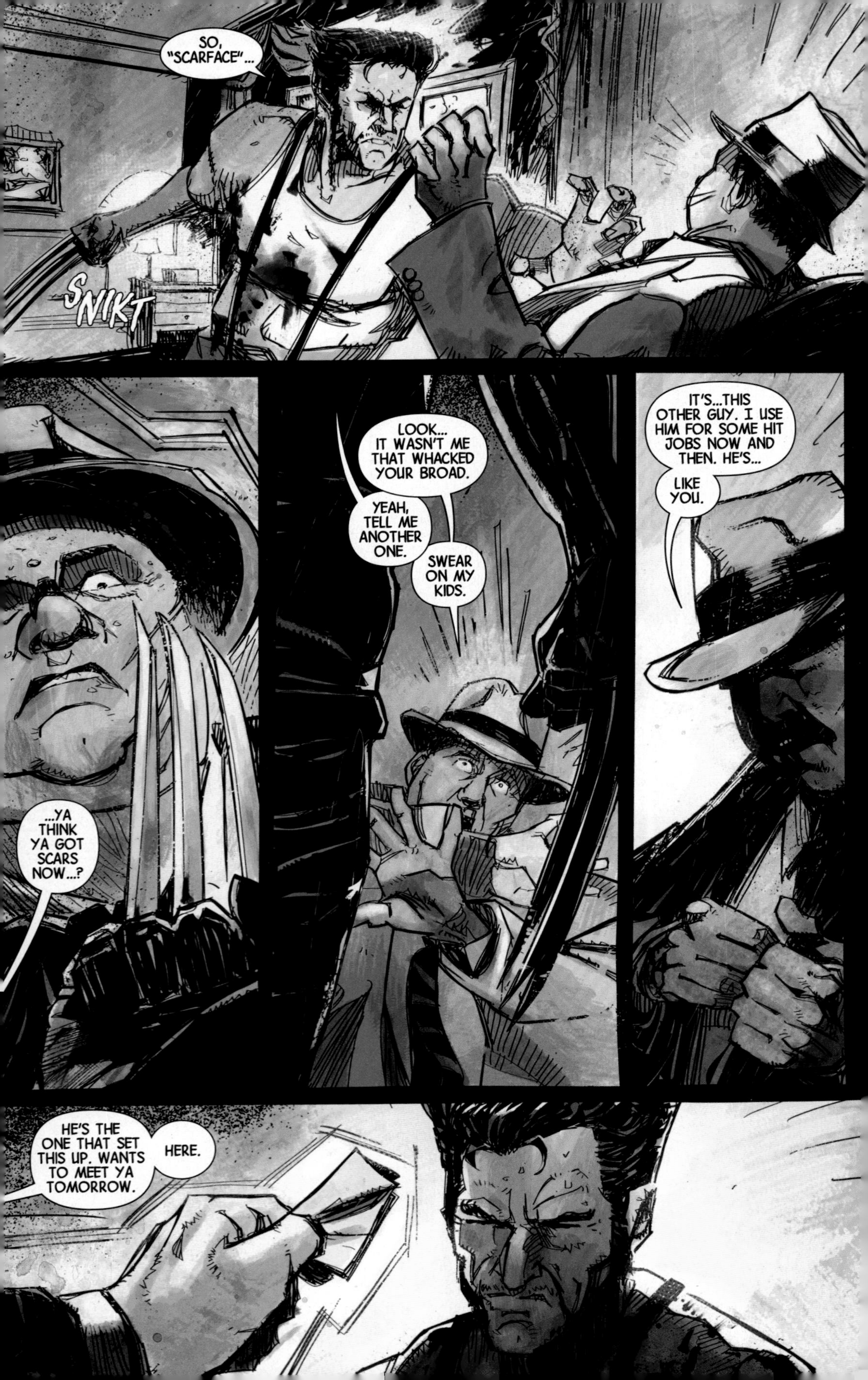
SO, "SCARFACE"...
SNIKT
...YA THINK YA GOT SCARS NOW...?
LOOK... IT WASN'T ME THAT WHACKED YOUR BROAD.
YEAH, TELL ME ANOTHER ONE.
SWEAR ON MY KIDS.
IT'S...THIS OTHER GUY. I USE HIM FOR SOME HIT JOBS NOW AND THEN. HE'S...
LIKE YOU.
HE'S THE ONE THAT SET THIS UP. WANTS TO MEET YA TOMORROW.
HERE.

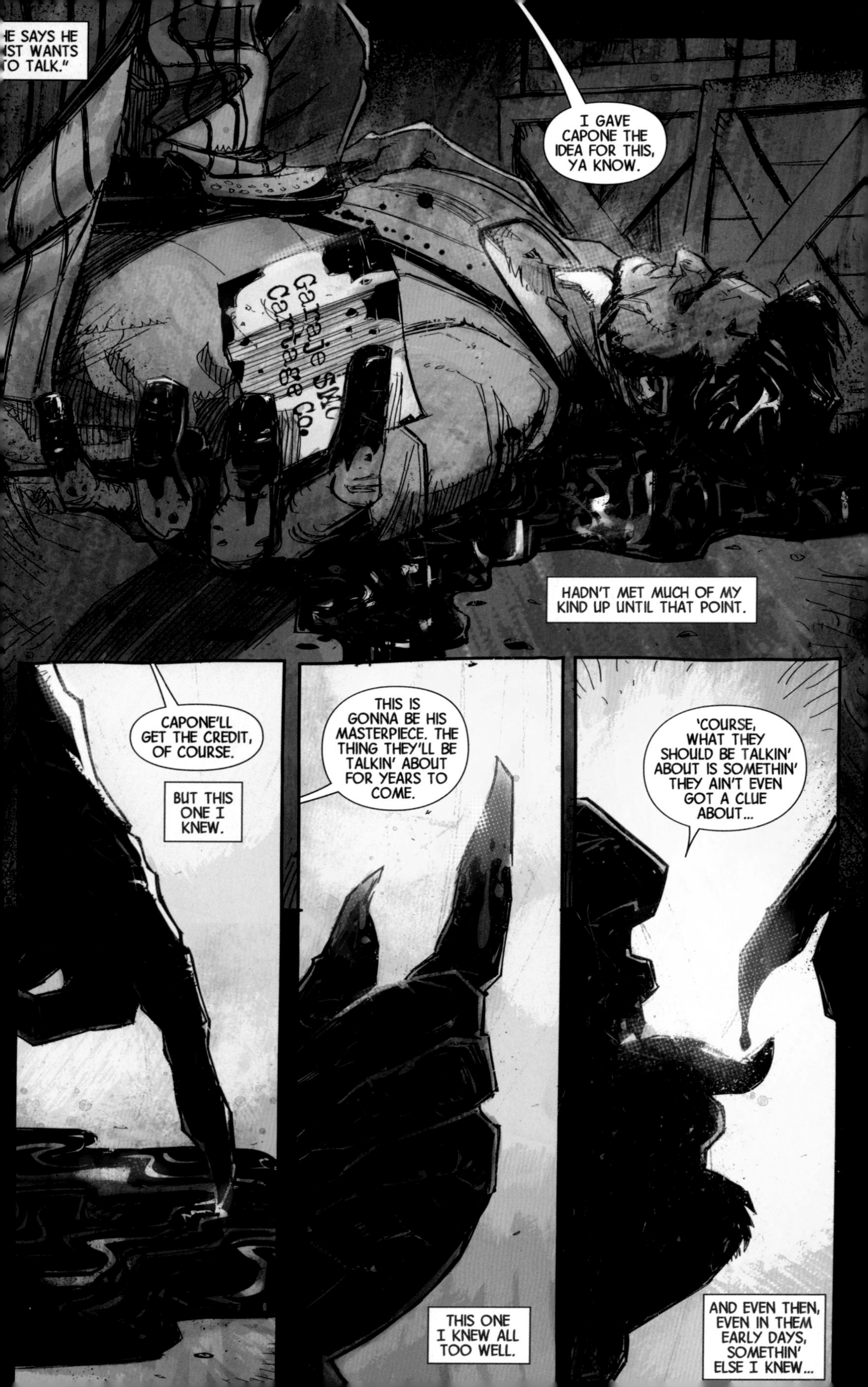
HE SAYS HE
JUST WANTS
TO TALK."
I GAVE CAPONE THE IDEA FOR THIS, YA KNOW.
Garaje SMC Cartage Co.
HADN'T MET MUCH OF MY KIND UP UNTIL THAT POINT.
CAPONE'LL GET THE CREDIT, OF COURSE.
BUT THIS ONE I KNEW.
THIS IS GONNA BE HIS MASTERPIECE. THE THING THEY'LL BE TALKIN' ABOUT FOR YEARS TO COME.
THIS ONE I KNEW ALL TOO WELL.
'COURSE, WHAT THEY SHOULD BE TALKIN' ABOUT IS SOMETHIN' THEY AIN'T EVEN GOT A CLUE ABOUT...
AND EVEN THEN, EVEN IN THEM EARLY DAYS, SOMETHIN' ELSE I KNEW...

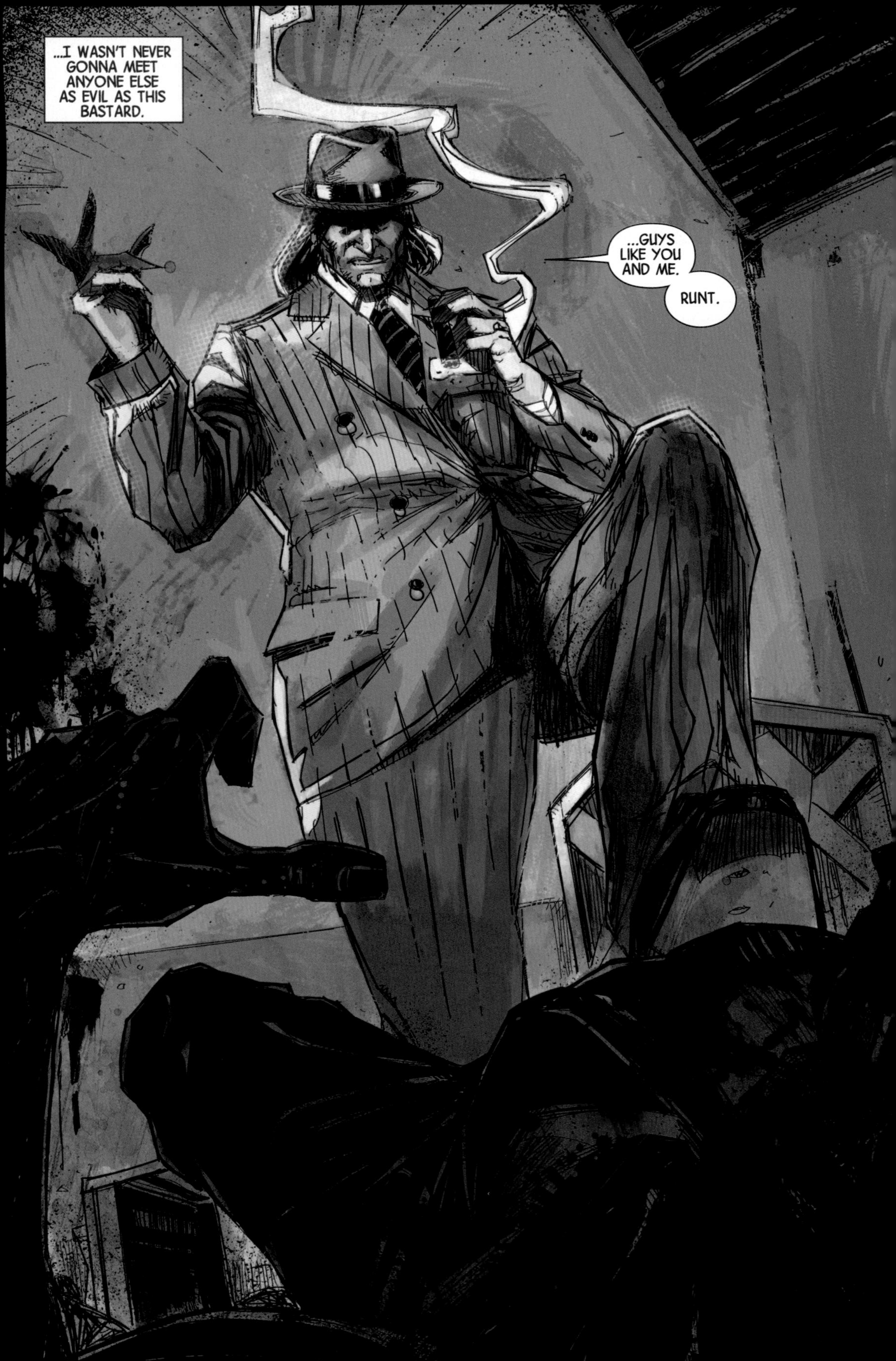
...I WASN'T NEVER GONNA MEET ANYONE ELSE AS EVIL AS THIS BASTARD.
...GUYS LIKE YOU AND ME.
RUNT.

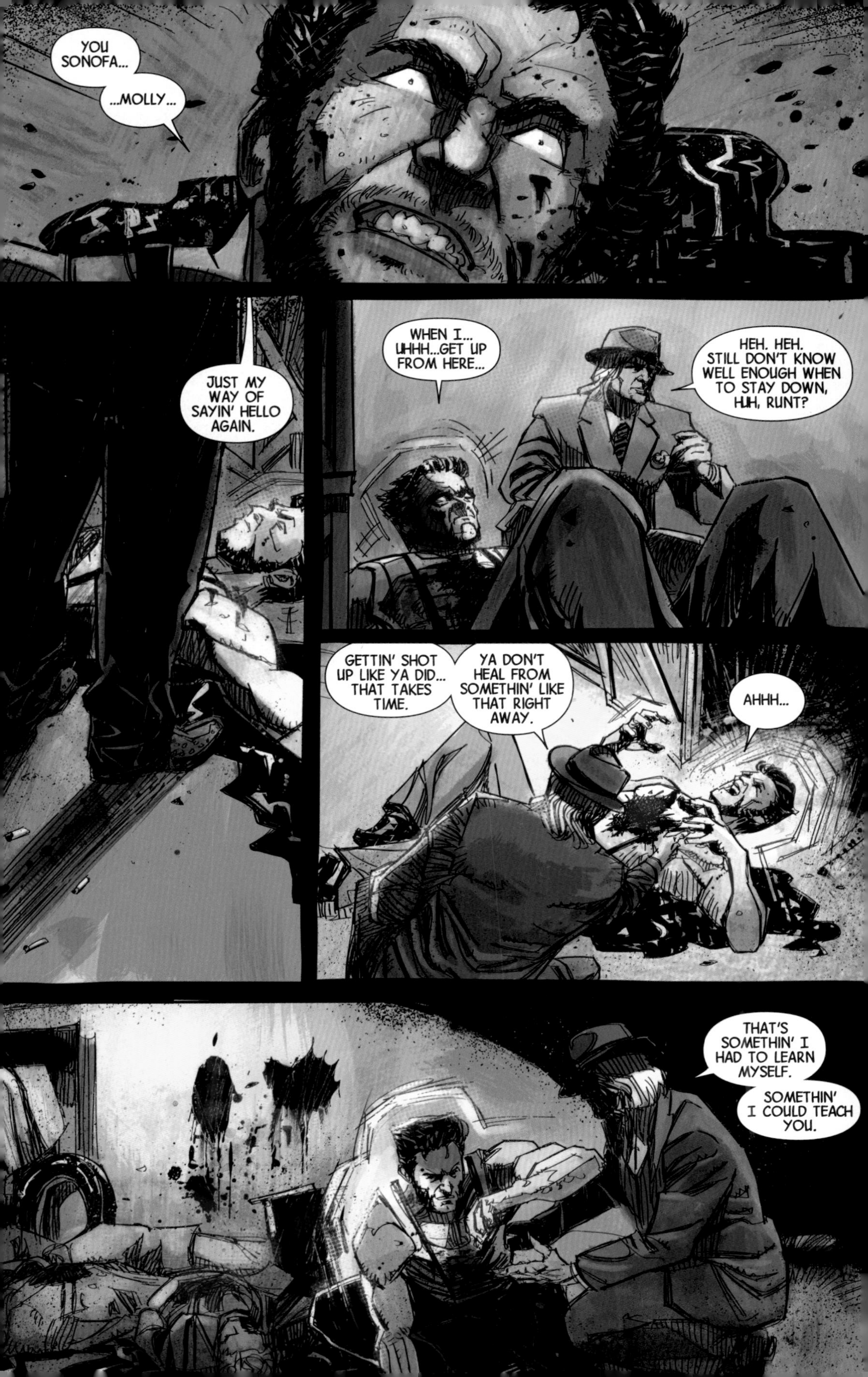
YOU SONOFA...
...MOLLY...
JUST MY WAY OF SAYIN' HELLO AGAIN.
WHEN I... UHHH...GET UP FROM HERE...
HEH. HEH. STILL DON'T KNOW WELL ENOUGH WHEN TO STAY DOWN, HUH, RUNT?
GETTIN' SHOT UP LIKE YA DID... THAT TAKES TIME.
YA DON'T HEAL FROM SOMETHIN' LIKE THAT RIGHT AWAY.
AHHH...
THAT'S SOMETHIN' I HAD TO LEARN MYSELF.
SOMETHIN' I COULD TEACH YOU.

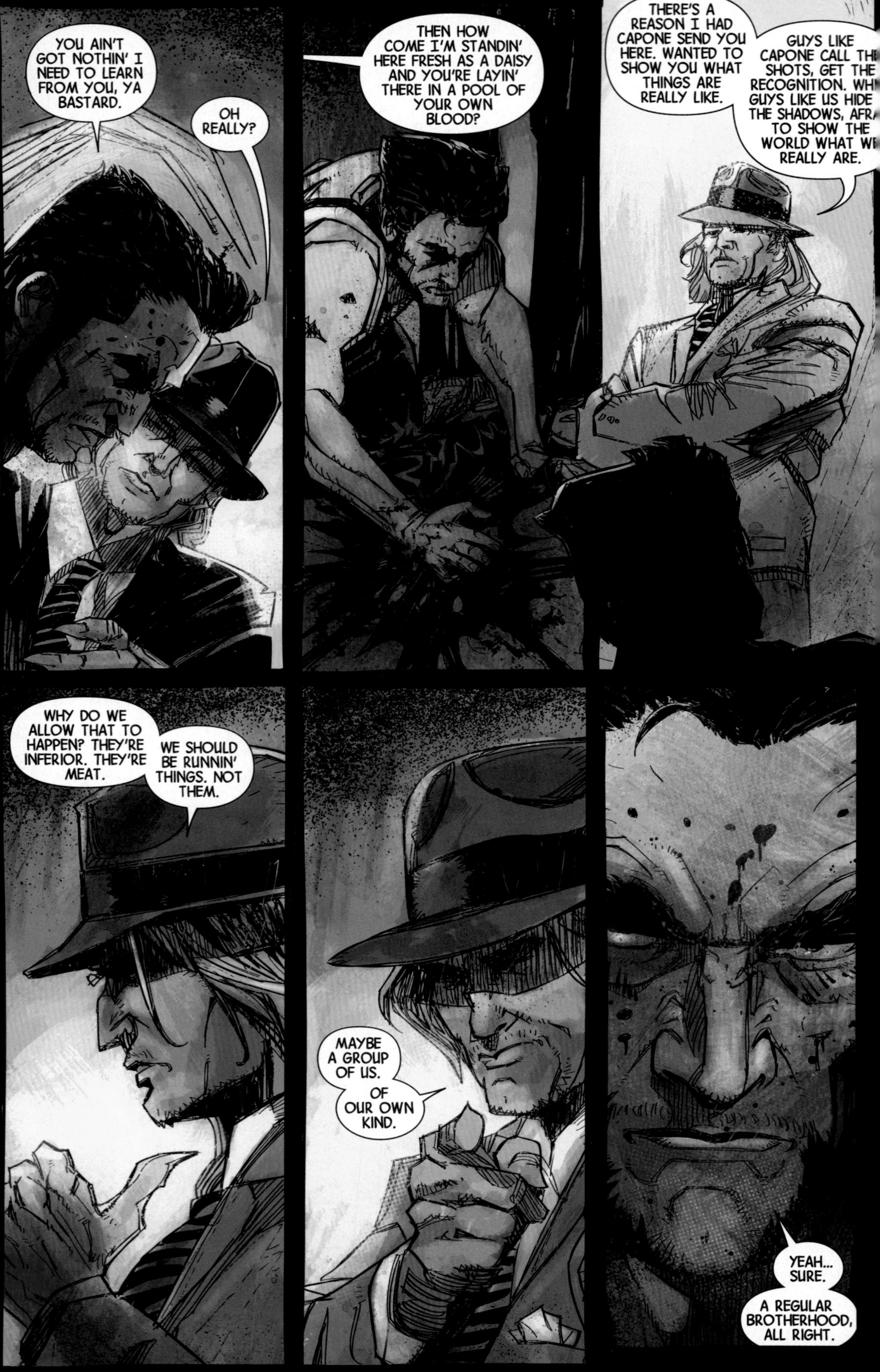

YOU AIN'T GOT NOTHIN' I NEED TO LEARN FROM YOU, YA BASTARD.
OH REALLY?
THEN HOW COME I'M STANDIN' HERE FRESH AS A DAISY AND YOU'RE LAYIN' THERE IN A POOL OF YOUR OWN BLOOD?
THERE'S A REASON I HAD CAPONE SEND YOU HERE. WANTED TO SHOW YOU WHAT THINGS ARE REALLY LIKE.
GUYS LIKE CAPONE CALL TH SHOTS, GET THE RECOGNITION. WH GUYS LIKE US HIDE THE SHADOWS, AFR TO SHOW THE WORLD WHAT W REALLY ARE.
WHY DO WE ALLOW THAT TO HAPPEN? THEY'RE INFERIOR. THEY'RE MEAT.
WE SHOULD BE RUNNIN' THINGS. NOT THEM.
MAYBE A GROUP OF US.
OF OUR OWN KIND.
YEAH... SURE.
A REGULAR BROTHERHOOD, ALL RIGHT.

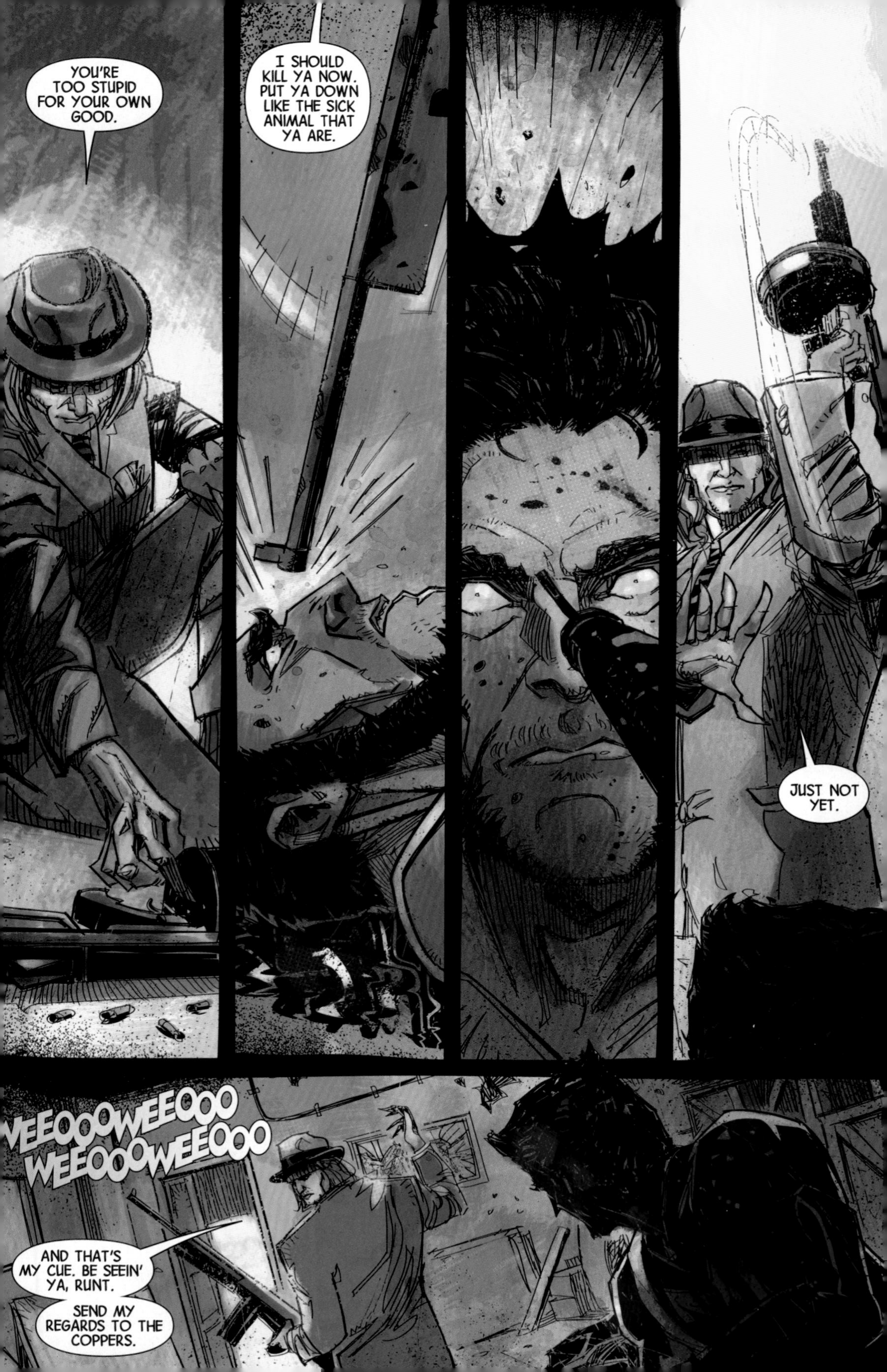
YOU'RE TOO STUPID FOR YOUR OWN GOOD.
I SHOULD KILL YA NOW. PUT YA DOWN LIKE THE SICK ANIMAL THAT YA ARE.
JUST NOT YET.
VEEOOOWEEOOO WEEOOOWEEOOO
AND THAT'S MY CUE. BE SEEIN' YA, RUNT.
SEND MY REGARDS TO THE COPPERS.

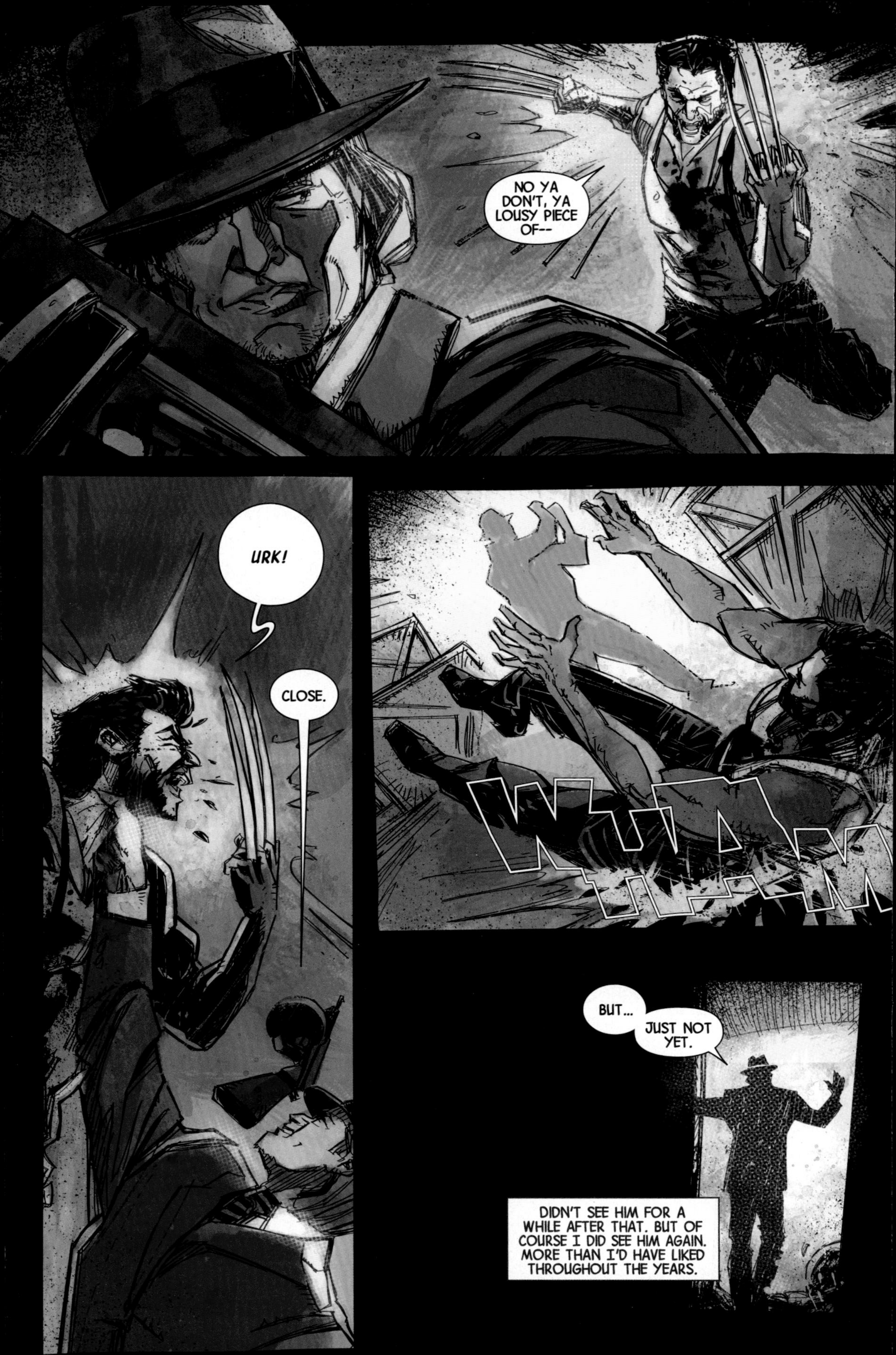
NO YA DON'T, YA LOUSY PIECE OF--
URK!
CLOSE.
WHAM
BUT...
JUST NOT YET.
DIDN'T SEE HIM FOR A WHILE AFTER THAT. BUT OF COURSE I DID SEE HIM AGAIN. MORE THAN I'D HAVE LIKED THROUGHOUT THE YEARS.

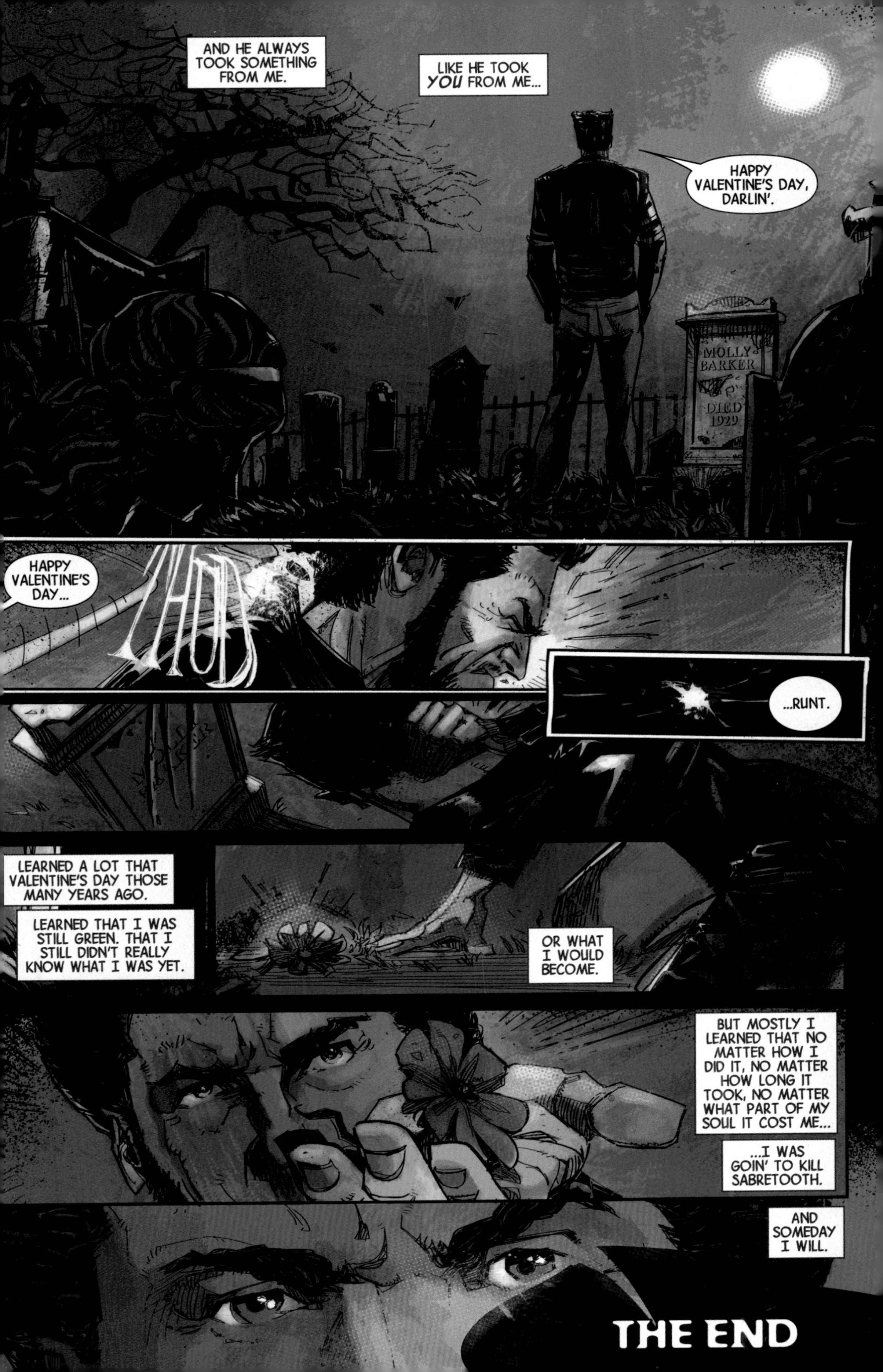
AND HE ALWAYS TOOK SOMETHING FROM ME.
LIKE HE TOOK YOU FROM ME...
HAPPY VALENTINE'S DAY, DARLIN'.
MOLLY BARKER
DIED 1929
HAPPY VALENTINE'S DAY...
THOD
...RUNT.
LEARNED A LOT THAT VALENTINE'S DAY THOSE MANY YEARS AGO.
LEARNED THAT I WAS STILL GREEN. THAT I STILL DIDN'T REALLY KNOW WHAT I WAS YET.
OR WHAT I WOULD BECOME.
BUT MOSTLY I LEARNED THAT NO MATTER HOW I DID IT, NO MATTER HOW LONG IT TOOK, NO MATTER WHAT PART OF MY SOUL IT COST ME...
...I WAS GOIN' TO KILL SABRETOOTH.
AND SOMEDAY I WILL.
THE END

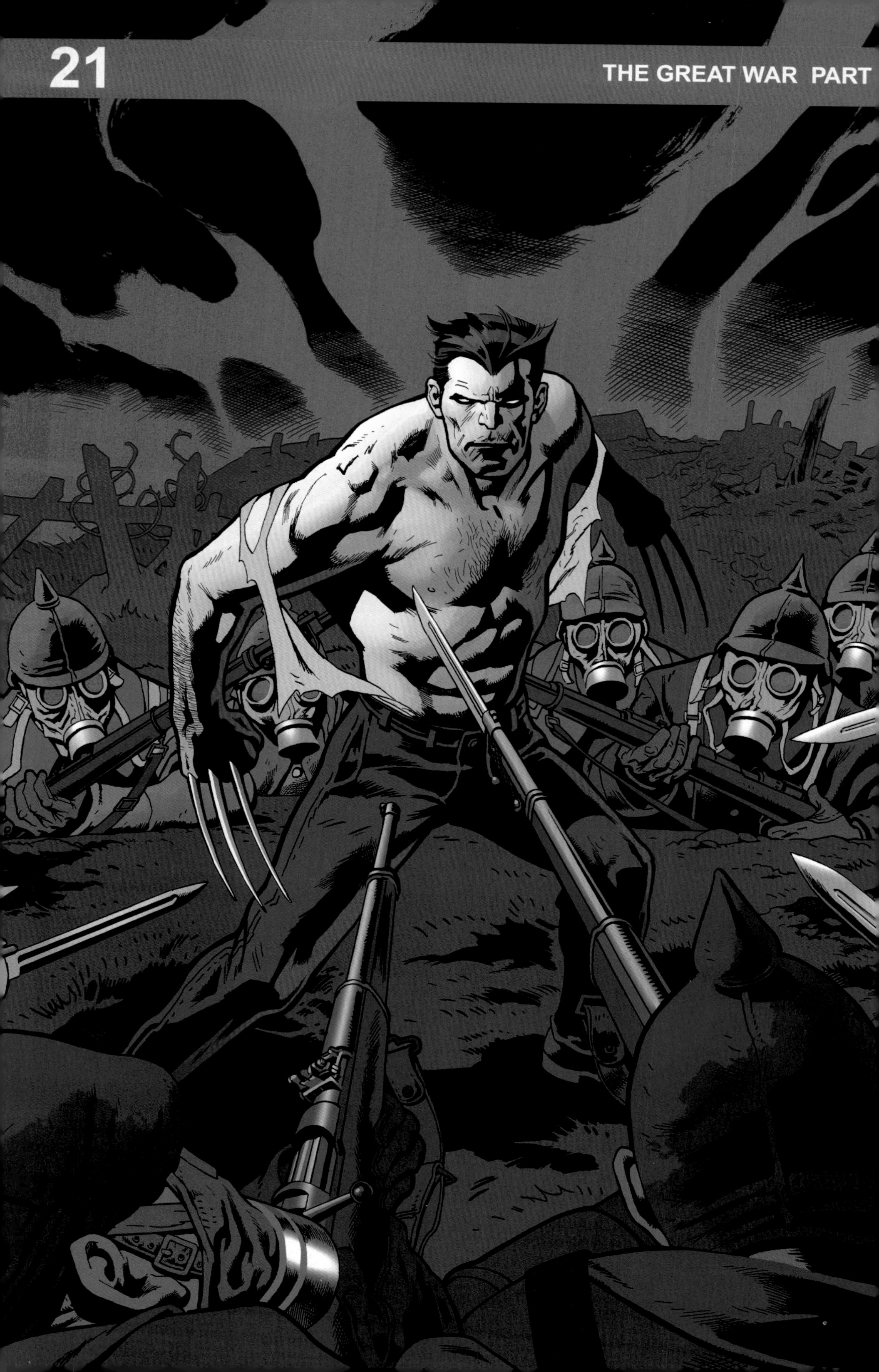

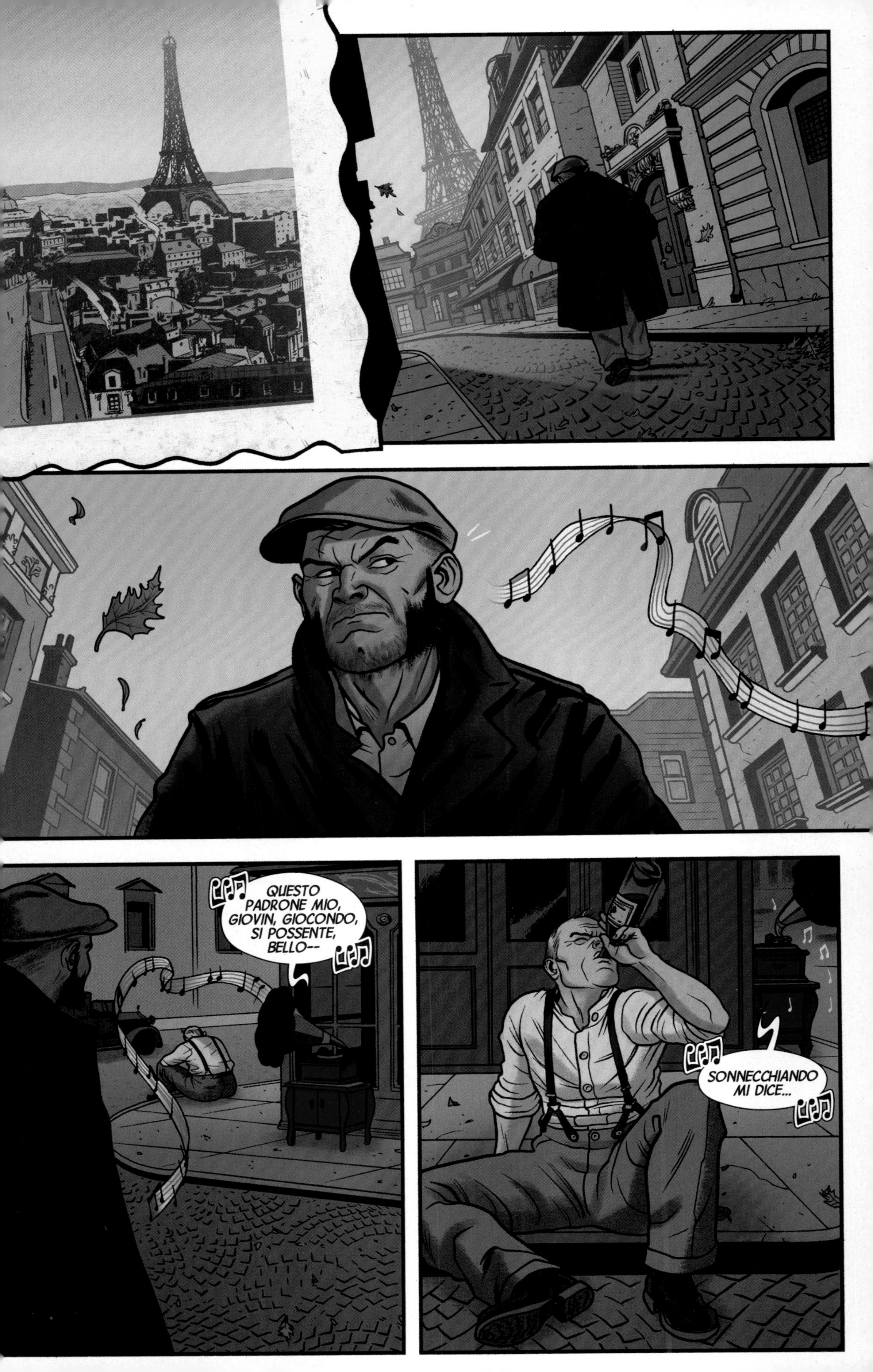
QUESTO PADRONE MIO, GIOVIN, GIOCONDO, SI POSSENTE, BELLO--
SONNECCHIANDO MI DICE...

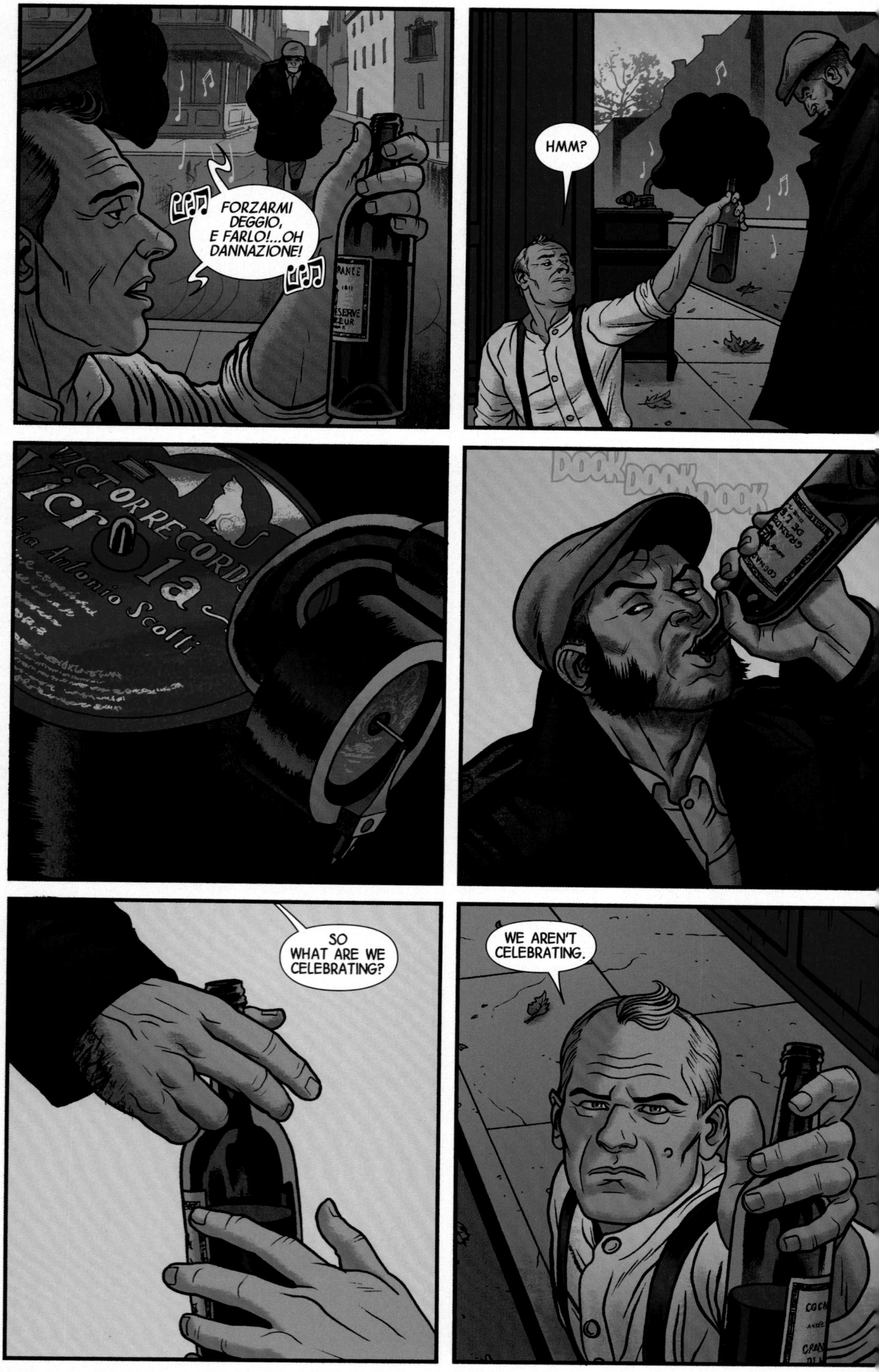

FORZARMI DEGGIO, E FARLO!...OH DANNAZIONE!
HMM?
DOOK DOOK DOOK
SO WHAT ARE WE CELEBRATING?
WE AREN'T CELEBRATING.

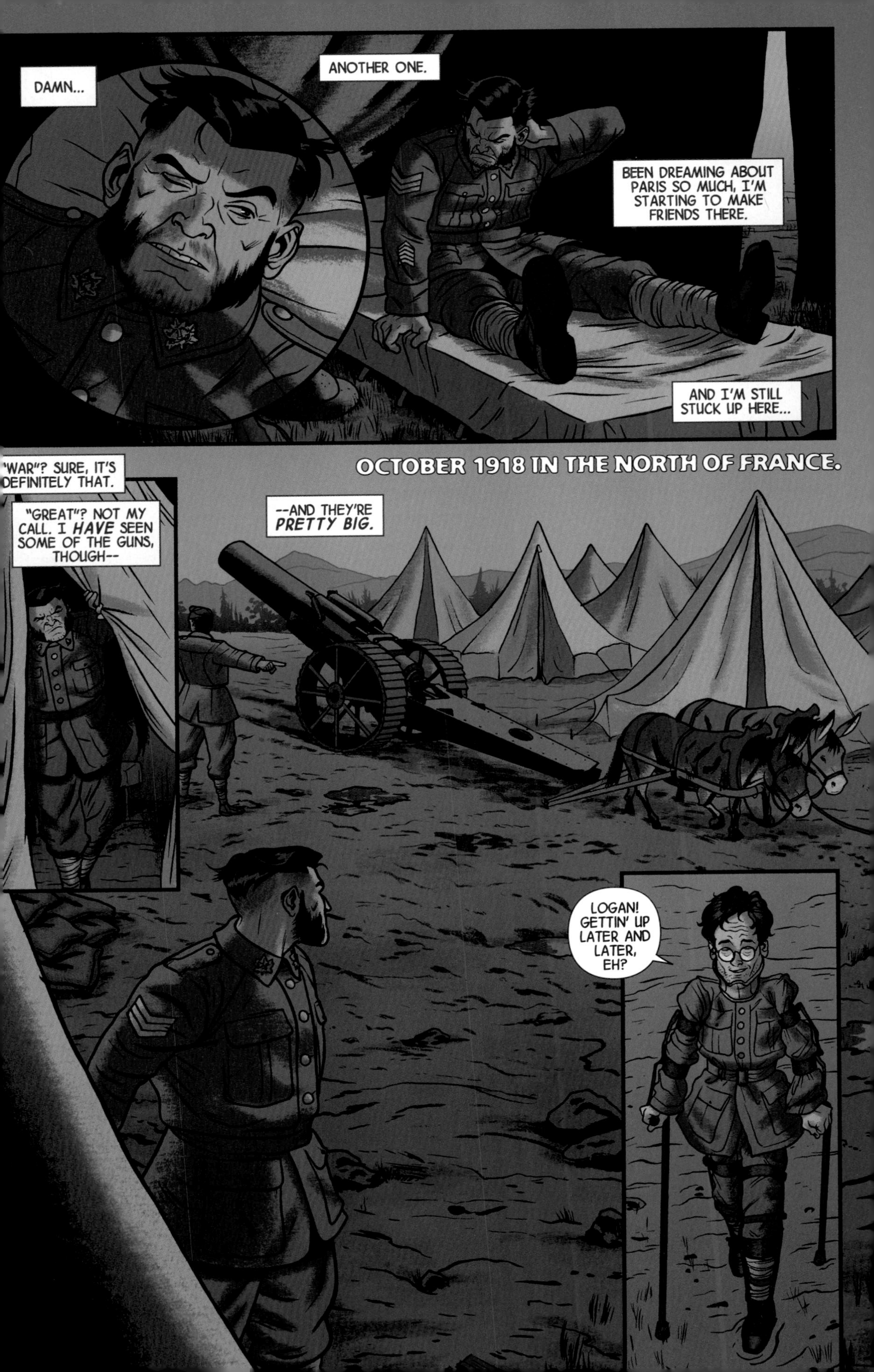
DAMN...
ANOTHER ONE.
BEEN DREAMING ABOUT PARIS SO MUCH, I'M STARTING TO MAKE FRIENDS THERE.
AND I'M STILL STUCK UP HERE...
OCTOBER 1918 IN THE NORTH OF FRANCE.
"WAR"? SURE, IT'S DEFINITELY THAT.
"GREAT"? NOT MY CALL. I HAVE SEEN SOME OF THE GUNS, THOUGH--
--AND THEY'RE PRETTY BIG.
LOGAN! GETTIN' UP LATER AND LATER, EH?

WHERE YOU OFF TO?

MESS. NEED A LITTLE BREAKFAST.

NO, NO, SERGEANT. BRIEFING IN FIVE MINUTES.

DAMN. I FORGOT.

LISTEN, LIEUTENANT, *YOU'RE* ALREADY IN THEIR HEADS. YOU KNOW WHAT THEY'RE GOING TO SAY, DON'T YOU?

HOW 'BO YOU AND SKIP T BRIEFING, SOME CH AND YOU ME IN

AND WHY WOULD I DO THAT?

WELL, YOU AN' ME, WE GOTTA STICK TOGETHER, WATCH EACH OTHER'S BACK.

JUST US TWO FREAKS AGAINST THE WORLD, EH?

I DIDN'T SAY "FREAK."

NOT OUT LOUD, NO. AND FOR THE RECORD, I'M *NOT* A FREAK. I'M CANADIAN, FIGHTIN' FOR MY COUNTRY.

IT'S MORE IMPORTANT FOR *YOU* TO BE DIFFERENT THOUGH, ISN'T IT?

YOU COULD BE PART OF SOMETHING BIGGER HERE, BUT YOU'D RATHER STICK OUT--BE "SPECIAL" WITH ME. WELL, I'M NOT HAVIN' IT!

SEE, I'M IN A BROTHERHOOD LARGER THAN TWO. MY MEN NEED ME-- AND MY TALENTS-- AND I NEED THEM. I *LIKE* THAT, LOGAN.

WE'RE LATE FOR THAT BRIEFING.

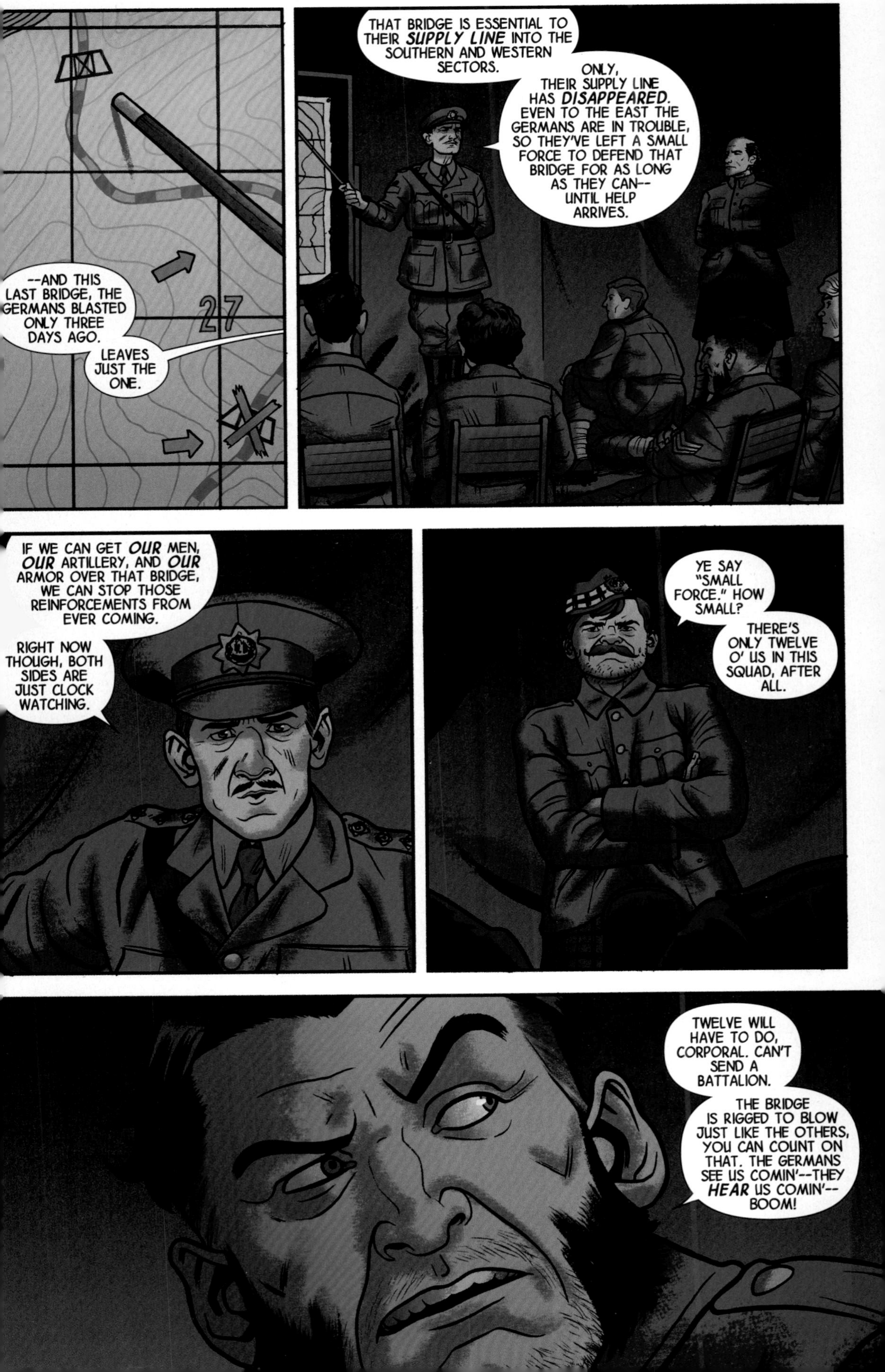
--AND THIS LAST BRIDGE, THE GERMANS BLASTED ONLY THREE DAYS AGO.
LEAVES JUST THE ONE.
THAT BRIDGE IS ESSENTIAL TO THEIR SUPPLY LINE INTO THE SOUTHERN AND WESTERN SECTORS.
ONLY, THEIR SUPPLY LINE HAS DISAPPEARED. EVEN TO THE EAST THE GERMANS ARE IN TROUBLE, SO THEY'VE LEFT A SMALL FORCE TO DEFEND THAT BRIDGE FOR AS LONG AS THEY CAN-- UNTIL HELP ARRIVES.
IF WE CAN GET OUR MEN, OUR ARTILLERY, AND OUR ARMOR OVER THAT BRIDGE, WE CAN STOP THOSE REINFORCEMENTS FROM EVER COMING.
RIGHT NOW THOUGH, BOTH SIDES ARE JUST CLOCK WATCHING.
YE SAY "SMALL FORCE." HOW SMALL?
THERE'S ONLY TWELVE O' US IN THIS SQUAD, AFTER ALL.
TWELVE WILL HAVE TO DO, CORPORAL. CAN'T SEND A BATTALION.
THE BRIDGE IS RIGGED TO BLOW JUST LIKE THE OTHERS, YOU CAN COUNT ON THAT. THE GERMANS SEE US COMIN'--THEY HEAR US COMIN'-- BOOM!

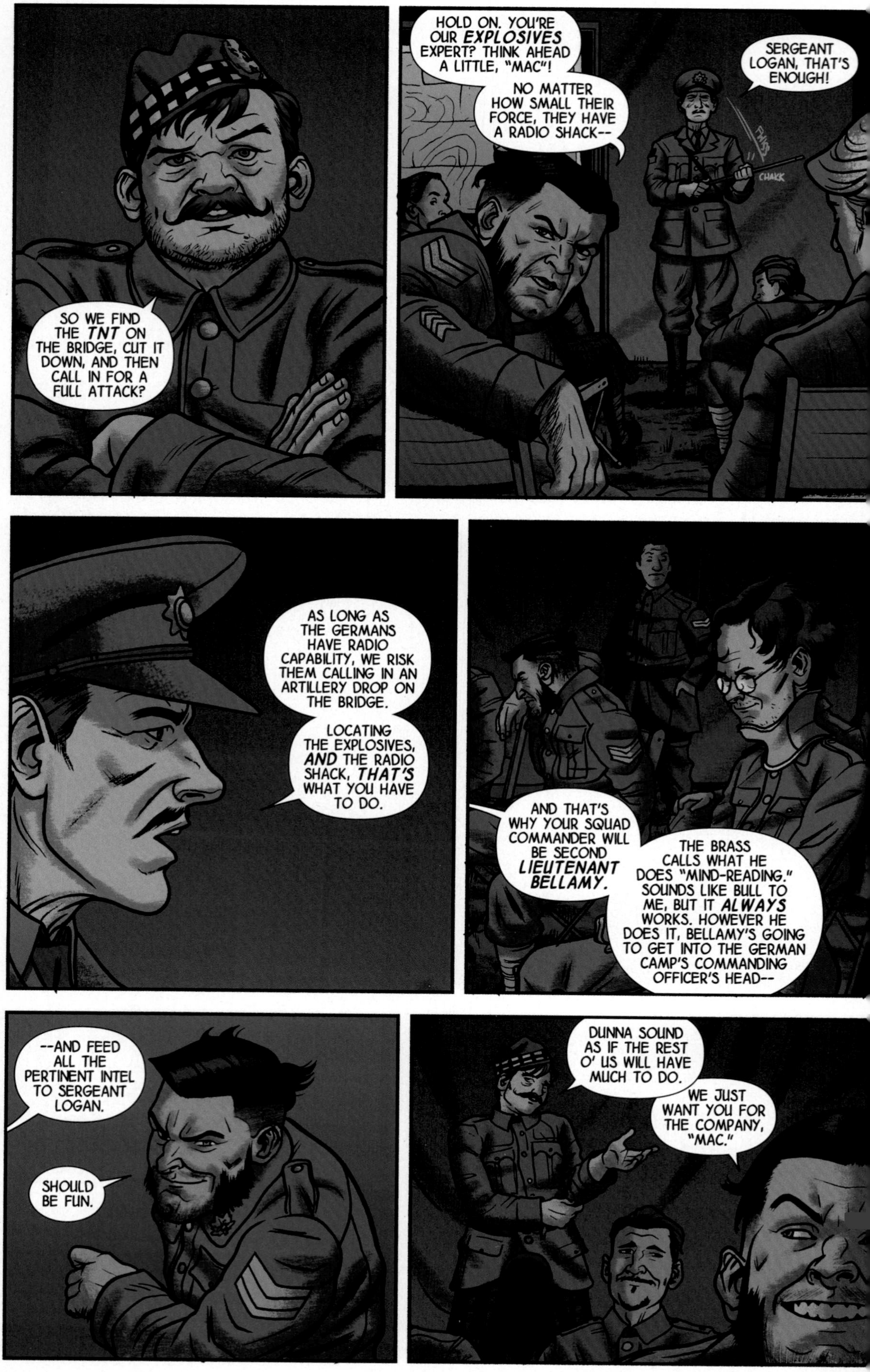
SO WE FIND THE *TNT* ON THE BRIDGE, CUT IT DOWN, AND THEN CALL IN FOR A FULL ATTACK?
HOLD ON. YOU'RE OUR *EXPLOSIVES* EXPERT? THINK AHEAD A LITTLE, "MAC"!
NO MATTER HOW SMALL THEIR FORCE, THEY HAVE A RADIO SHACK--
FWISS
CHAKK
SERGEANT LOGAN, THAT'S ENOUGH!
AS LONG AS THE GERMANS HAVE RADIO CAPABILITY, WE RISK THEM CALLING IN AN ARTILLERY DROP ON THE BRIDGE.
LOCATING THE EXPLOSIVES, *AND* THE RADIO SHACK, *THAT'S* WHAT YOU HAVE TO DO.
AND THAT'S WHY YOUR SQUAD COMMANDER WILL BE SECOND *LIEUTENANT BELLAMY.*
THE BRASS CALLS WHAT HE DOES "MIND-READING." SOUNDS LIKE BULL TO ME, BUT IT *ALWAYS* WORKS. HOWEVER HE DOES IT, BELLAMY'S GOING TO GET INTO THE GERMAN CAMP'S COMMANDING OFFICER'S HEAD--
--AND FEED ALL THE PERTINENT INTEL TO SERGEANT LOGAN.
SHOULD BE FUN.
DUNNA SOUND AS IF THE REST O' US WILL HAVE MUCH TO DO.
WE JUST WANT YOU FOR THE COMPANY, "MAC."

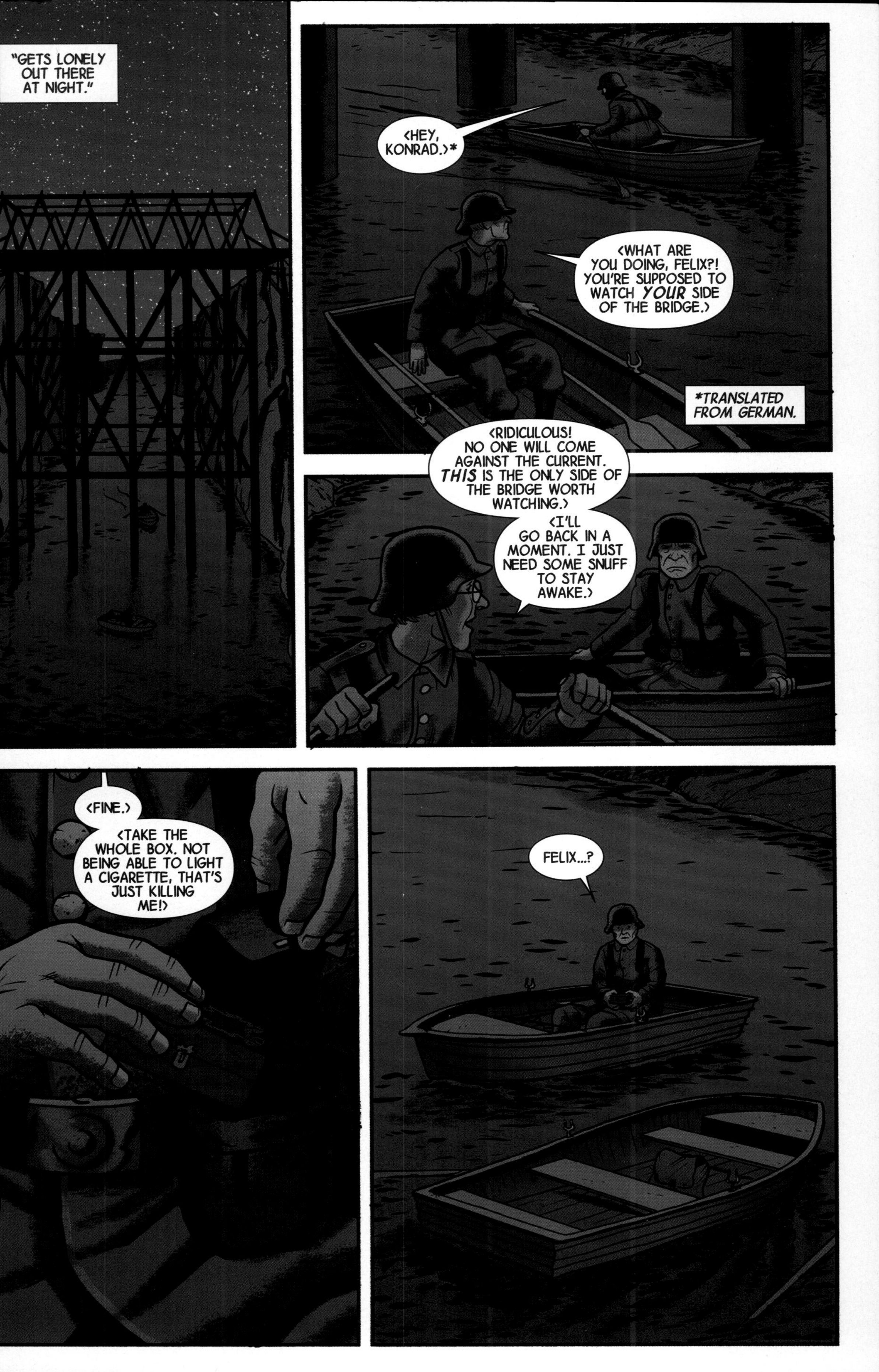
"GETS LONELY OUT THERE AT NIGHT."
<HEY, KONRAD.>*
<WHAT ARE YOU DOING, FELIX?! YOU'RE SUPPOSED TO WATCH YOUR SIDE OF THE BRIDGE.>
*TRANSLATED FROM GERMAN.
<RIDICULOUS! NO ONE WILL COME AGAINST THE CURRENT. THIS IS THE ONLY SIDE OF THE BRIDGE WORTH WATCHING.>
<I'LL GO BACK IN A MOMENT. I JUST NEED SOME SNUFF TO STAY AWAKE.>
<FINE.>
<TAKE THE WHOLE BOX. NOT BEING ABLE TO LIGHT A CIGARETTE, THAT'S JUST KILLING ME!>
FELIX...?

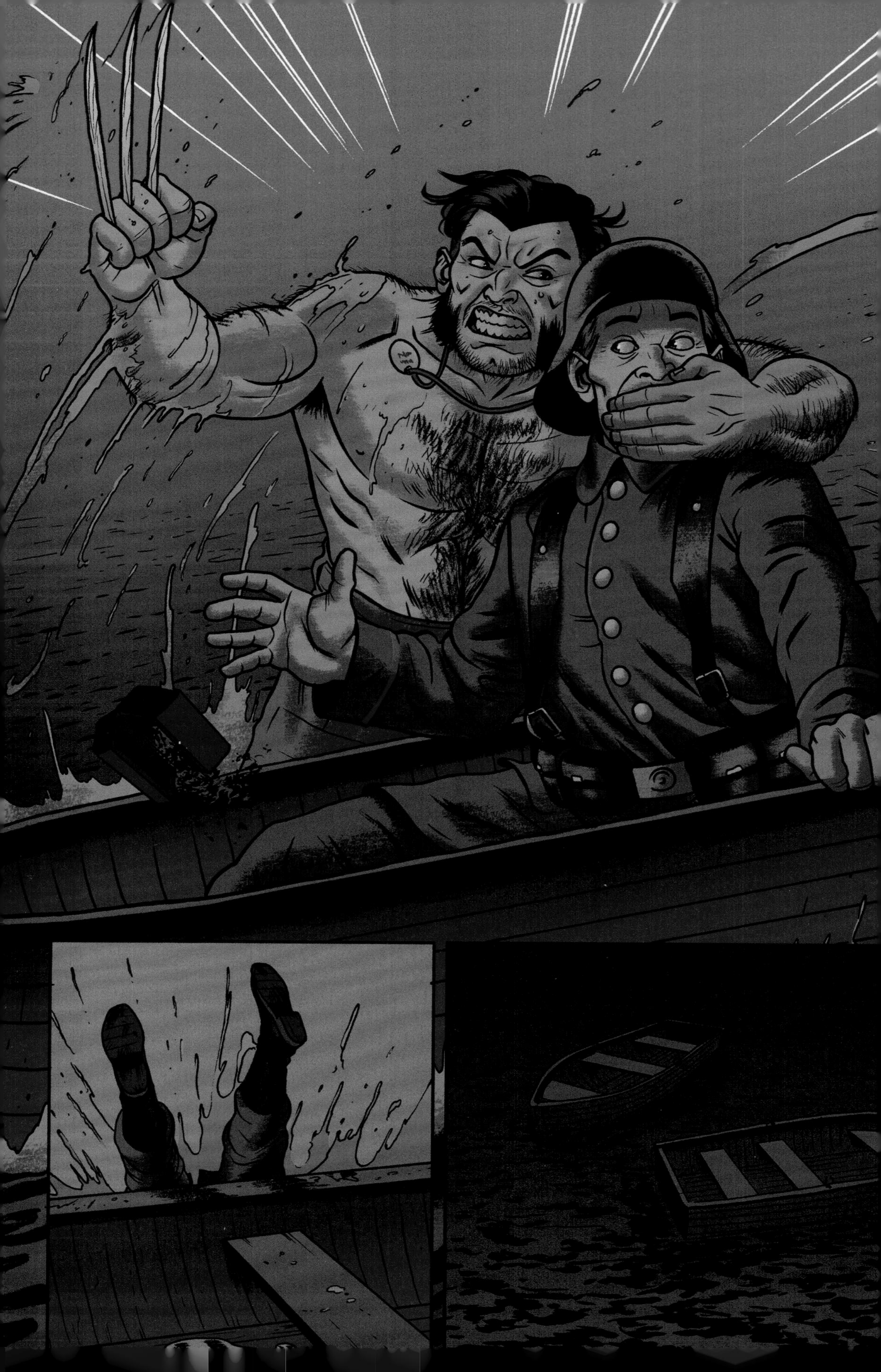

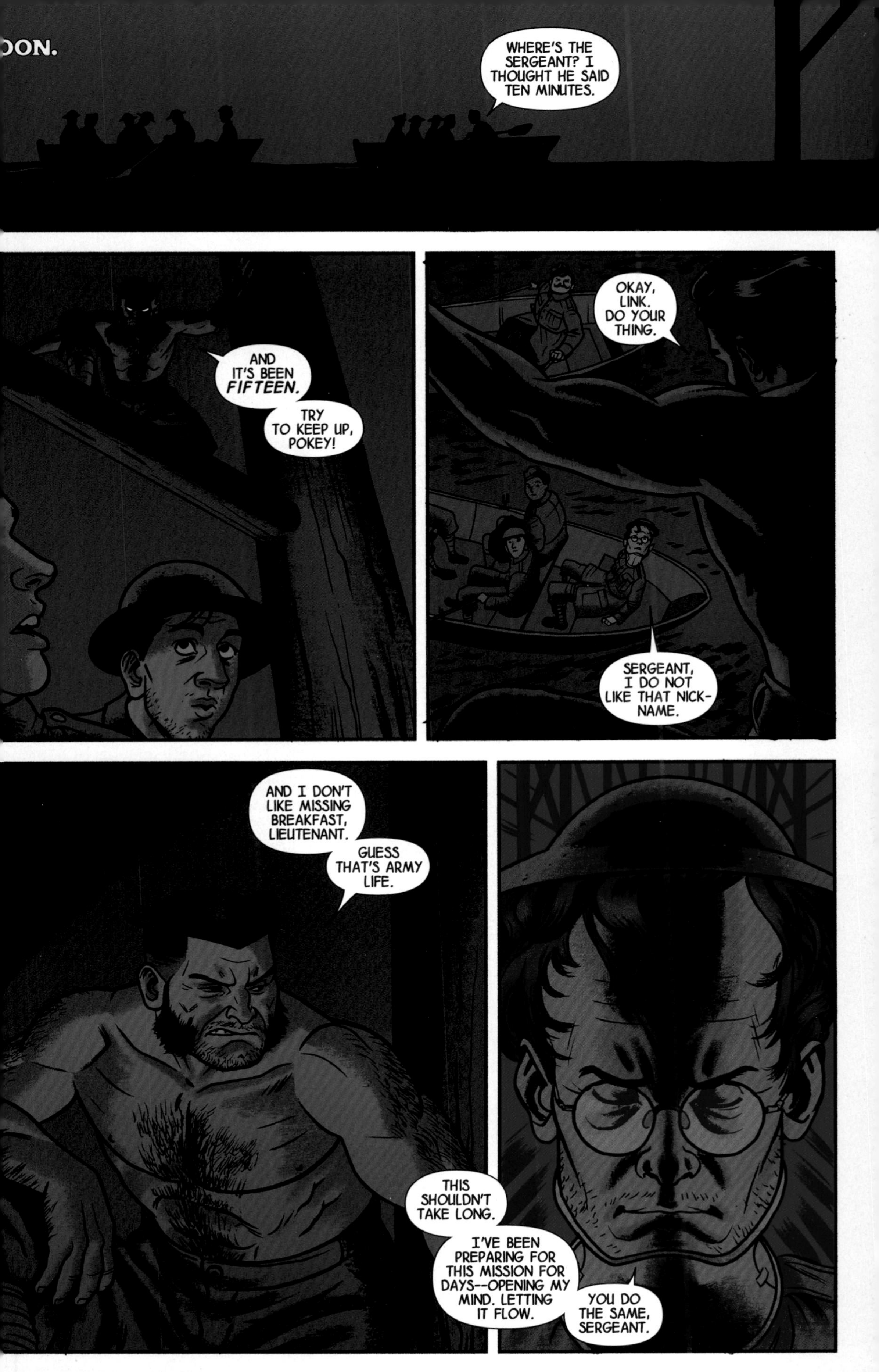
OON.
WHERE'S THE SERGEANT? I THOUGHT HE SAID TEN MINUTES.
AND IT'S BEEN *FIFTEEN.*
TRY TO KEEP UP, POKEY!
OKAY, LINK. DO YOUR THING.
SERGEANT, I DO NOT LIKE THAT NICK-NAME.
AND I DON'T LIKE MISSING BREAKFAST, LIEUTENANT.
GUESS THAT'S ARMY LIFE.
THIS SHOULDN'T TAKE LONG.
I'VE BEEN PREPARING FOR THIS MISSION FOR DAYS--OPENING MY MIND. LETTING IT FLOW.
YOU DO THE SAME, SERGEANT.

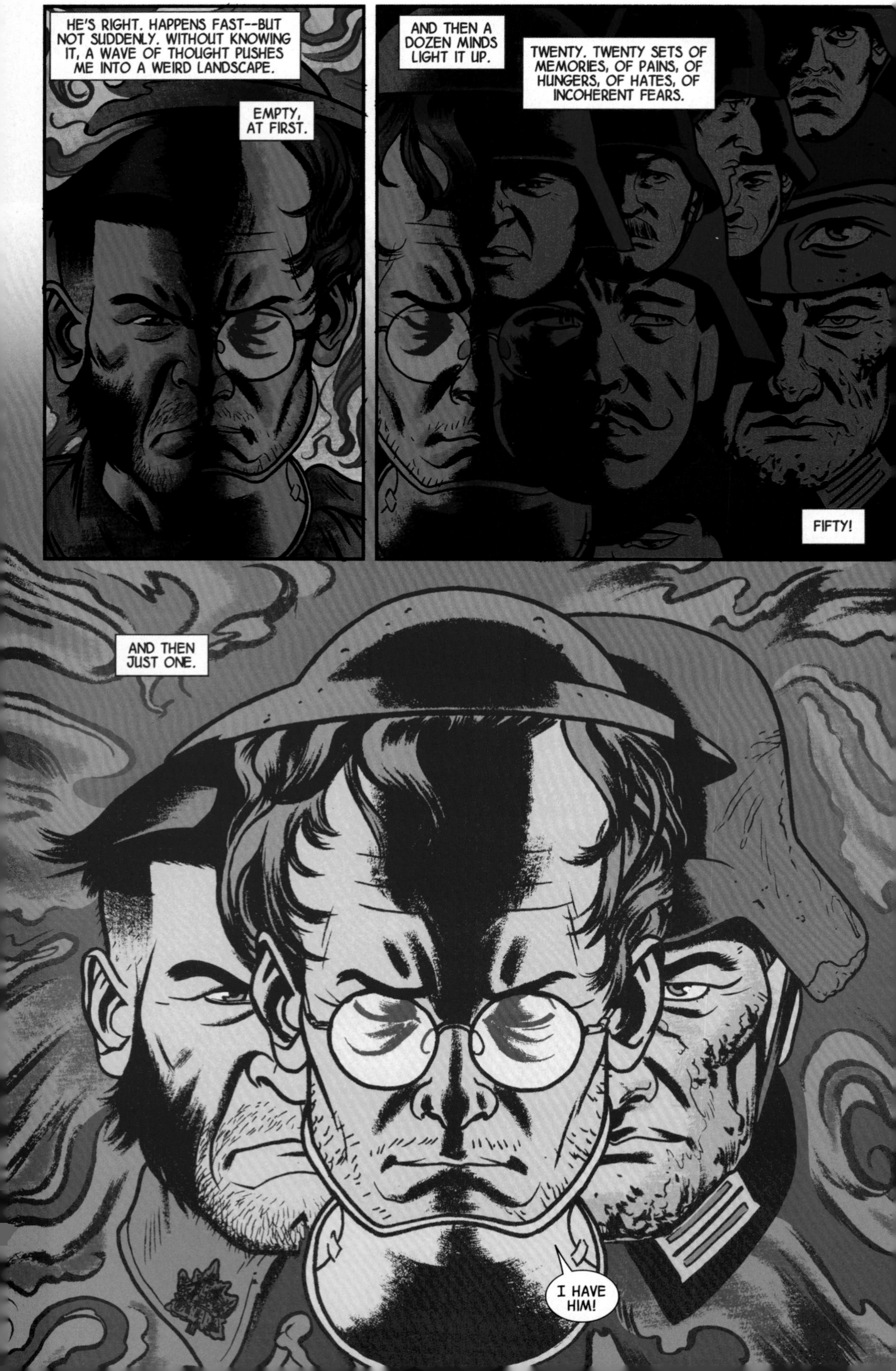
HE'S RIGHT. HAPPENS FAST--BUT NOT SUDDENLY. WITHOUT KNOWING IT, A WAVE OF THOUGHT PUSHES ME INTO A WEIRD LANDSCAPE.
EMPTY, AT FIRST.
AND THEN A DOZEN MINDS LIGHT IT UP.
TWENTY. TWENTY SETS OF MEMORIES, OF PAINS, OF HUNGERS, OF HATES, OF INCOHERENT FEARS.
FIFTY!
AND THEN JUST ONE.
I HAVE HIM!

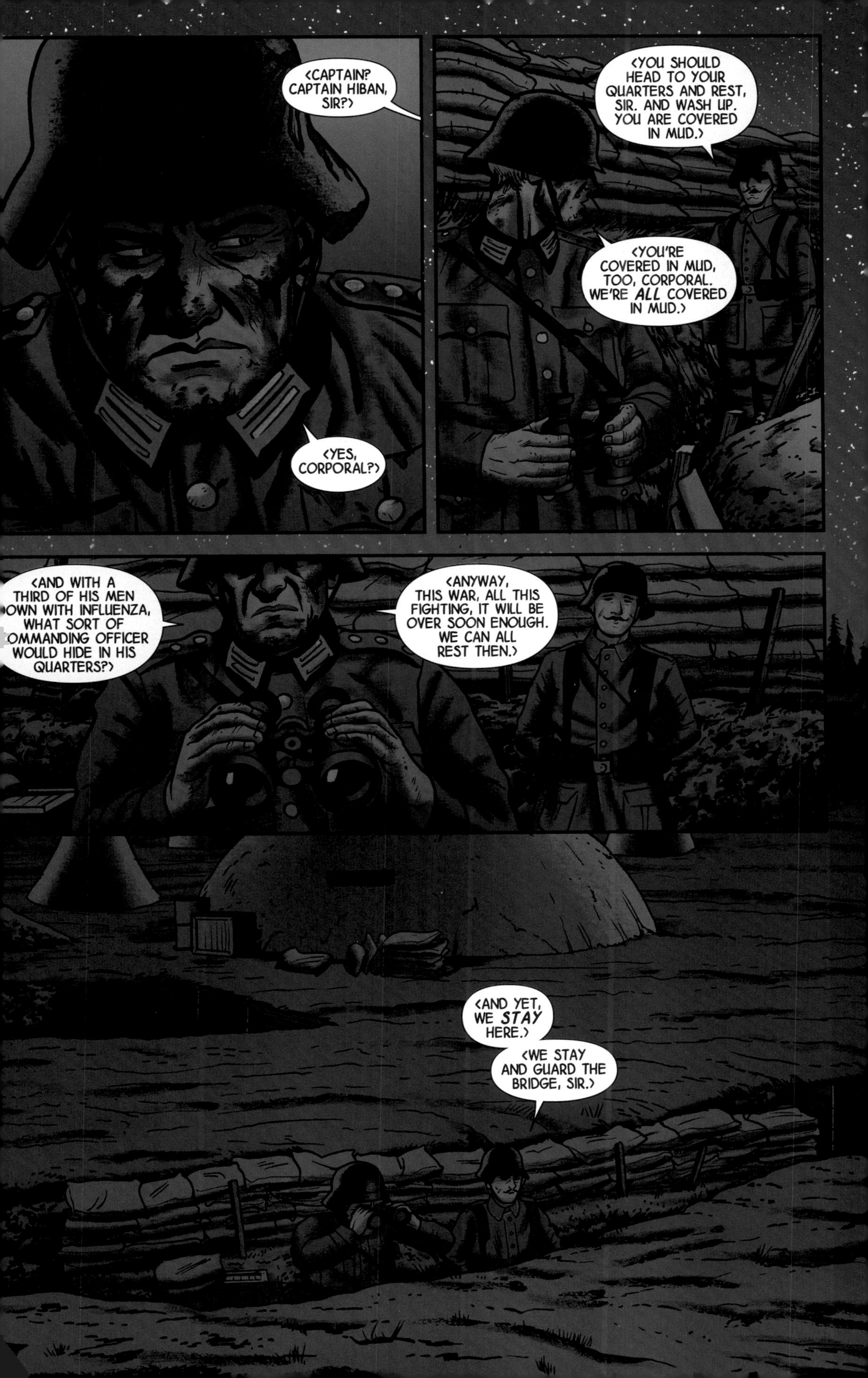
<CAPTAIN? CAPTAIN HIBAN, SIR?>
<YES, CORPORAL?>
<YOU SHOULD HEAD TO YOUR QUARTERS AND REST, SIR. AND WASH UP. YOU ARE COVERED IN MUD.>
<YOU'RE COVERED IN MUD, TOO, CORPORAL. WE'RE ALL COVERED IN MUD.>
<AND WITH A THIRD OF HIS MEN OWN WITH INFLUENZA, WHAT SORT OF OMMANDING OFFICER WOULD HIDE IN HIS QUARTERS?>
<ANYWAY, THIS WAR, ALL THIS FIGHTING, IT WILL BE OVER SOON ENOUGH. WE CAN ALL REST THEN.>
<AND YET, WE STAY HERE.>
<WE STAY AND GUARD THE BRIDGE, SIR.>

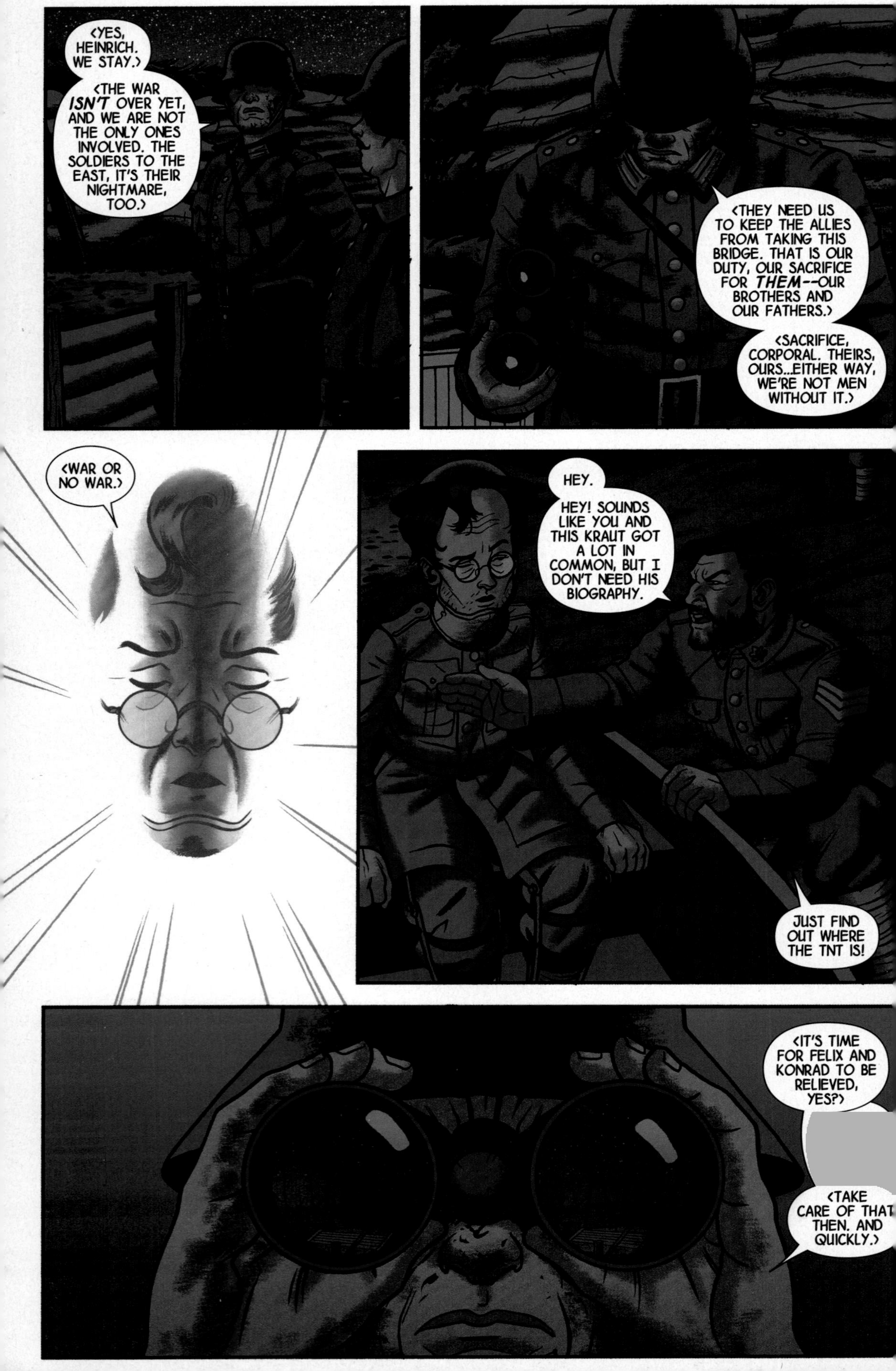

<YES, HEINRICH. WE STAY.>
<THE WAR ISN'T OVER YET, AND WE ARE NOT THE ONLY ONES INVOLVED. THE SOLDIERS TO THE EAST, IT'S THEIR NIGHTMARE, TOO.>
<THEY NEED US TO KEEP THE ALLIES FROM TAKING THIS BRIDGE. THAT IS OUR DUTY, OUR SACRIFICE FOR THEM--OUR BROTHERS AND OUR FATHERS.>
<SACRIFICE, CORPORAL. THEIRS, OURS...EITHER WAY, WE'RE NOT MEN WITHOUT IT.>
<WAR OR NO WAR.>
HEY.
HEY! SOUNDS LIKE YOU AND THIS KRAUT GOT A LOT IN COMMON, BUT I DON'T NEED HIS BIOGRAPHY.
JUST FIND OUT WHERE THE TNT IS!
<IT'S TIME FOR FELIX AND KONRAD TO BE RELIEVED, YES?>
<TAKE CARE OF THAT THEN. AND QUICKLY.>

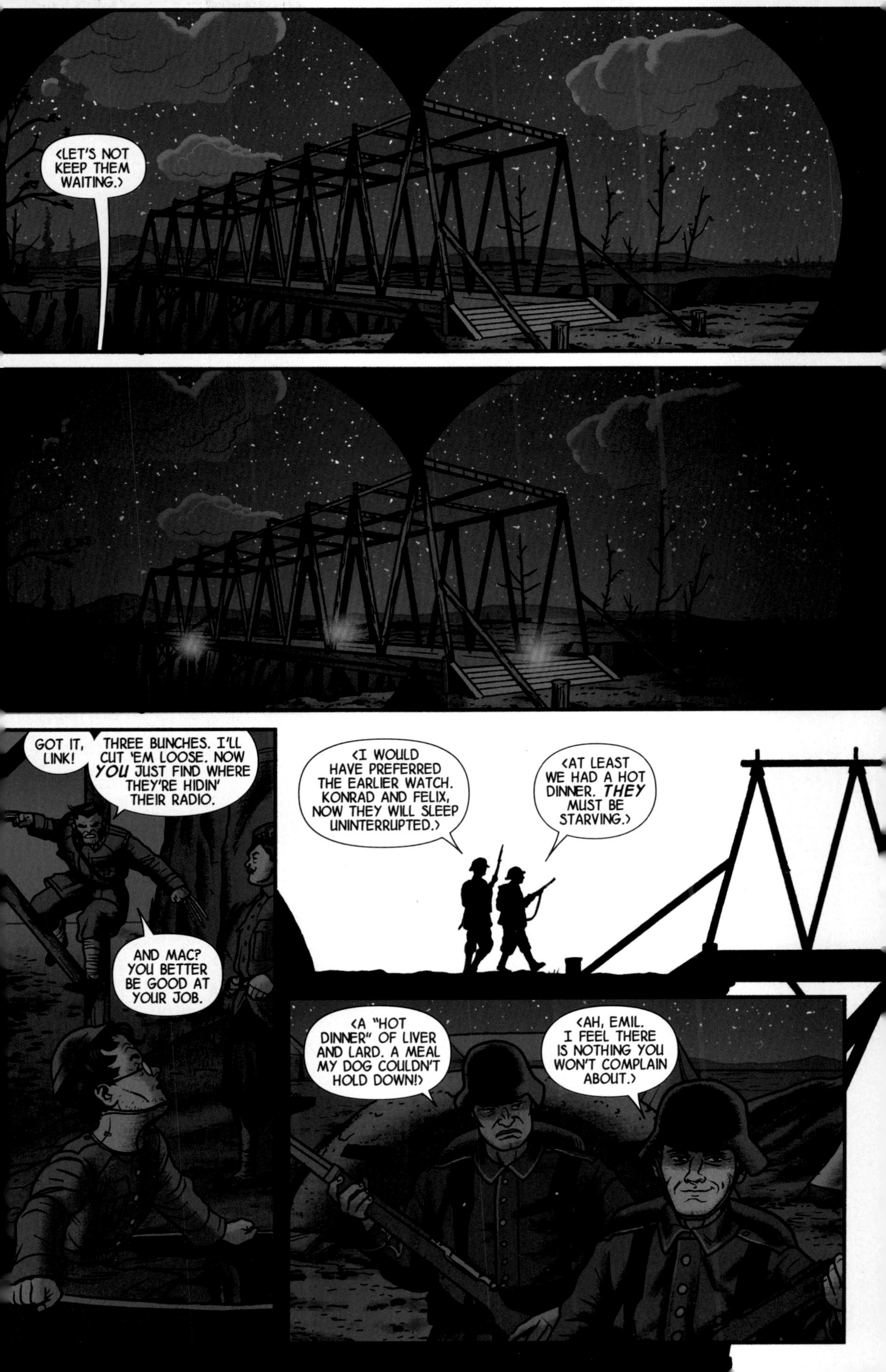

<LET'S NOT KEEP THEM WAITING.>
GOT IT, LINK!
THREE BUNCHES. I'LL CUT 'EM LOOSE. NOW YOU JUST FIND WHERE THEY'RE HIDIN' THEIR RADIO.
AND MAC? YOU BETTER BE GOOD AT YOUR JOB.
<I WOULD HAVE PREFERRED THE EARLIER WATCH. KONRAD AND FELIX, NOW THEY WILL SLEEP UNINTERRUPTED.>
<AT LEAST WE HAD A HOT DINNER. THEY MUST BE STARVING.>
<A "HOT DINNER" OF LIVER AND LARD. A MEAL MY DOG COULDN'T HOLD DOWN!>
<AH, EMIL. I FEEL THERE IS NOTHING YOU WON'T COMPLAIN ABOUT.>

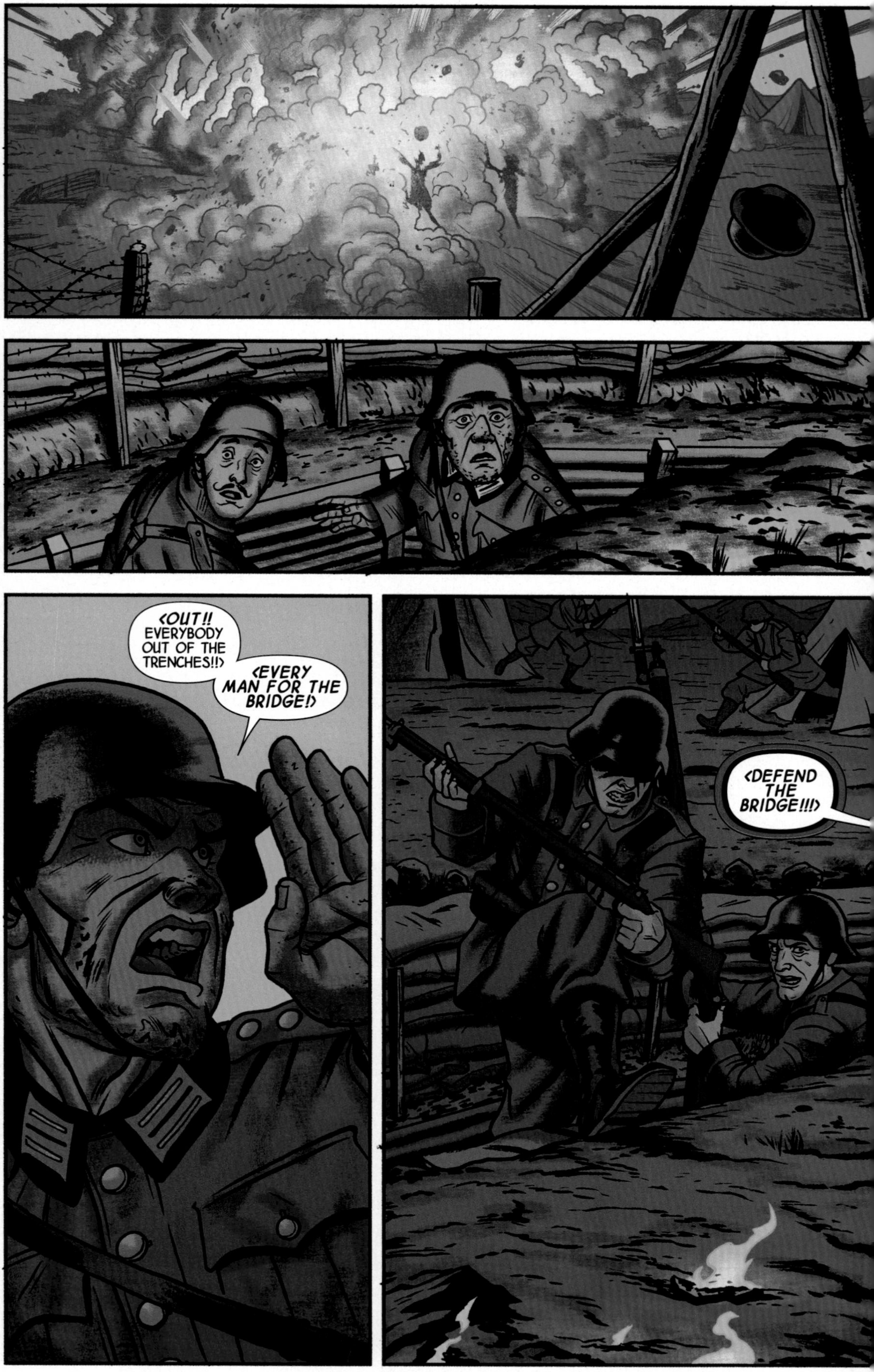
<OUT!! EVERYBODY OUT OF THE TRENCHES!!>
<EVERY MAN FOR THE BRIDGE!>
<DEFEND THE BRIDGE!!!>

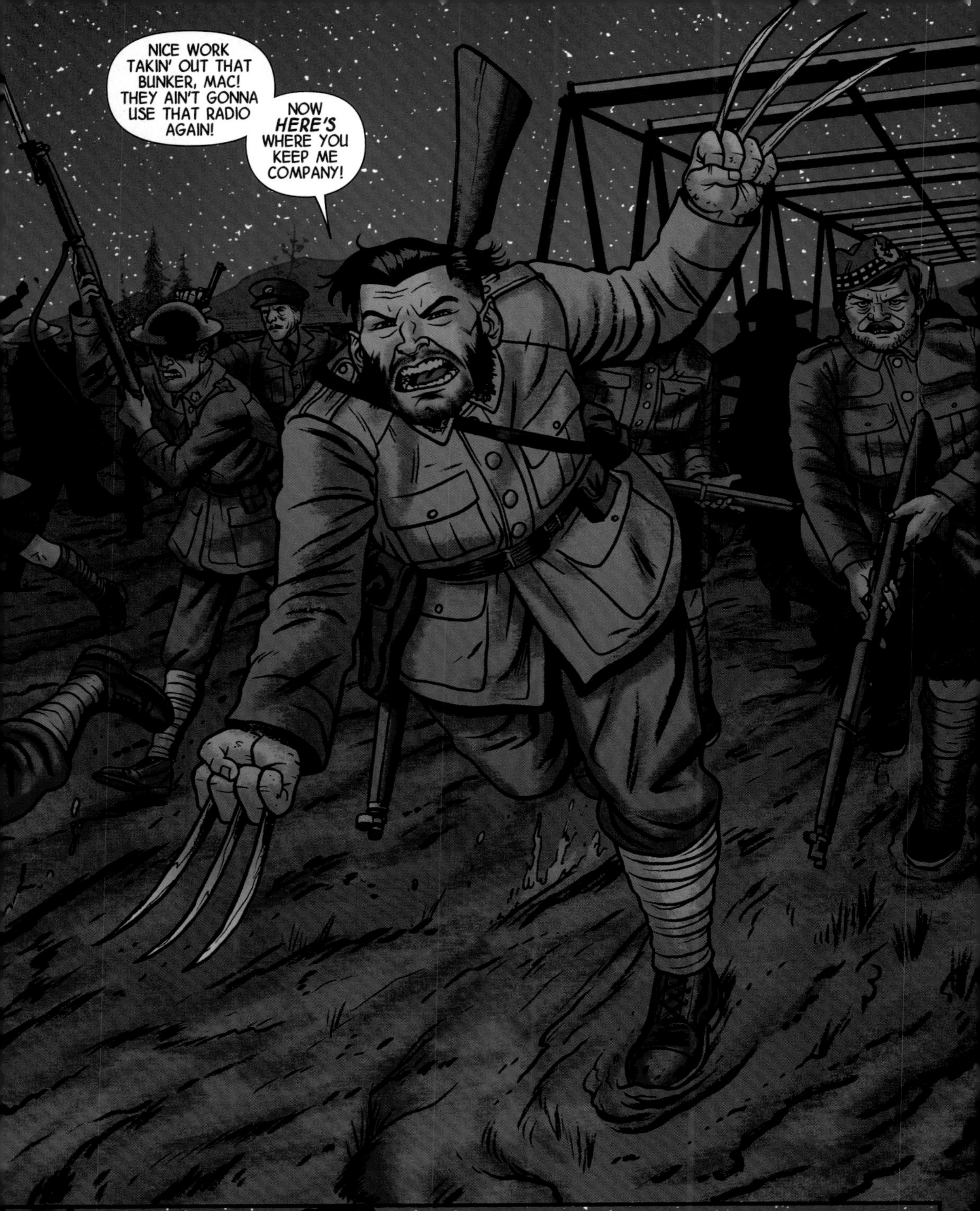
NICE WORK TAKIN' OUT THAT BUNKER, MAC! THEY AIN'T GONNA USE THAT RADIO AGAIN!
NOW *HERE'S* WHERE YOU KEEP ME COMPANY!

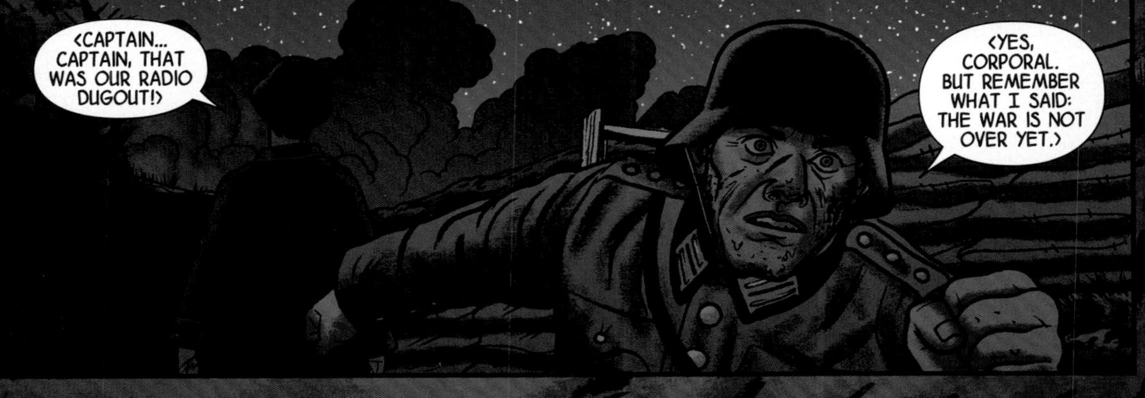
<CAPTAIN... CAPTAIN, THAT WAS OUR RADIO DUGOUT!>
<YES, CORPORAL. BUT REMEMBER WHAT I SAID: THE WAR IS NOT OVER YET.>

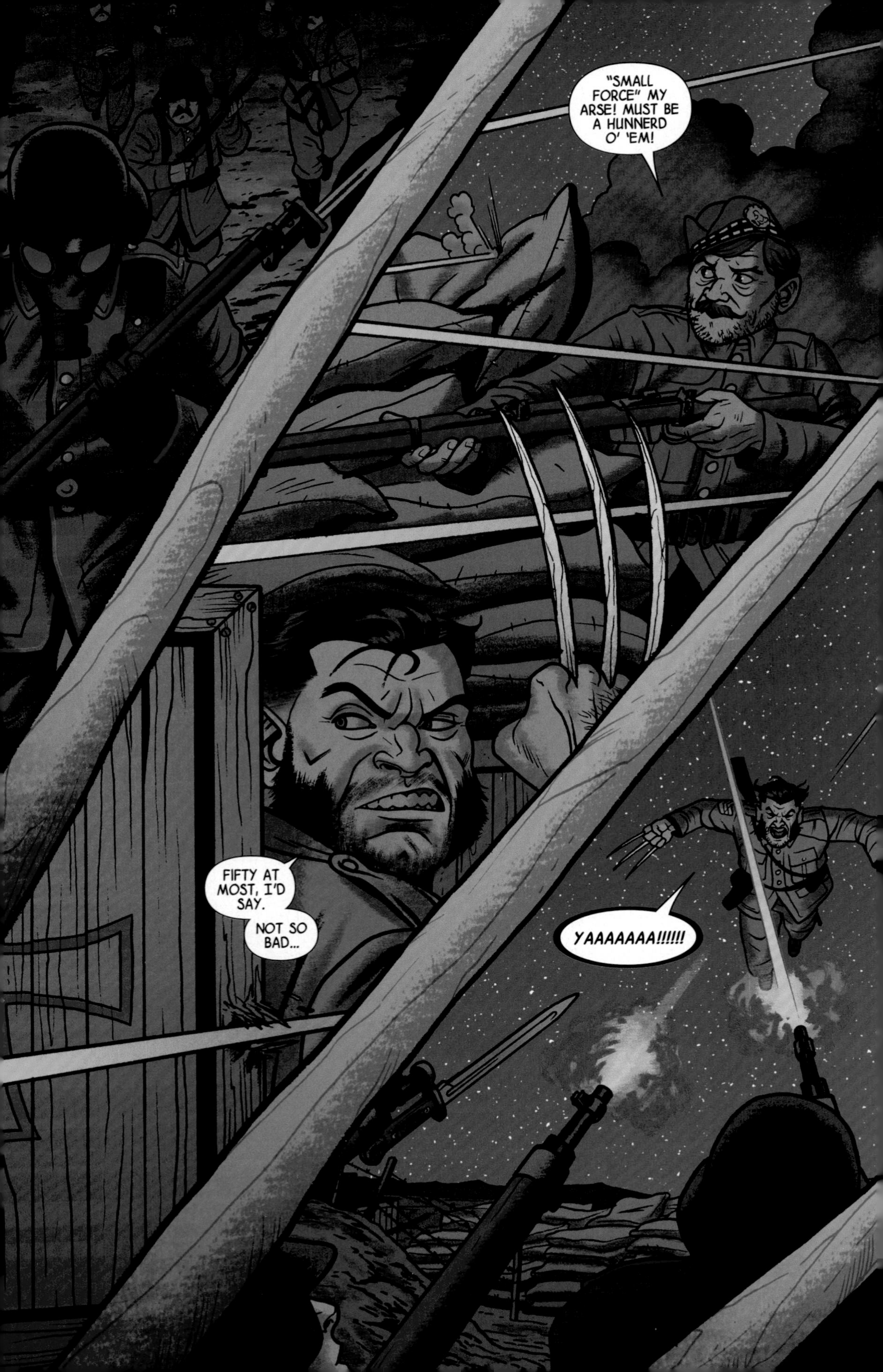
"SMALL FORCE" MY ARSE! MUST BE A HUNNERD O' 'EM!
FIFTY AT MOST, I'D SAY.
NOT SO BAD...
YAAAAAAA!!!!!!

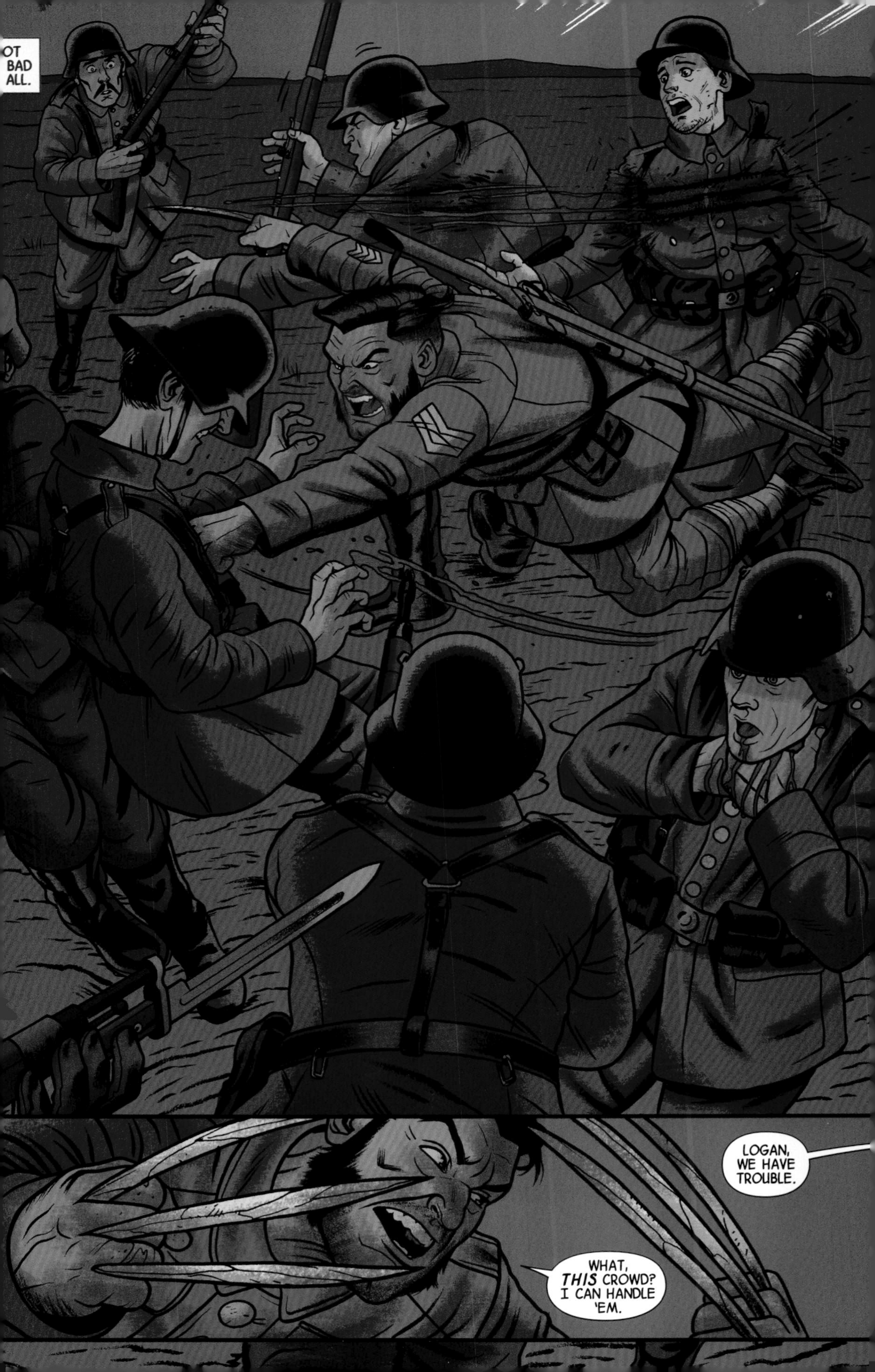
OT BAD ALL.
LOGAN, WE HAVE TROUBLE.
WHAT, THIS CROWD? I CAN HANDLE 'EM.

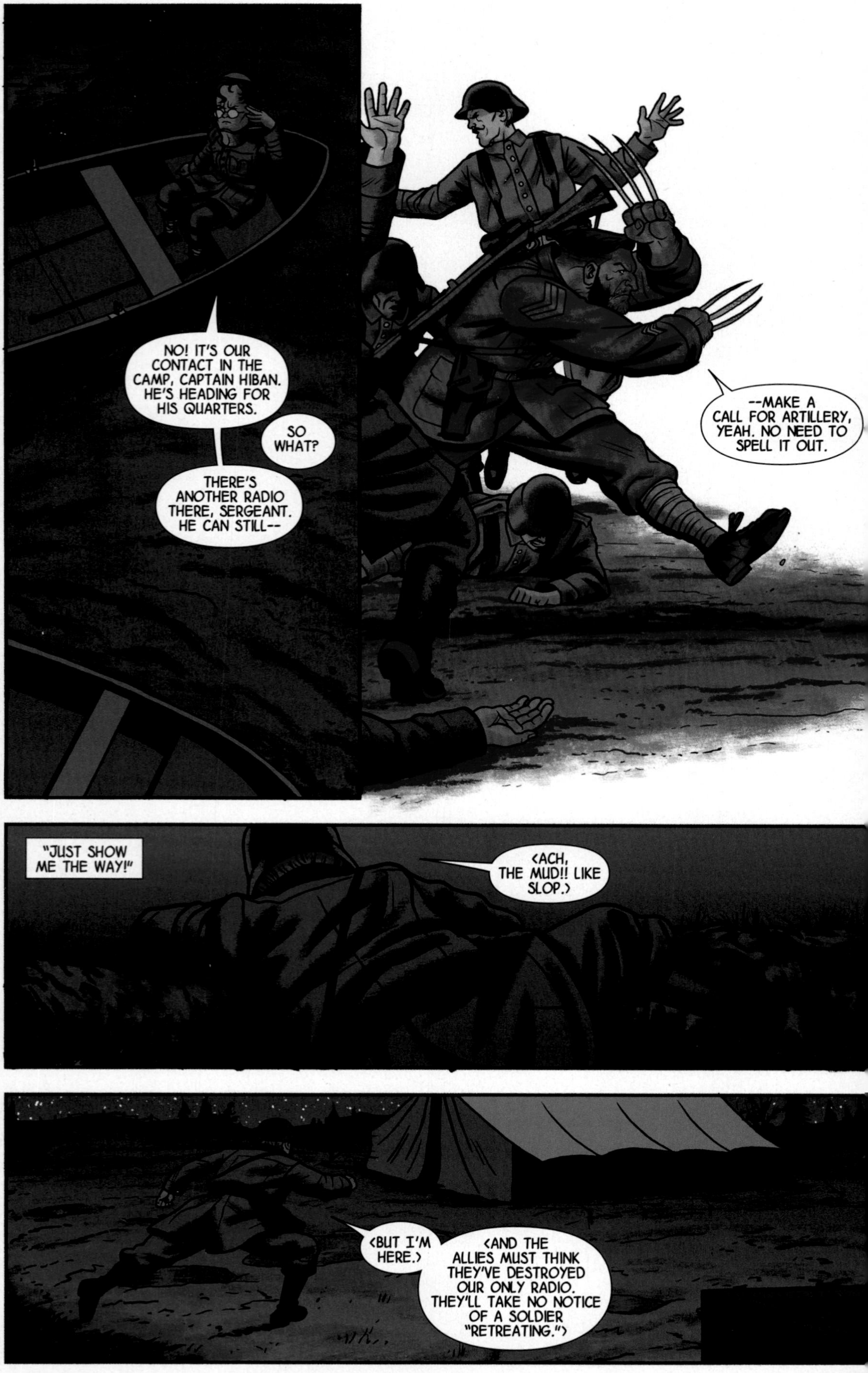
NO! IT'S OUR CONTACT IN THE CAMP, CAPTAIN HIBAN. HE'S HEADING FOR HIS QUARTERS.
SO WHAT?
THERE'S ANOTHER RADIO THERE, SERGEANT. HE CAN STILL--
--MAKE A CALL FOR ARTILLERY, YEAH. NO NEED TO SPELL IT OUT.
"JUST SHOW ME THE WAY!"
<ACH, THE MUD!! LIKE SLOP.>
<BUT I'M HERE.>
<AND THE ALLIES MUST THINK THEY'VE DESTROYED OUR ONLY RADIO. THEY'LL TAKE NO NOTICE OF A SOLDIER "RETREATING.">

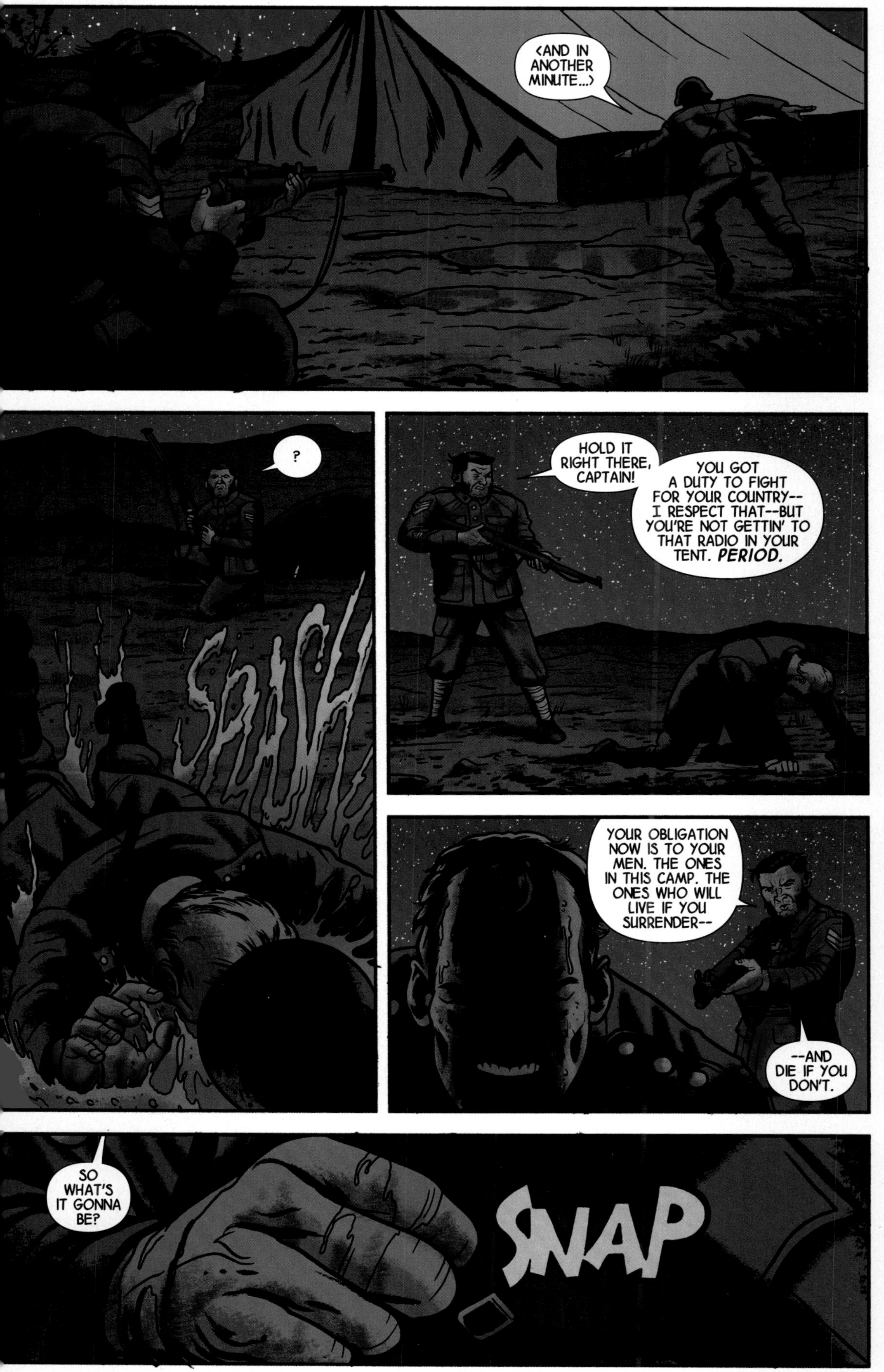

<AND IN ANOTHER MINUTE...>
?
SPASH
HOLD IT RIGHT THERE, CAPTAIN!
YOU GOT A DUTY TO FIGHT FOR YOUR COUNTRY-- I RESPECT THAT--BUT YOU'RE NOT GETTIN' TO THAT RADIO IN YOUR TENT. PERIOD.
YOUR OBLIGATION NOW IS TO YOUR MEN. THE ONES IN THIS CAMP. THE ONES WHO WILL LIVE IF YOU SURRENDER--
--AND DIE IF YOU DON'T.
SO WHAT'S IT GONNA BE?
SNAP

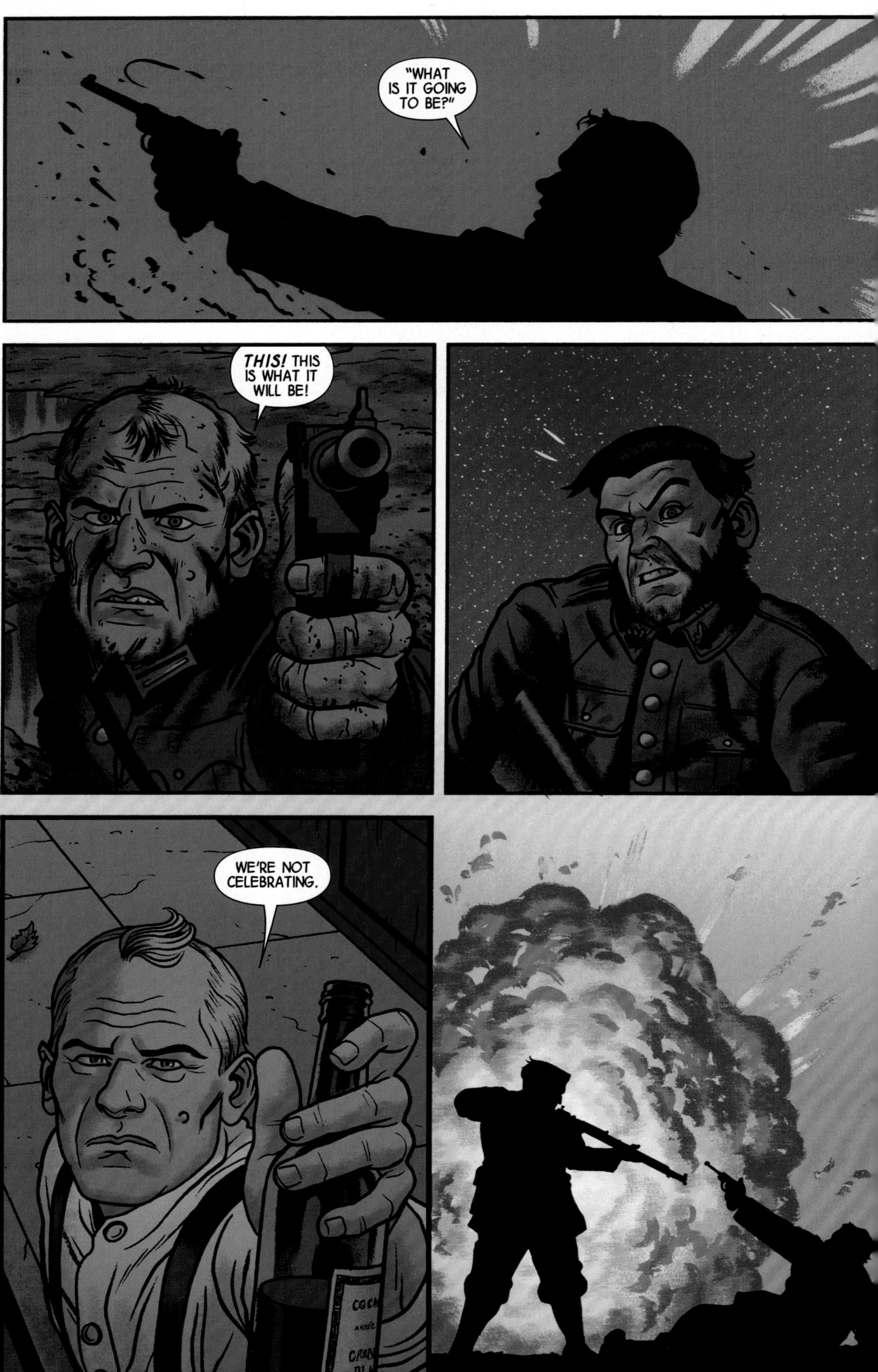
"WHAT IS IT GOING TO BE?"
THIS! THIS IS WHAT IT WILL BE!
WE'RE NOT CELEBRATING.

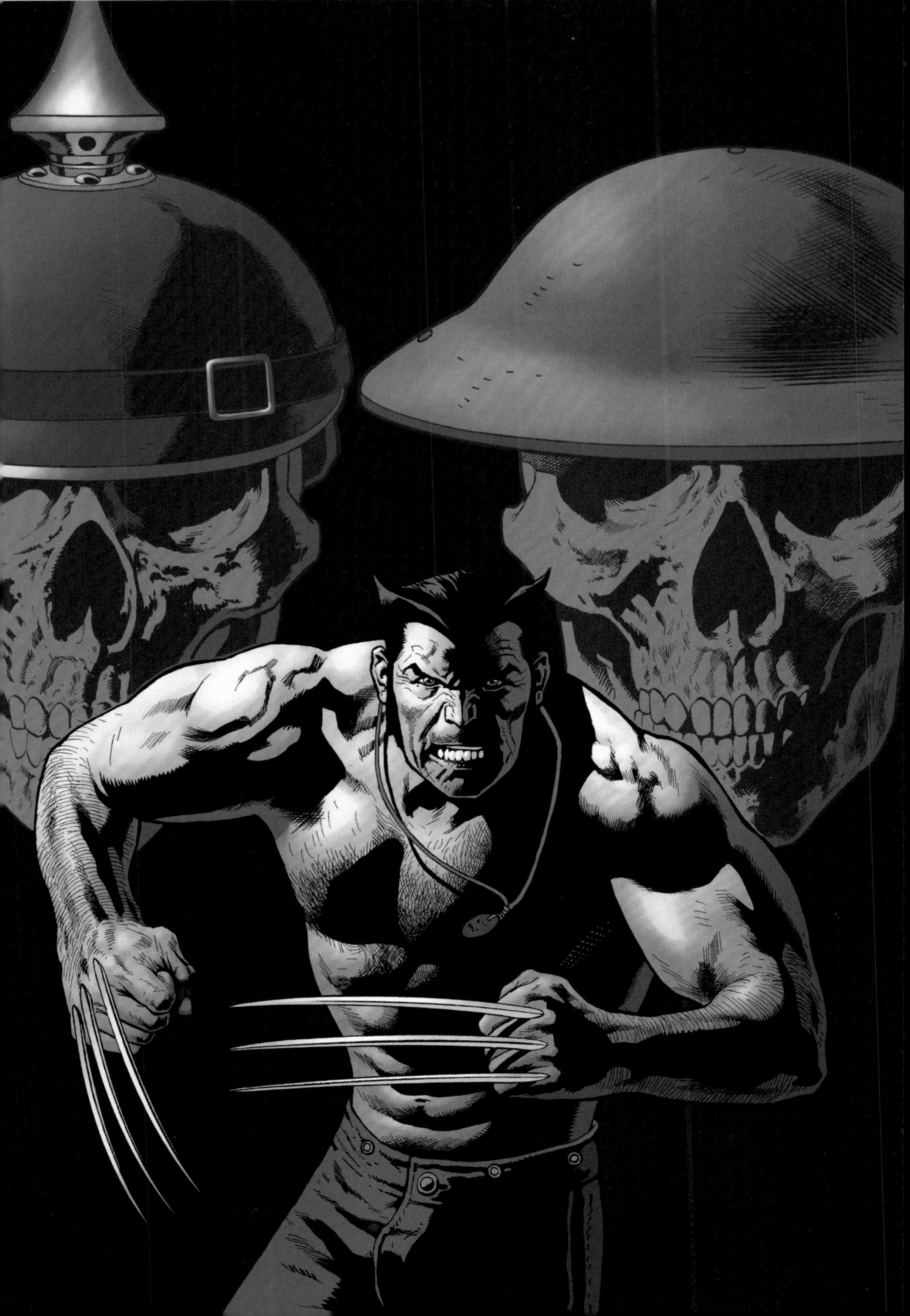

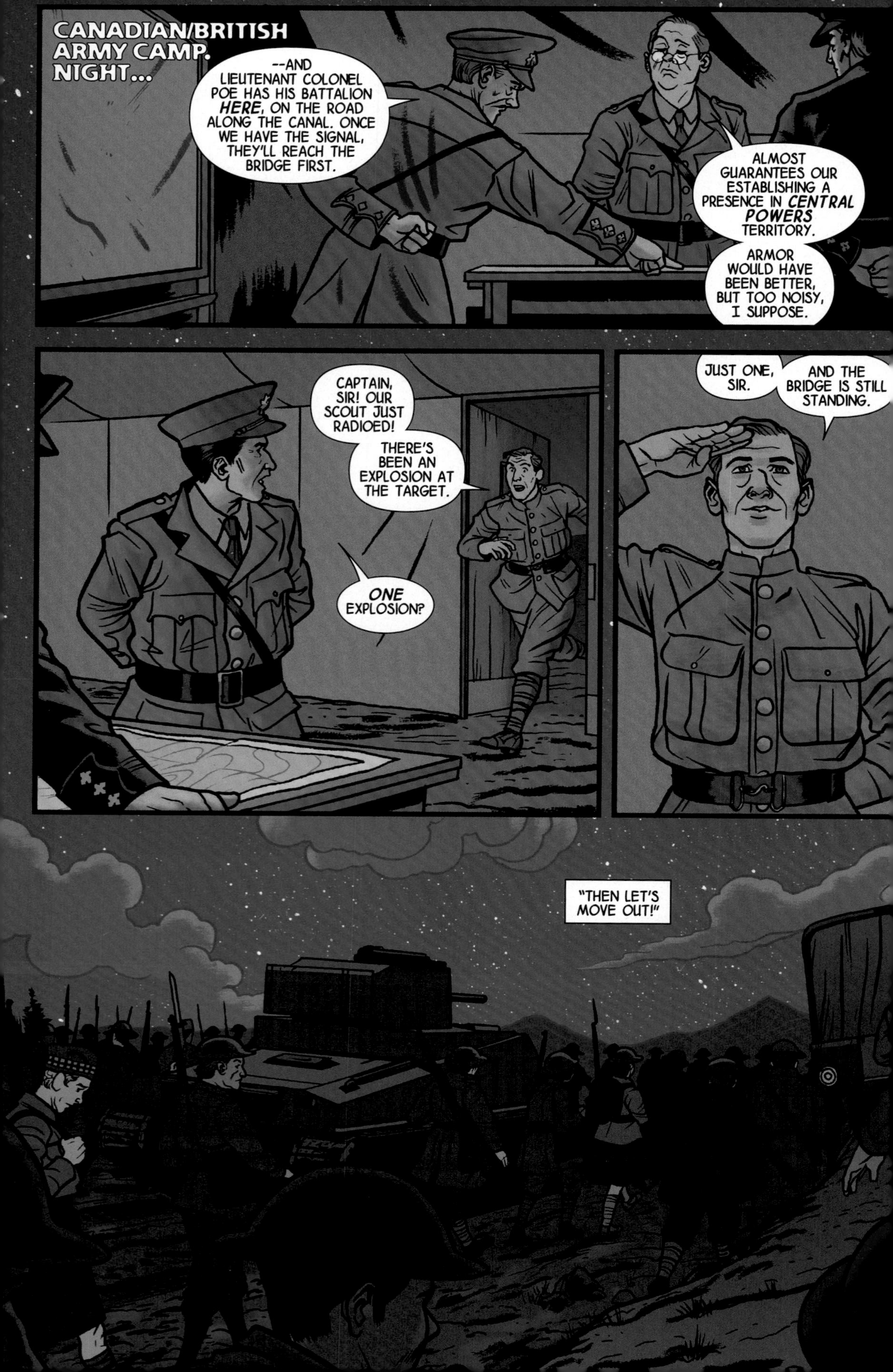
CANADIAN/BRITISH ARMY CAMP. NIGHT...
--AND LIEUTENANT COLONEL POE HAS HIS BATTALION *HERE*, ON THE ROAD ALONG THE CANAL. ONCE WE HAVE THE SIGNAL, THEY'LL REACH THE BRIDGE FIRST.
ALMOST GUARANTEES OUR ESTABLISHING A PRESENCE IN *CENTRAL POWERS* TERRITORY.
ARMOR WOULD HAVE BEEN BETTER, BUT TOO NOISY, I SUPPOSE.
CAPTAIN, SIR! OUR SCOUT JUST RADIOED!
THERE'S BEEN AN EXPLOSION AT THE TARGET.
ONE EXPLOSION?
JUST ONE, SIR.
AND THE BRIDGE IS STILL STANDING.
"THEN LET'S MOVE OUT!"

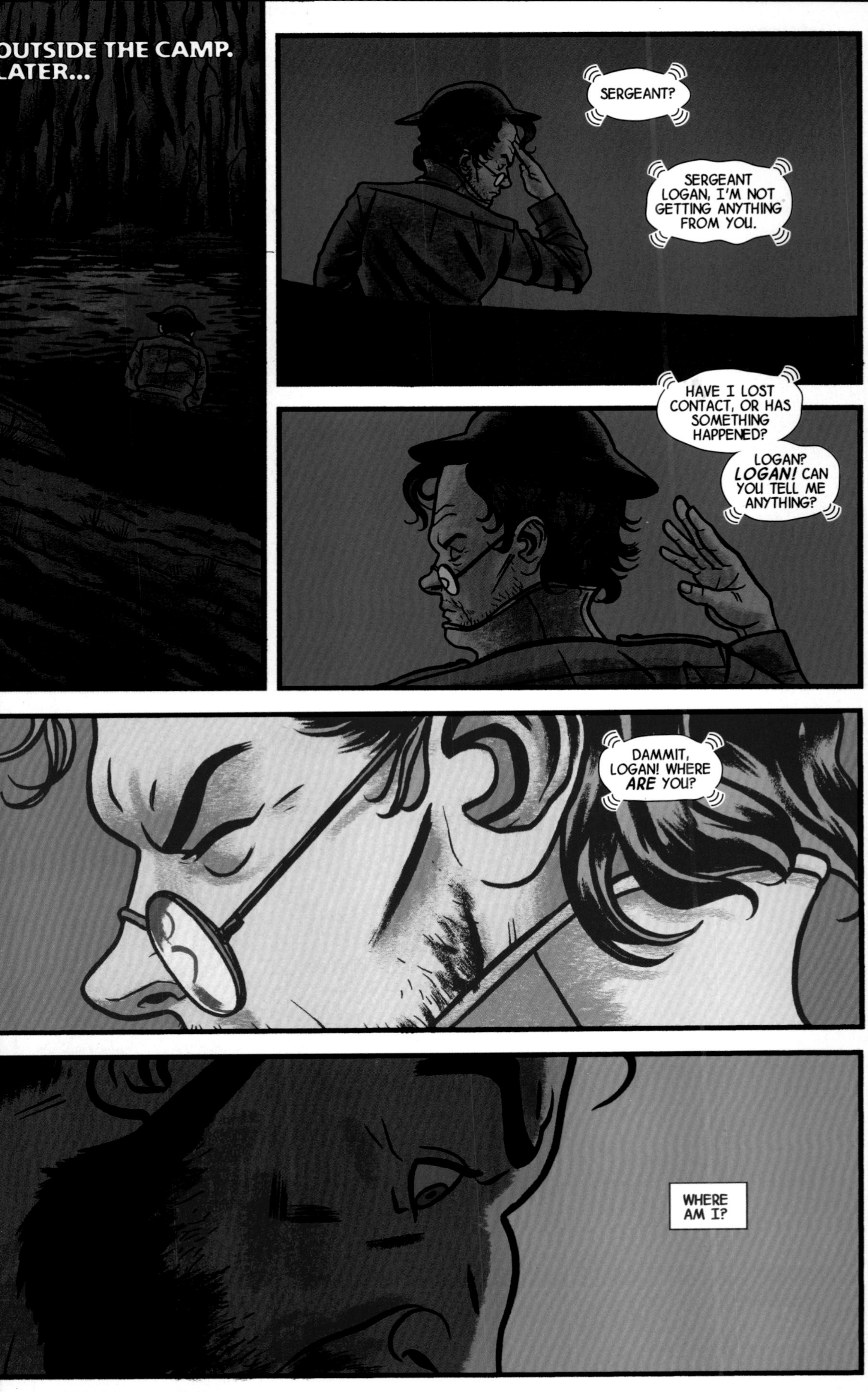
OUTSIDE THE CAMP.
LATER...
SERGEANT?
SERGEANT LOGAN, I'M NOT GETTING ANYTHING FROM YOU.
HAVE I LOST CONTACT, OR HAS SOMETHING HAPPENED?
LOGAN? LOGAN! CAN YOU TELL ME ANYTHING?
DAMMIT, LOGAN! WHERE ARE YOU?
WHERE AM I?

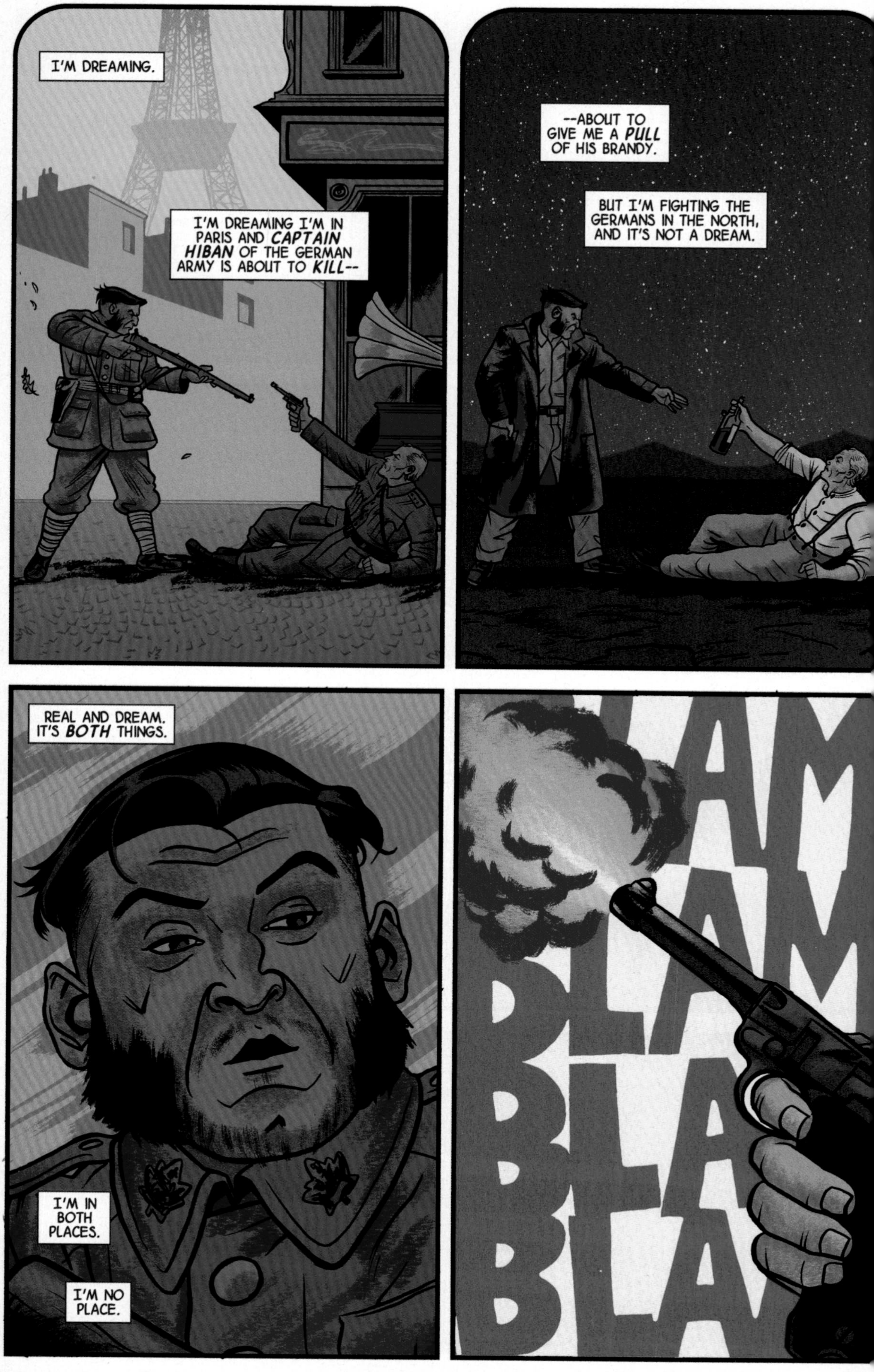
I'M DREAMING.
I'M DREAMING I'M IN PARIS AND CAPTAIN HIBAN OF THE GERMAN ARMY IS ABOUT TO KILL--
--ABOUT TO GIVE ME A PULL OF HIS BRANDY.
BUT I'M FIGHTING THE GERMANS IN THE NORTH, AND IT'S NOT A DREAM.
REAL AND DREAM. IT'S BOTH THINGS.
I'M IN BOTH PLACES.
I'M NO PLACE.
BLAM

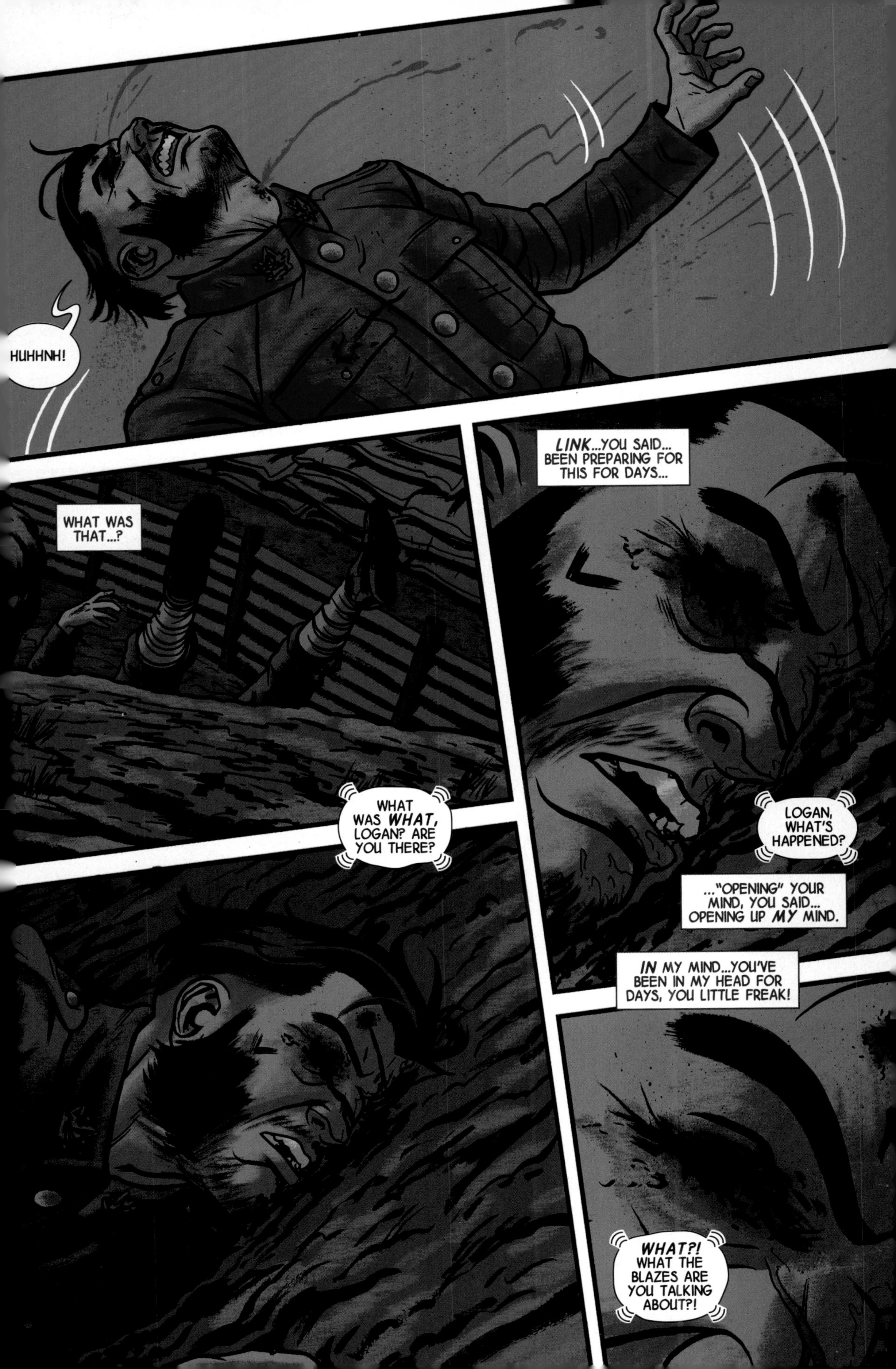
HUHHHNH!
WHAT WAS THAT...?
LINK...YOU SAID... BEEN PREPARING FOR THIS FOR DAYS...
WHAT WAS WHAT, LOGAN? ARE YOU THERE?
LOGAN, WHAT'S HAPPENED?
..."OPENING" YOUR MIND, YOU SAID... OPENING UP MY MIND.
IN MY MIND...YOU'VE BEEN IN MY HEAD FOR DAYS, YOU LITTLE FREAK!
WHAT?! WHAT THE BLAZES ARE YOU TALKING ABOUT?!

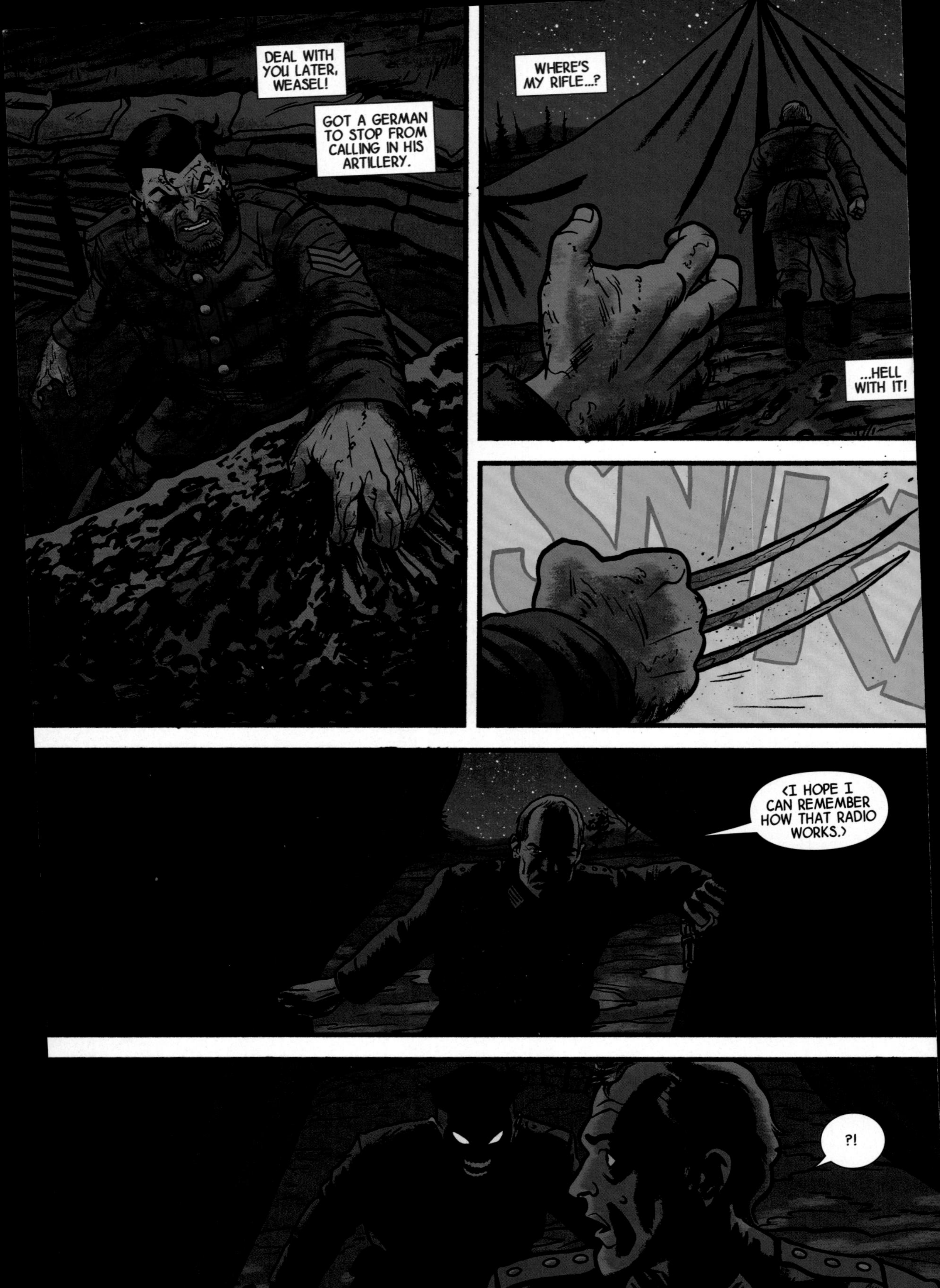
DEAL WITH YOU LATER, WEASEL!
GOT A GERMAN TO STOP FROM CALLING IN HIS ARTILLERY.
WHERE'S MY RIFLE...?
...HELL WITH IT!
<I HOPE I CAN REMEMBER HOW THAT RADIO WORKS.>
?!

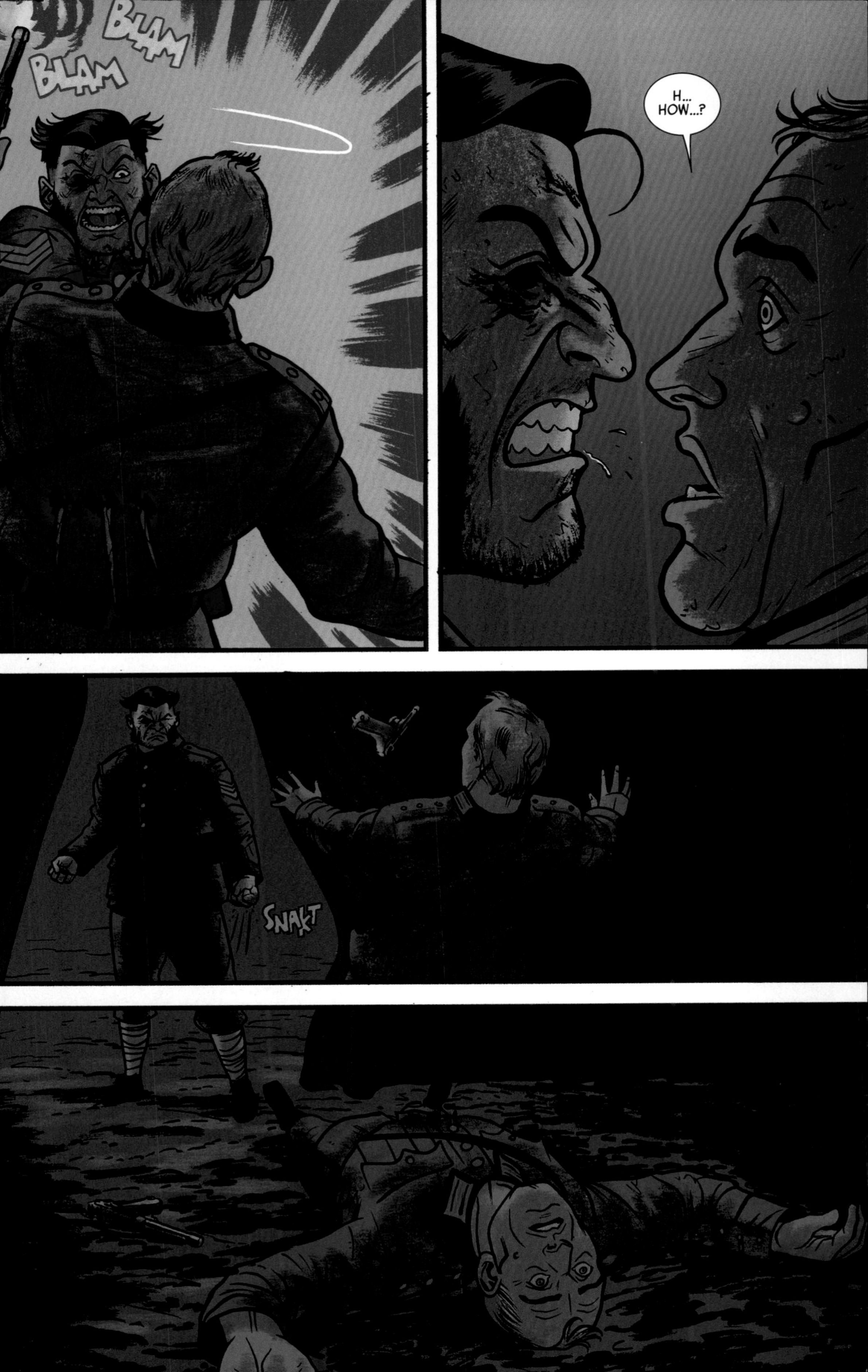
BLAM
BLAM
H... HOW...?
SNAKT

TATATATATATATATATATATATATAT

STERBEN, ENGLISCH FEIGLINGE!

HELL, DOC, WHEN'S THE REST O' 'EM COMIN'?! I MUSTA BLOWN OFF THAT *TNT* TEN MINUTES AGO. THAT *WAS* THE SIGNAL, WASN'T IT?

PAFF

YOU CAN'T MOVE THAT MANY MEN VERY FAST. THEY'LL BE HERE. STOP SQUIRMING SO I CAN FINISH THIS UP.

WE'RE JUST LUCKY YOU'RE OUR ONLY CASUALTY, MAC.

NOT SO SURE O' THAT. WHERE'S SERGEANT LOGAN?

HERE.

GOOD GOD, SERGEANT!

SIT DOWN! LET ME TEND TO YOU.

UH-UH.

BUT YOU'RE WOUNDED, MAN!

UH-HUH.

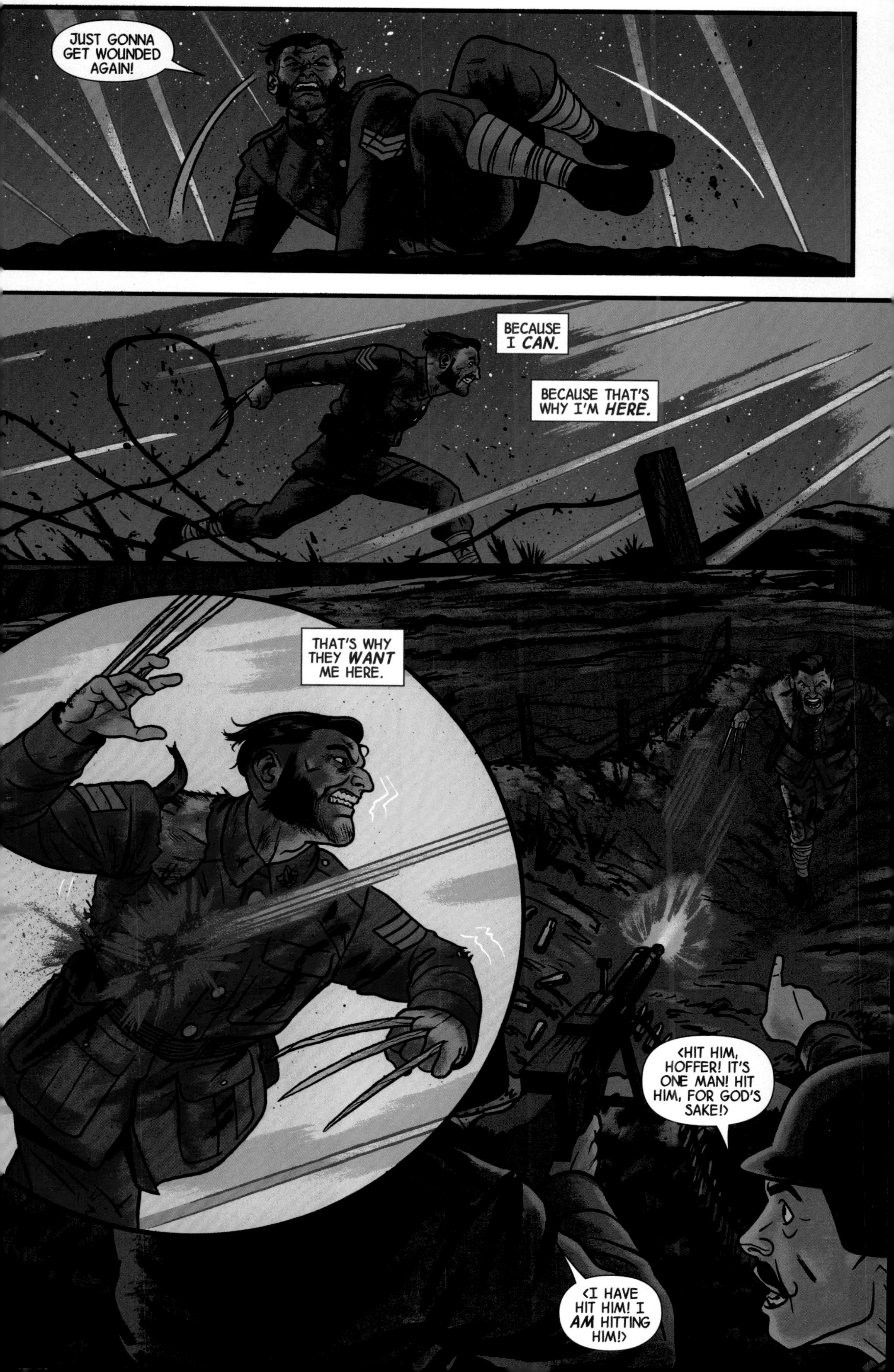
JUST GONNA GET WOUNDED AGAIN!
BECAUSE I *CAN*.
BECAUSE THAT'S WHY I'M ***HERE***.
THAT'S WHY THEY ***WANT*** ME HERE.
<HIT HIM, HOFFER! IT'S ONE MAN! HIT HIM, FOR GOD'S SAKE!>
<I HAVE HIT HIM! I ***AM*** HITTING HIM!>

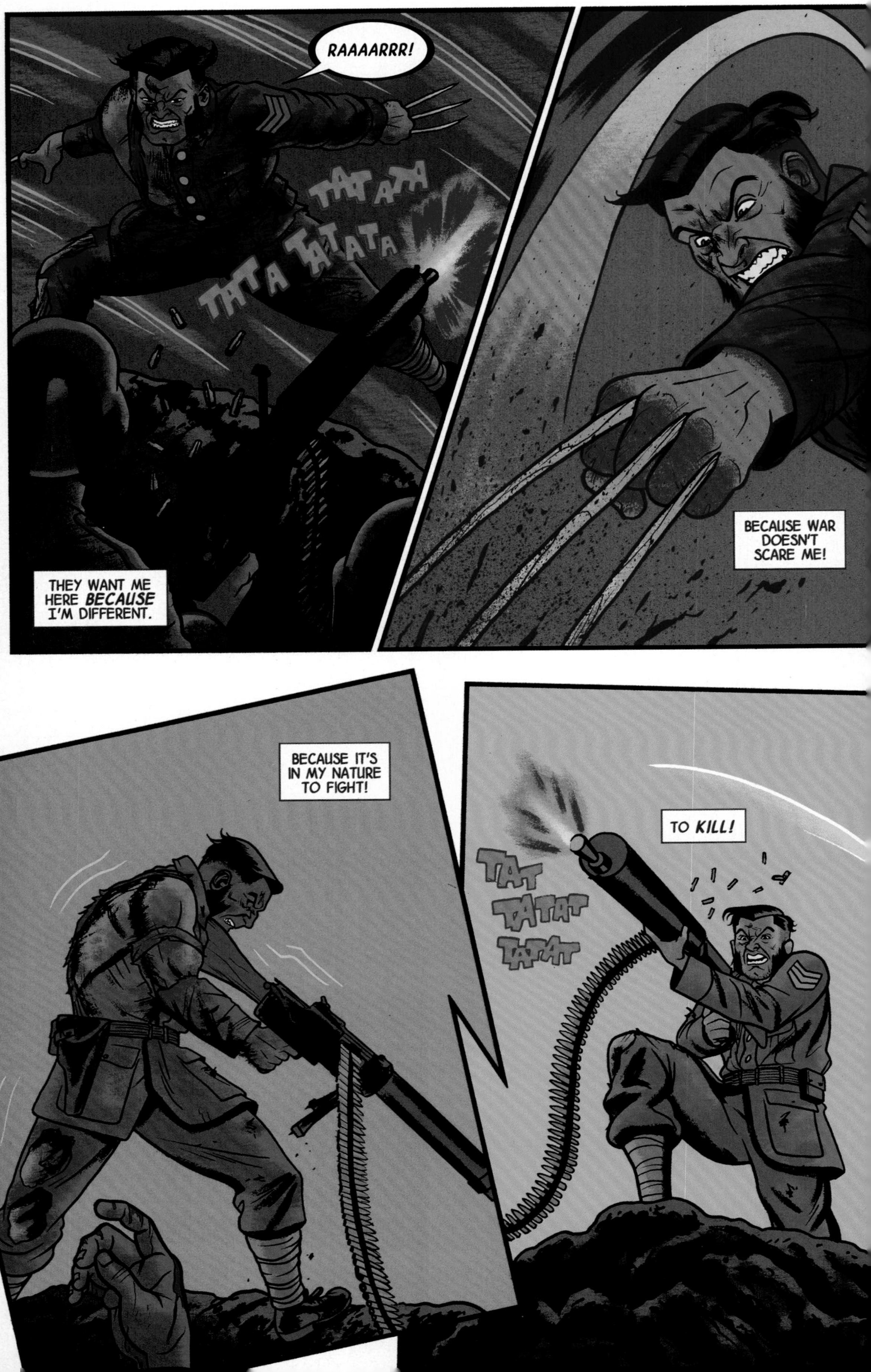
RAAAARRR!
TATATA
TATA TATATA
TATA
THEY WANT ME HERE *BECAUSE* I'M DIFFERENT.
BECAUSE WAR DOESN'T SCARE ME!
BECAUSE IT'S IN MY NATURE TO FIGHT!
TO *KILL!*
TAT
TATAT
TATAT

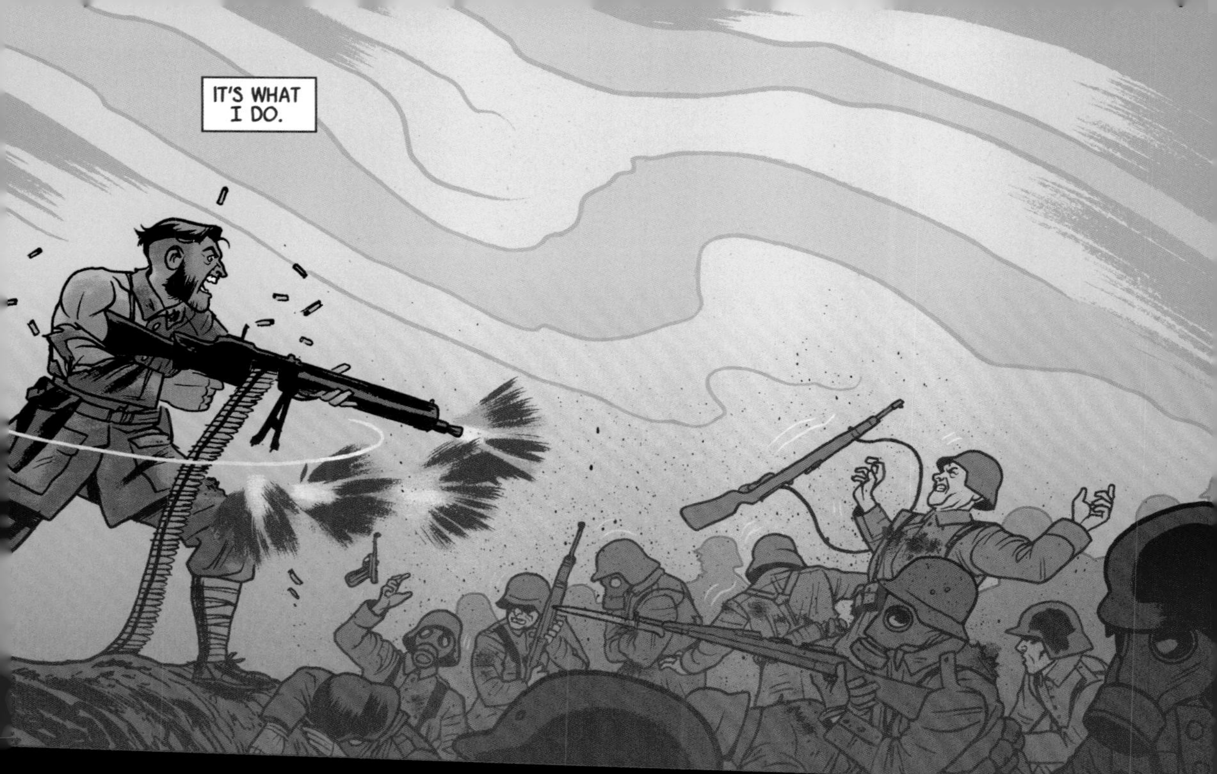
IT'S WHAT I DO.

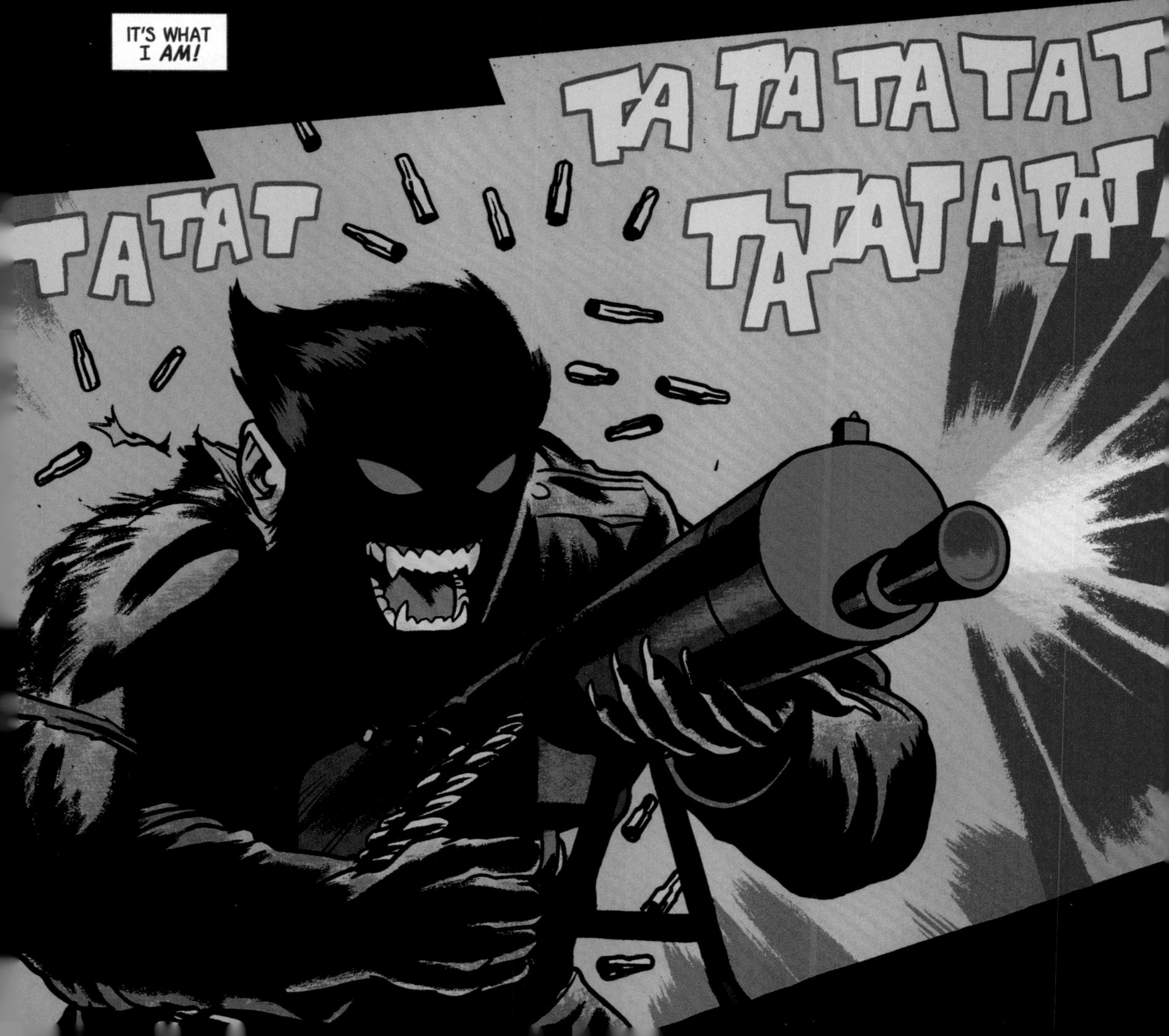
IT'S WHAT I *AM!*
TA TA TA TAT
TATAT
TATATATATAT

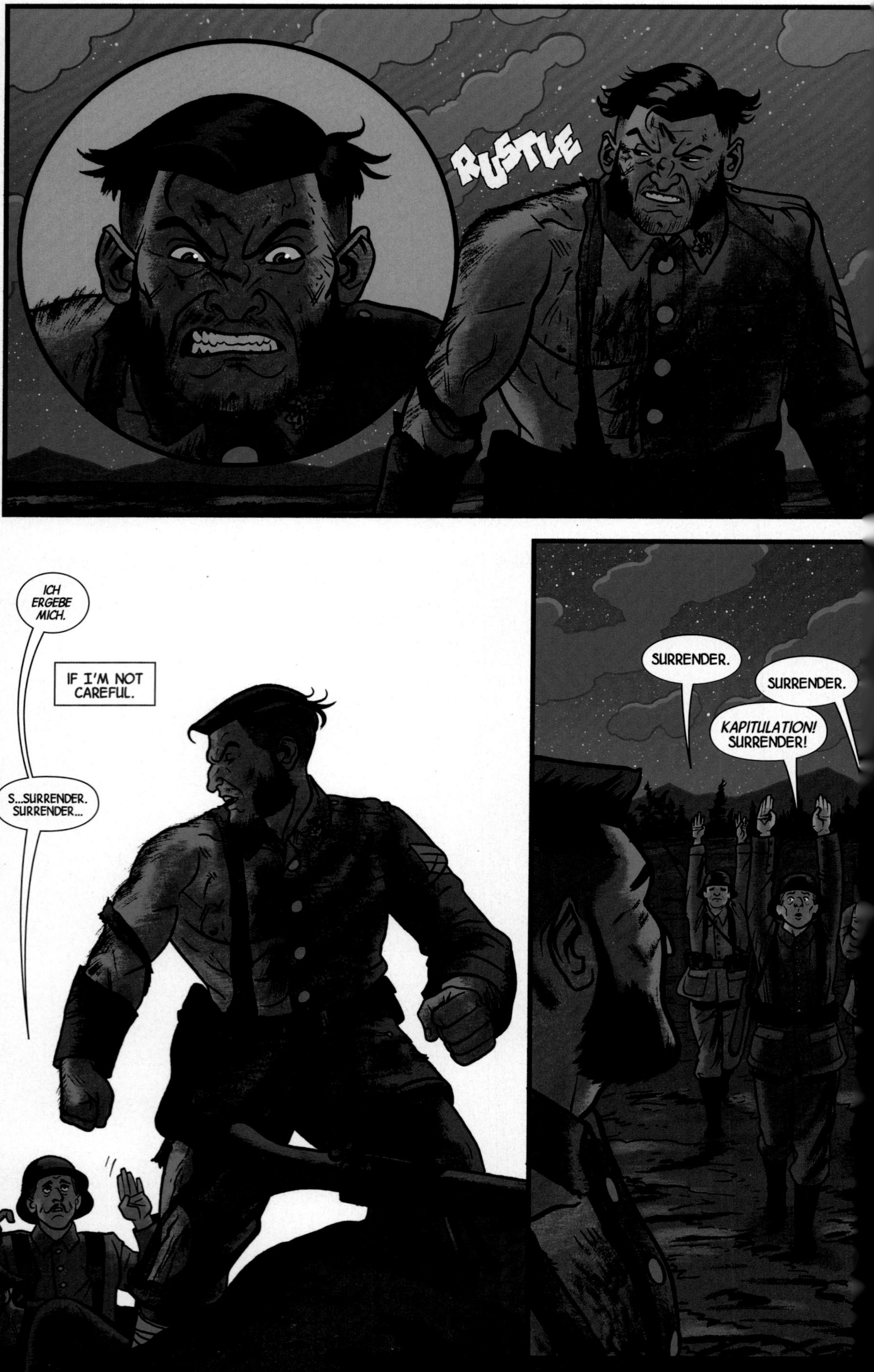
RUSTLE
ICH ERGEBE MICH.
IF I'M NOT CAREFUL.
S...SURRENDER. SURRENDER...
SURRENDER.
SURRENDER.
KAPITULATION! SURRENDER!

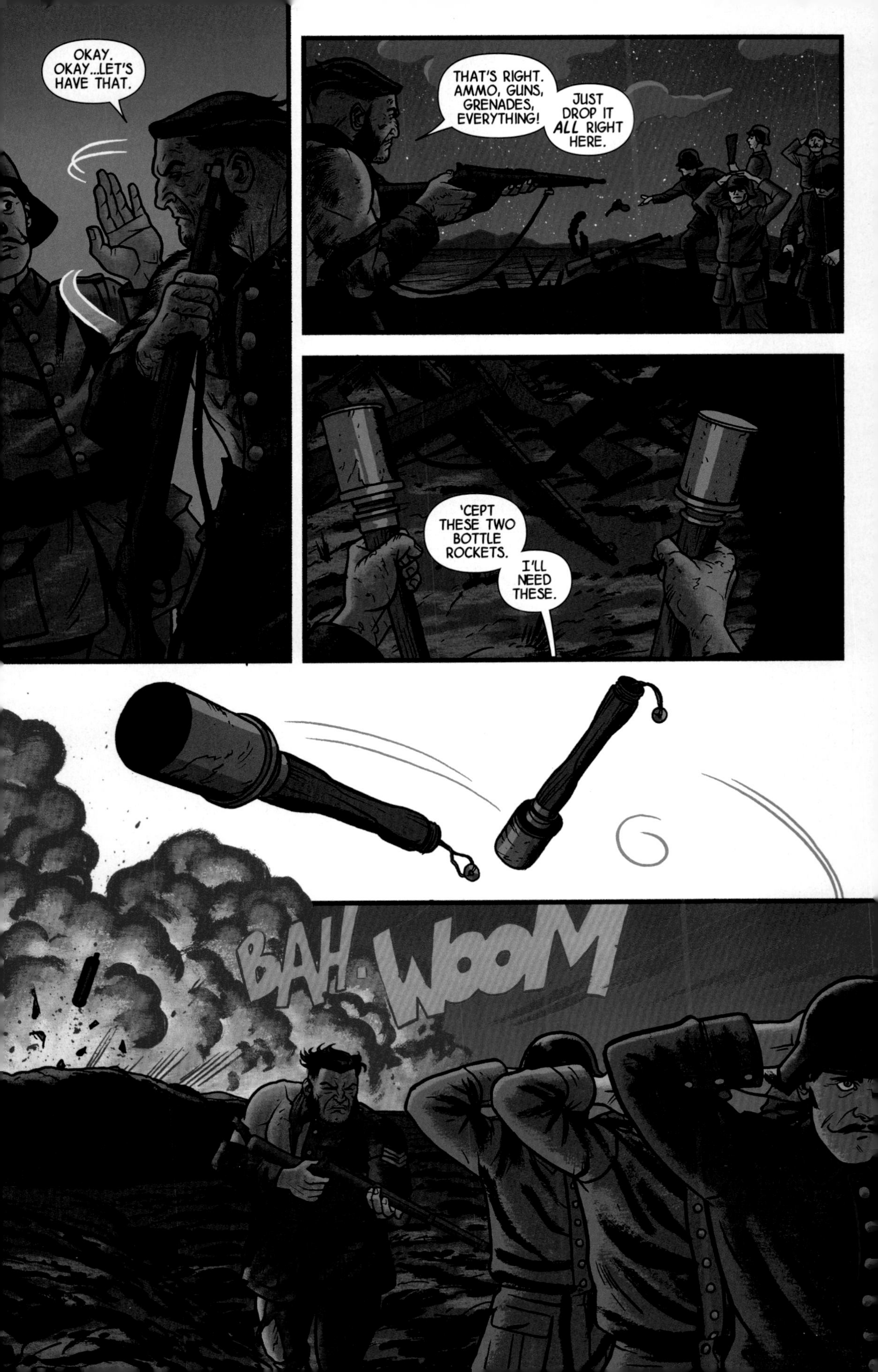
OKAY. OKAY...LET'S HAVE THAT.
THAT'S RIGHT. AMMO, GUNS, GRENADES, EVERYTHING!
JUST DROP IT ALL RIGHT HERE.
'CEPT THESE TWO BOTTLE ROCKETS.
I'LL NEED THESE.
BAH-WOOM

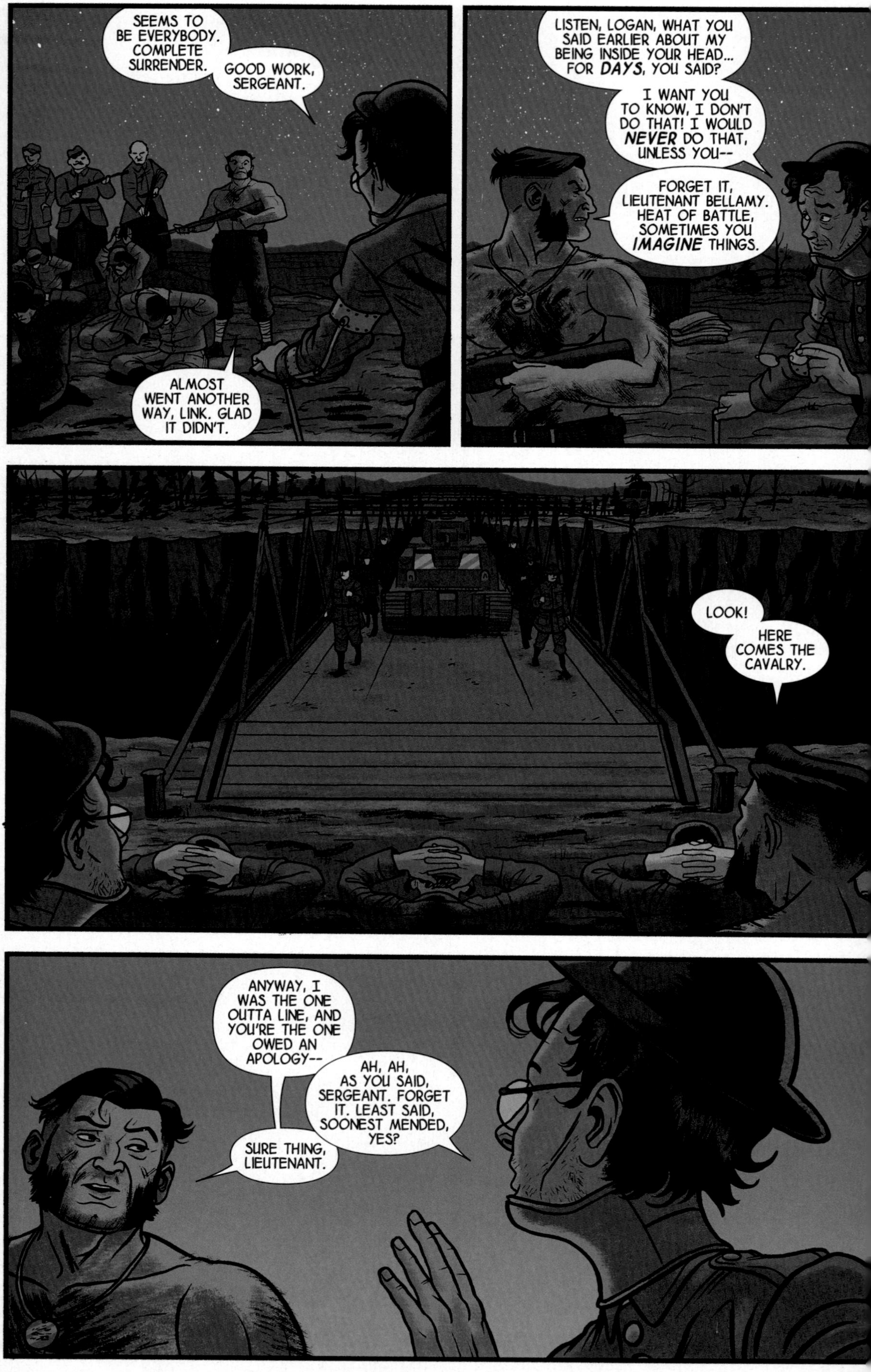
SEEMS TO BE EVERYBODY. COMPLETE SURRENDER.
GOOD WORK, SERGEANT.
ALMOST WENT ANOTHER WAY, LINK. GLAD IT DIDN'T.
LISTEN, LOGAN, WHAT YOU SAID EARLIER ABOUT MY BEING INSIDE YOUR HEAD... FOR DAYS, YOU SAID?
I WANT YOU TO KNOW, I DON'T DO THAT! I WOULD NEVER DO THAT, UNLESS YOU--
FORGET IT, LIEUTENANT BELLAMY. HEAT OF BATTLE, SOMETIMES YOU IMAGINE THINGS.
LOOK!
HERE COMES THE CAVALRY.
ANYWAY, I WAS THE ONE OUTTA LINE, AND YOU'RE THE ONE OWED AN APOLOGY--
AH, AH, AS YOU SAID, SERGEANT. FORGET IT. LEAST SAID, SOONEST MENDED, YES?
SURE THING, LIEUTENANT.

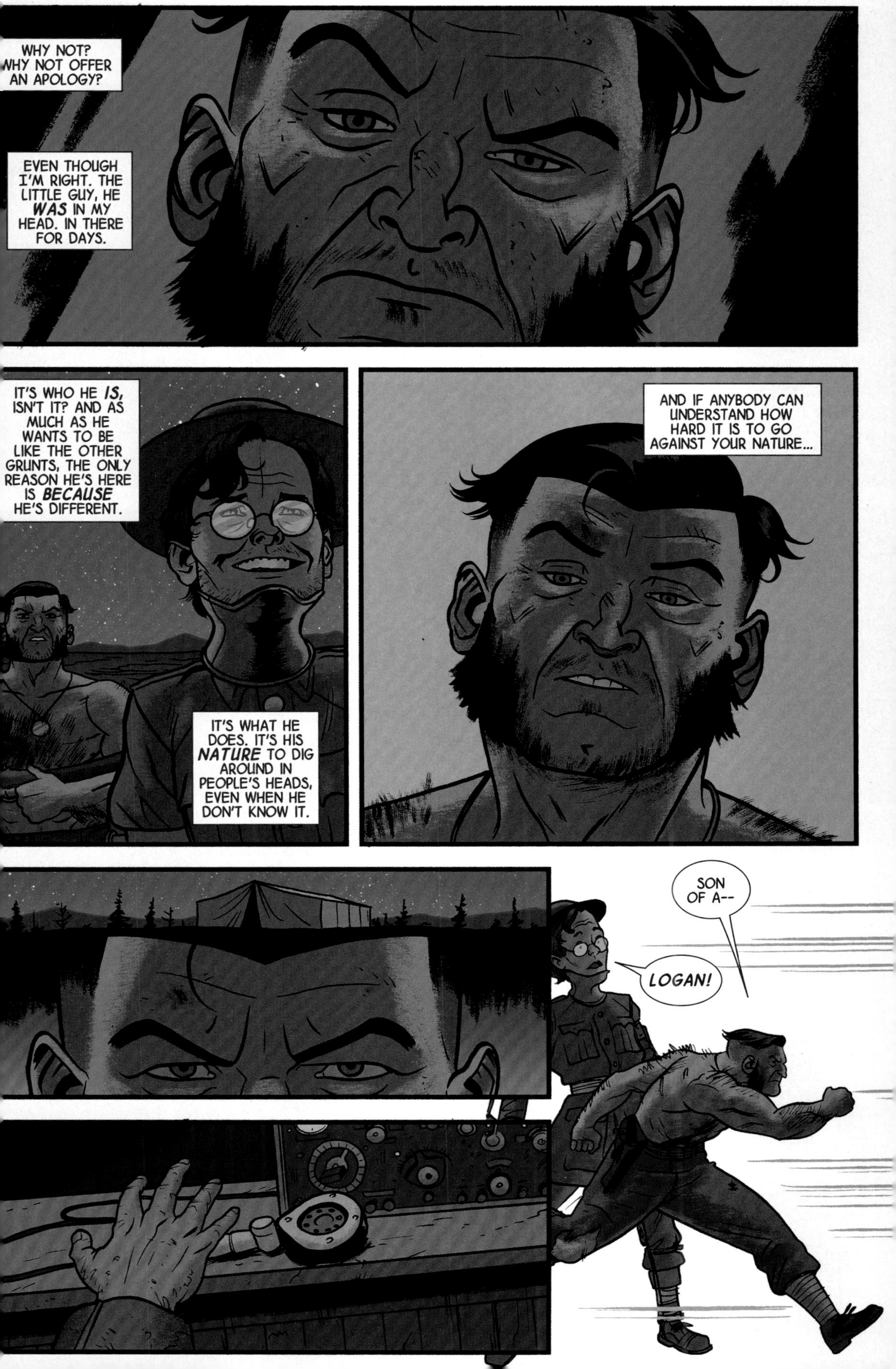
WHY NOT? WHY NOT OFFER AN APOLOGY?
EVEN THOUGH I'M RIGHT. THE LITTLE GUY, HE WAS IN MY HEAD. IN THERE FOR DAYS.
IT'S WHO HE IS, ISN'T IT? AND AS MUCH AS HE WANTS TO BE LIKE THE OTHER GRUNTS, THE ONLY REASON HE'S HERE IS BECAUSE HE'S DIFFERENT.
IT'S WHAT HE DOES. IT'S HIS NATURE TO DIG AROUND IN PEOPLE'S HEADS, EVEN WHEN HE DON'T KNOW IT.
AND IF ANYBODY CAN UNDERSTAND HOW HARD IT IS TO GO AGAINST YOUR NATURE...
SON OF A--
LOGAN!

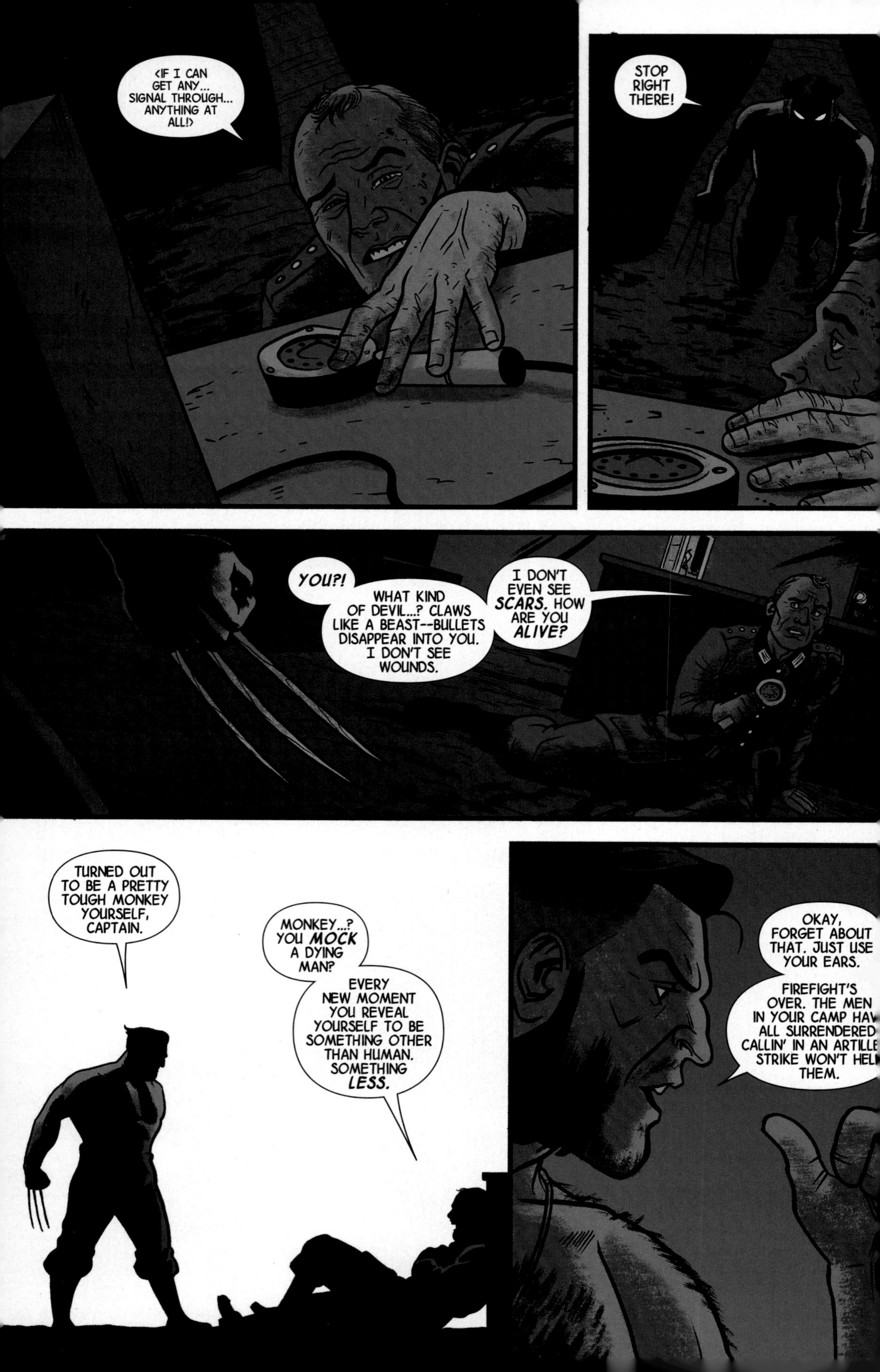
<IF I CAN GET ANY... SIGNAL THROUGH... ANYTHING AT ALL!>
STOP RIGHT THERE!
YOU?!
WHAT KIND OF DEVIL...? CLAWS LIKE A BEAST--BULLETS DISAPPEAR INTO YOU. I DON'T SEE WOUNDS.
I DON'T EVEN SEE SCARS. HOW ARE YOU ALIVE?
TURNED OUT TO BE A PRETTY TOUGH MONKEY YOURSELF, CAPTAIN.
MONKEY...? YOU MOCK A DYING MAN?
EVERY NEW MOMENT YOU REVEAL YOURSELF TO BE SOMETHING OTHER THAN HUMAN. SOMETHING LESS.
OKAY, FORGET ABOUT THAT. JUST USE YOUR EARS.
FIREFIGHT'S OVER. THE MEN IN YOUR CAMP HAV ALL SURRENDERED CALLIN' IN AN ARTILLE STRIKE WON'T HEL THEM.

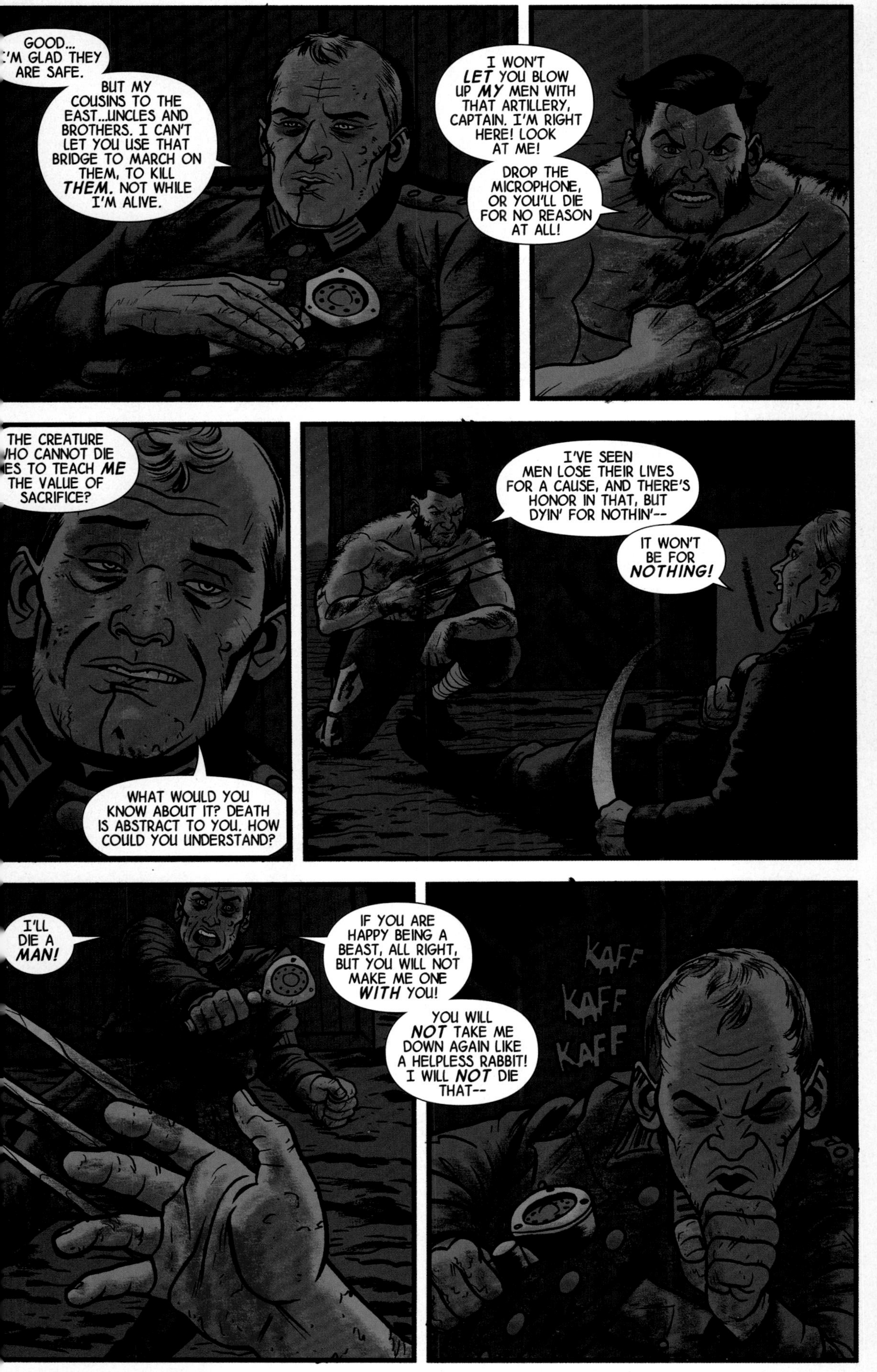
GOOD... I'M GLAD THEY ARE SAFE.
BUT MY COUSINS TO THE EAST...UNCLES AND BROTHERS. I CAN'T LET YOU USE THAT BRIDGE TO MARCH ON THEM, TO KILL THEM. NOT WHILE I'M ALIVE.
I WON'T LET YOU BLOW UP MY MEN WITH THAT ARTILLERY, CAPTAIN. I'M RIGHT HERE! LOOK AT ME!
DROP THE MICROPHONE, OR YOU'LL DIE FOR NO REASON AT ALL!
THE CREATURE WHO CANNOT DIE ES TO TEACH ME THE VALUE OF SACRIFICE?
WHAT WOULD YOU KNOW ABOUT IT? DEATH IS ABSTRACT TO YOU. HOW COULD YOU UNDERSTAND?
I'VE SEEN MEN LOSE THEIR LIVES FOR A CAUSE, AND THERE'S HONOR IN THAT, BUT DYIN' FOR NOTHIN'--
IT WON'T BE FOR NOTHING!
I'LL DIE A MAN!
IF YOU ARE HAPPY BEING A BEAST, ALL RIGHT, BUT YOU WILL NOT MAKE ME ONE WITH YOU!
YOU WILL NOT TAKE ME DOWN AGAIN LIKE A HELPLESS RABBIT! I WILL NOT DIE THAT--
KAFF
KAFF
KAFF

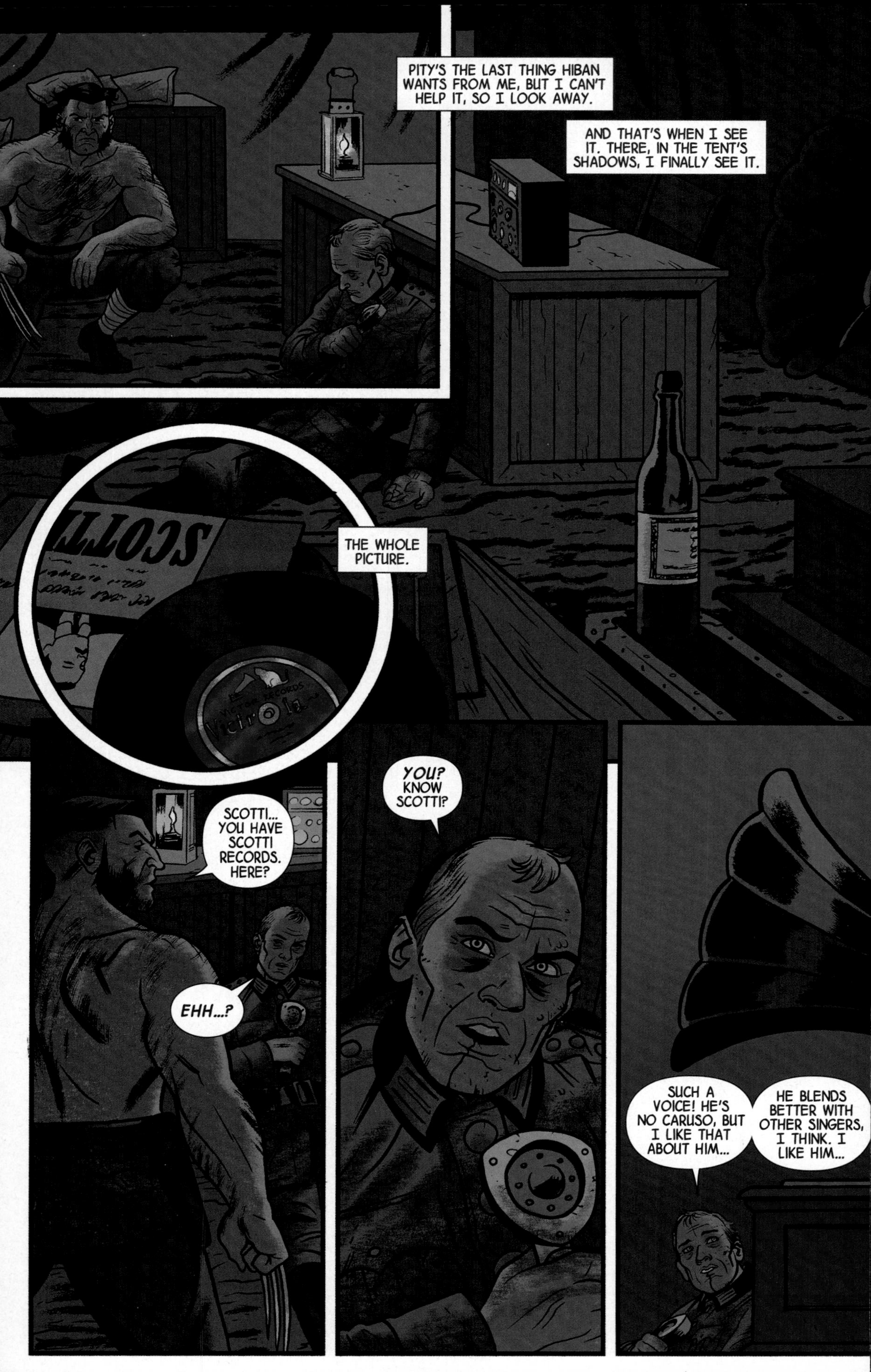
PITY'S THE LAST THING HIBAN WANTS FROM ME, BUT I CAN'T HELP IT, SO I LOOK AWAY.
AND THAT'S WHEN I SEE IT. THERE, IN THE TENT'S SHADOWS, I FINALLY SEE IT.
SCOTTI
THE WHOLE PICTURE.
SCOTTI... YOU HAVE SCOTTI RECORDS. HERE?
EHH...?
YOU? KNOW SCOTTI?
SUCH A VOICE! HE'S NO CARUSO, BUT I LIKE THAT ABOUT HIM...
HE BLENDS BETTER WITH OTHER SINGERS, I THINK. I LIKE HIM...

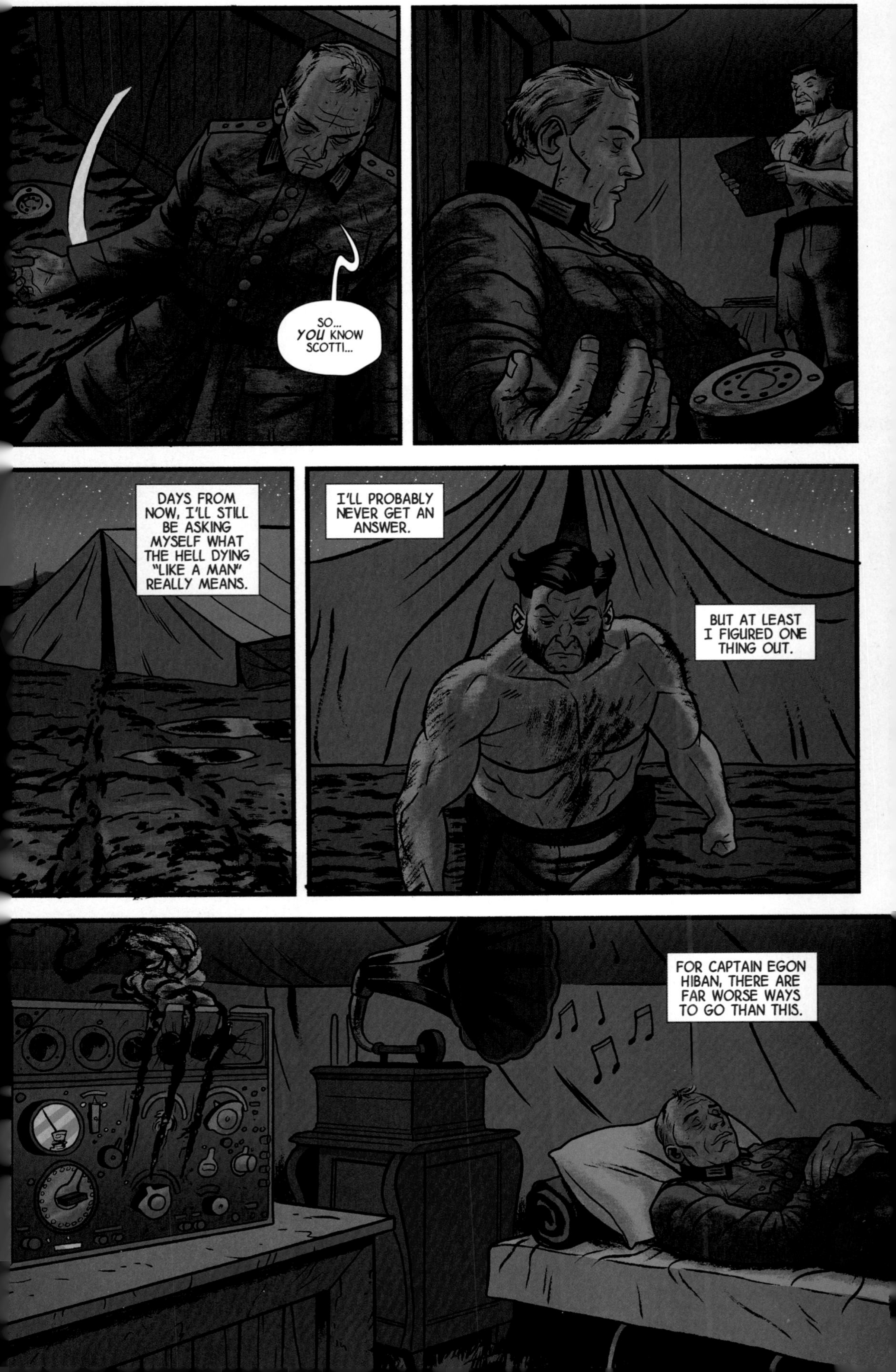
SO... YOU KNOW SCOTTI...
DAYS FROM NOW, I'LL STILL BE ASKING MYSELF WHAT THE HELL DYING "LIKE A MAN" REALLY MEANS.
I'LL PROBABLY NEVER GET AN ANSWER.
BUT AT LEAST I FIGURED ONE THING OUT.
FOR CAPTAIN EGON HIBAN, THERE ARE FAR WORSE WAYS TO GO THAN THIS.

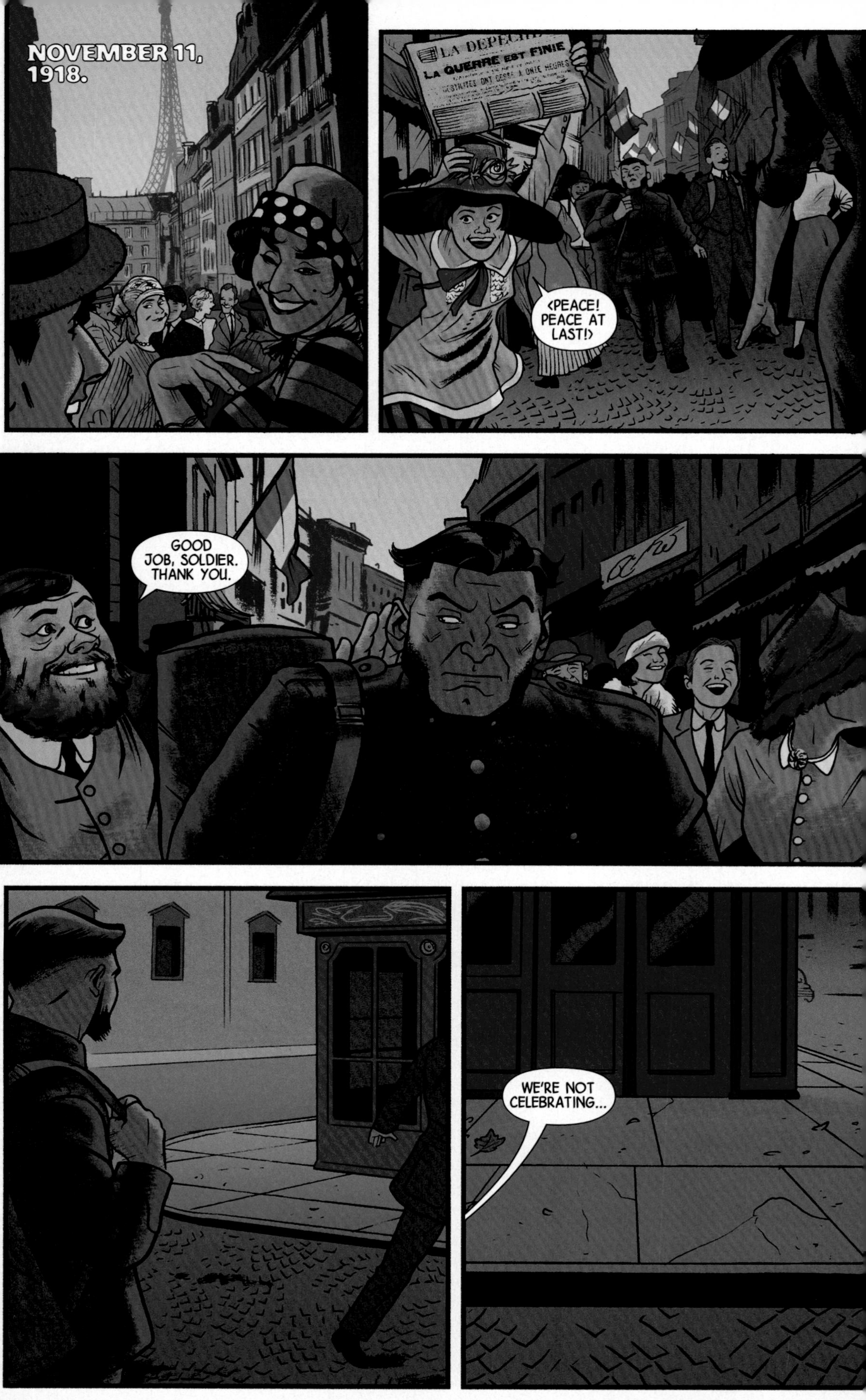
NOVEMBER 11, 1918.
LA GUERRE EST FINIE
<PEACE! PEACE AT LAST!>
GOOD JOB, SOLDIER. THANK YOU.
WE'RE NOT CELEBRATING...

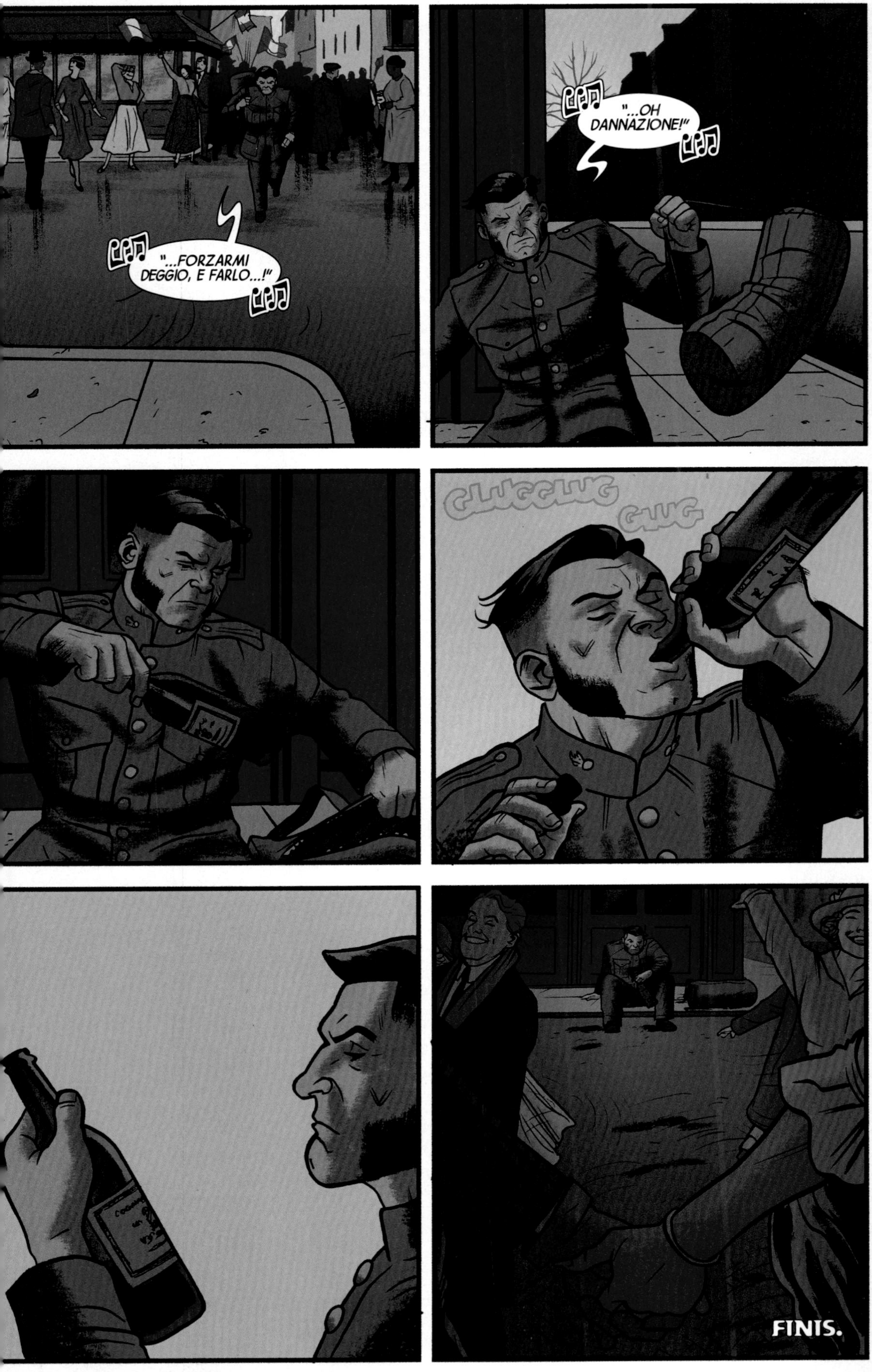
"...FORZARMI DEGGIO, E FARLO...!"
"...OH DANNAZIONE!"
GLUGGLUG
GLUG
FINIS.

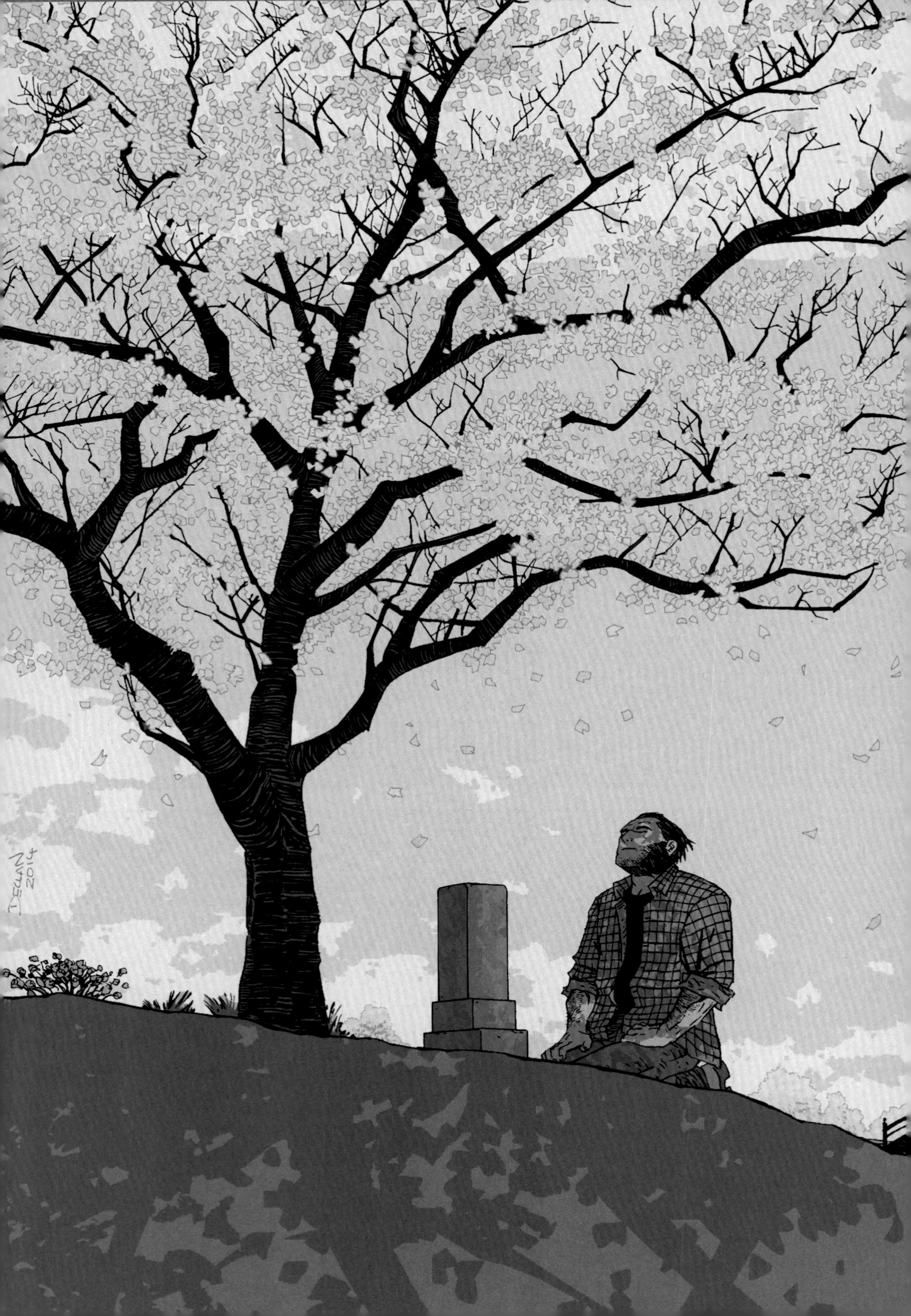
DECLAN 2014

Human. Animal.

Hunter. Hunted.

Since his long-ago mysterious origins, Wolverine has been torn between two violently different worlds, always on the move, pursued as much as searching, never knowing rest or peace.

Now a savage twist of circumstance drives him back to the primal mountains of his youth, where he once lived as an animal, in a desperate effort to come to terms with his powers.

Perhaps at last he'll understand what or who he truly is—and what it means to be. . .

WOLVERINE

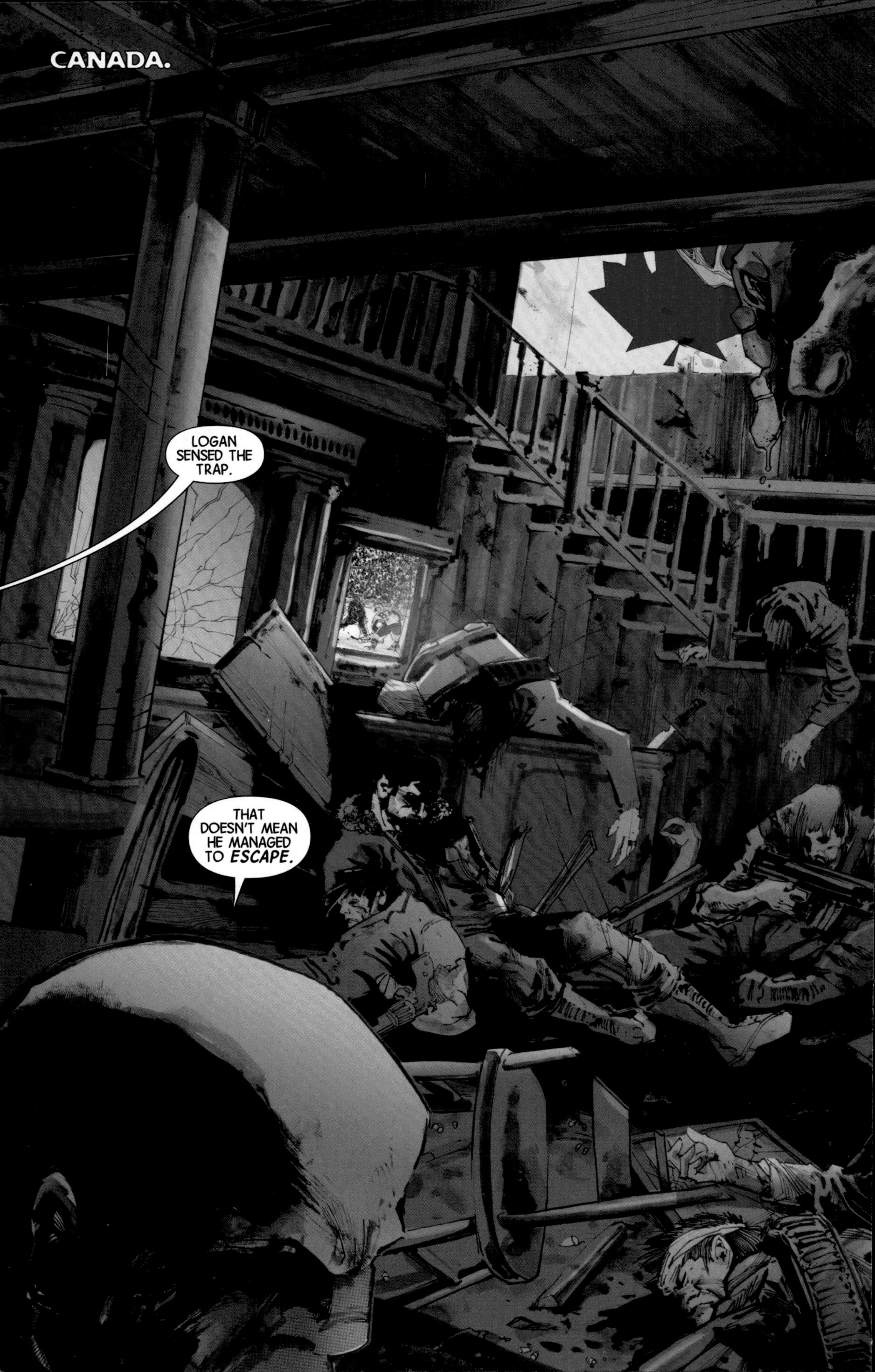
CANADA.
LOGAN SENSED THE TRAP.
THAT DOESN'T MEAN HE MANAGED TO *ESCAPE.*

WE DON'T GET *PAID* IF WE DON'T DELIVER LOGAN'S *BODY!*

LOOK *HARDER*, VIC!

I CAN'T FIND IT!

ALL THE BLADES HAD THE *DRUG* ON THEM, BUT WE CAN'T ASSUME THIS IS LOGAN'S *BLOOD.*

YES, WE CAN. I'D BET MY SHARE OF THE *BOUNTY* ON IT.

WHAT MAKES YOU SO SURE?

THESE.

HE CAN'T HAVE GONE FAR. HIS WOUNDS NORMALLY HEAL FAST, BUT THE DRUG CHANGES THAT. IF WE GET TO HIM BEFORE IT WEARS OFF...

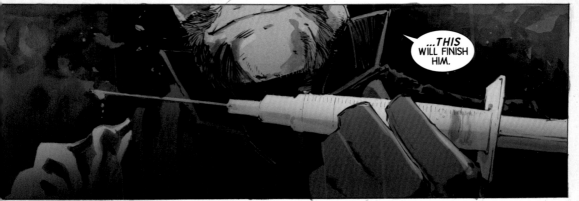

...*THIS* WILL FINISH HIM.

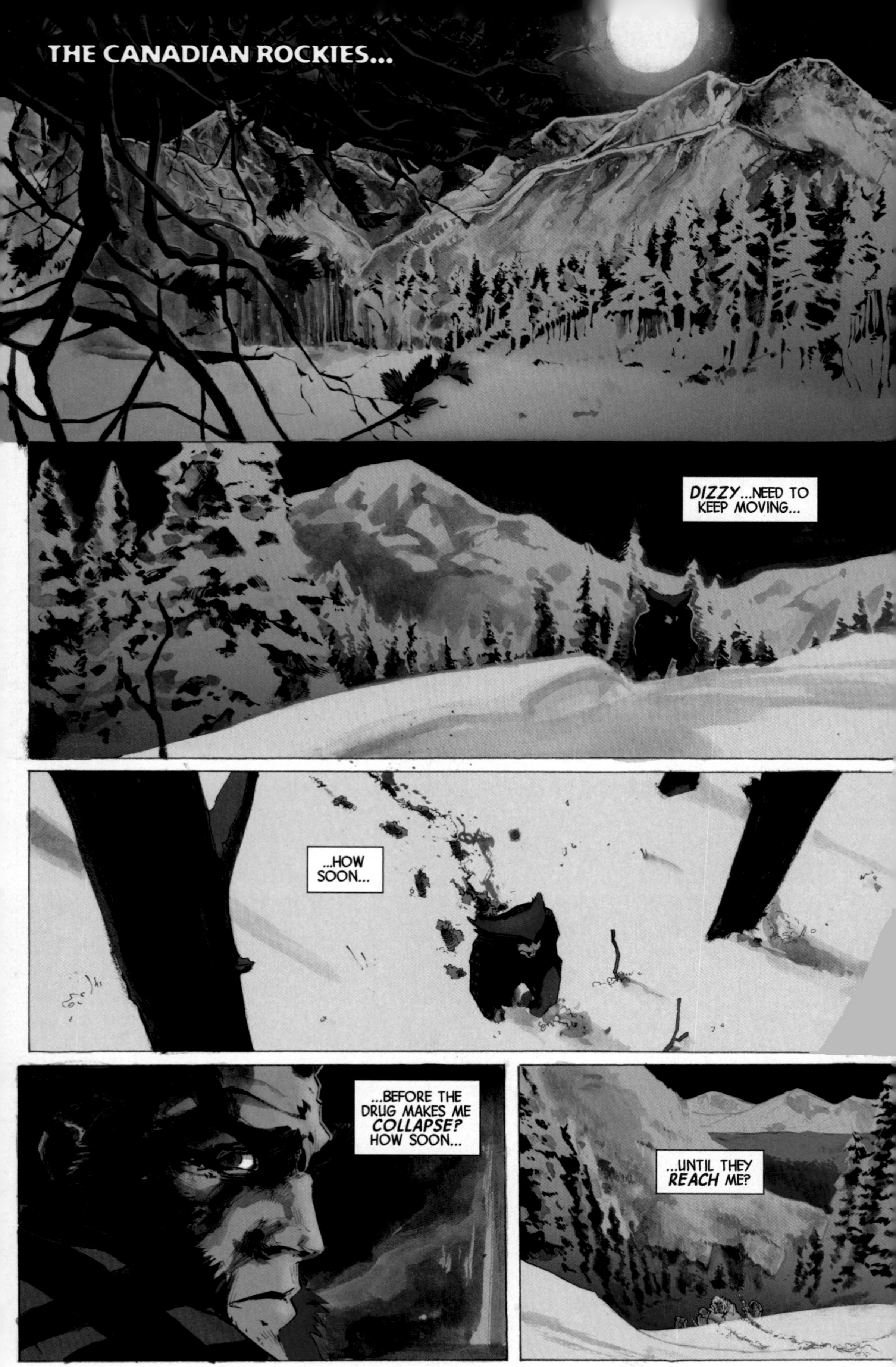
THE CANADIAN ROCKIES...
DIZZY...NEED TO KEEP MOVING...
...HOW SOON...
...BEFORE THE DRUG MAKES ME COLLAPSE? HOW SOON...
...UNTIL THEY REACH ME?

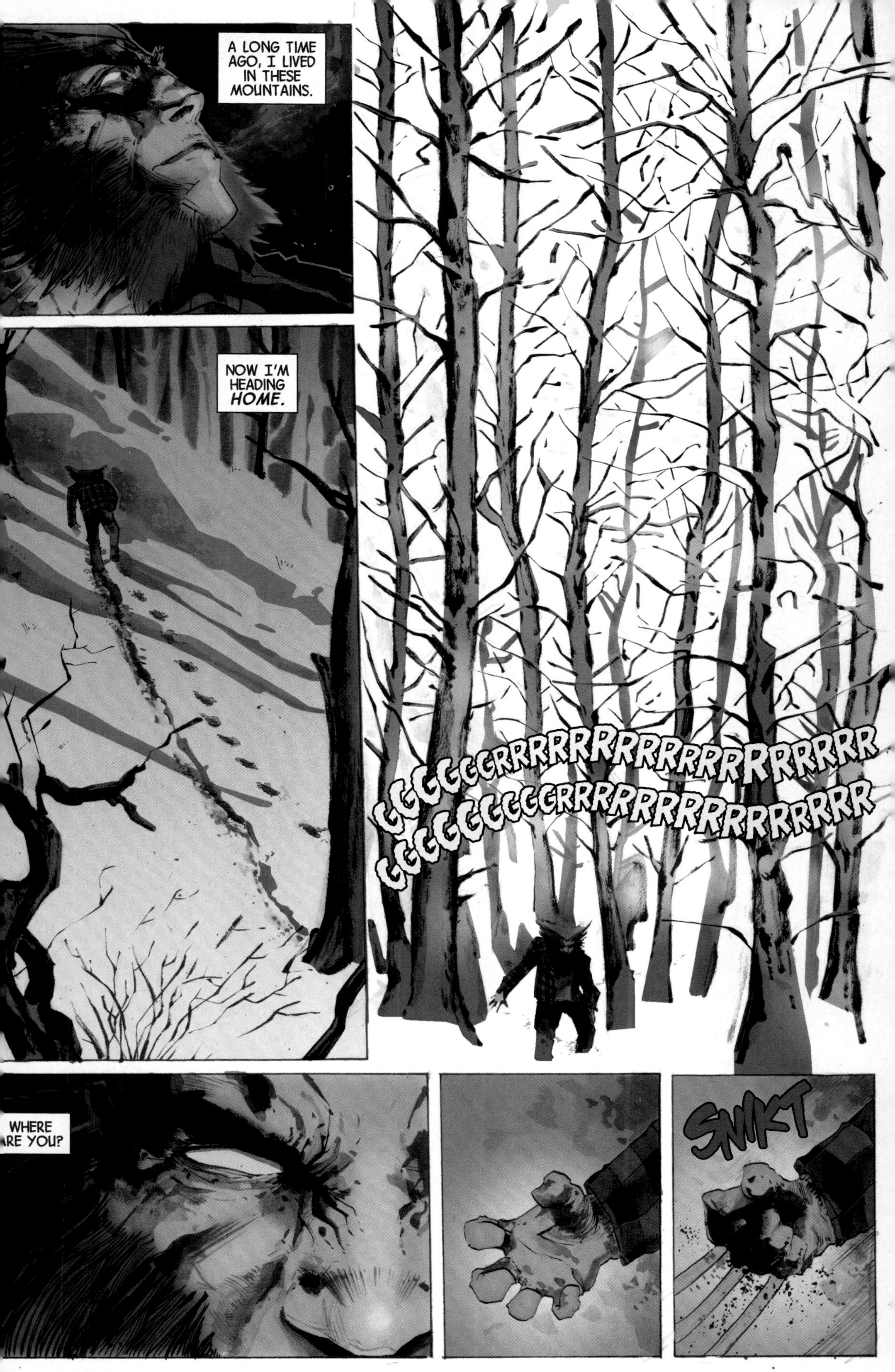

A LONG TIME AGO, I LIVED IN THESE MOUNTAINS.
NOW I'M HEADING HOME.
GGGGGGRRRRRRRRRRRRRRRRRRRRRR
GGGGGGGGGGRRRRRRRRRRRRRRRRRRRR
WHERE ARE YOU?
SNIKT

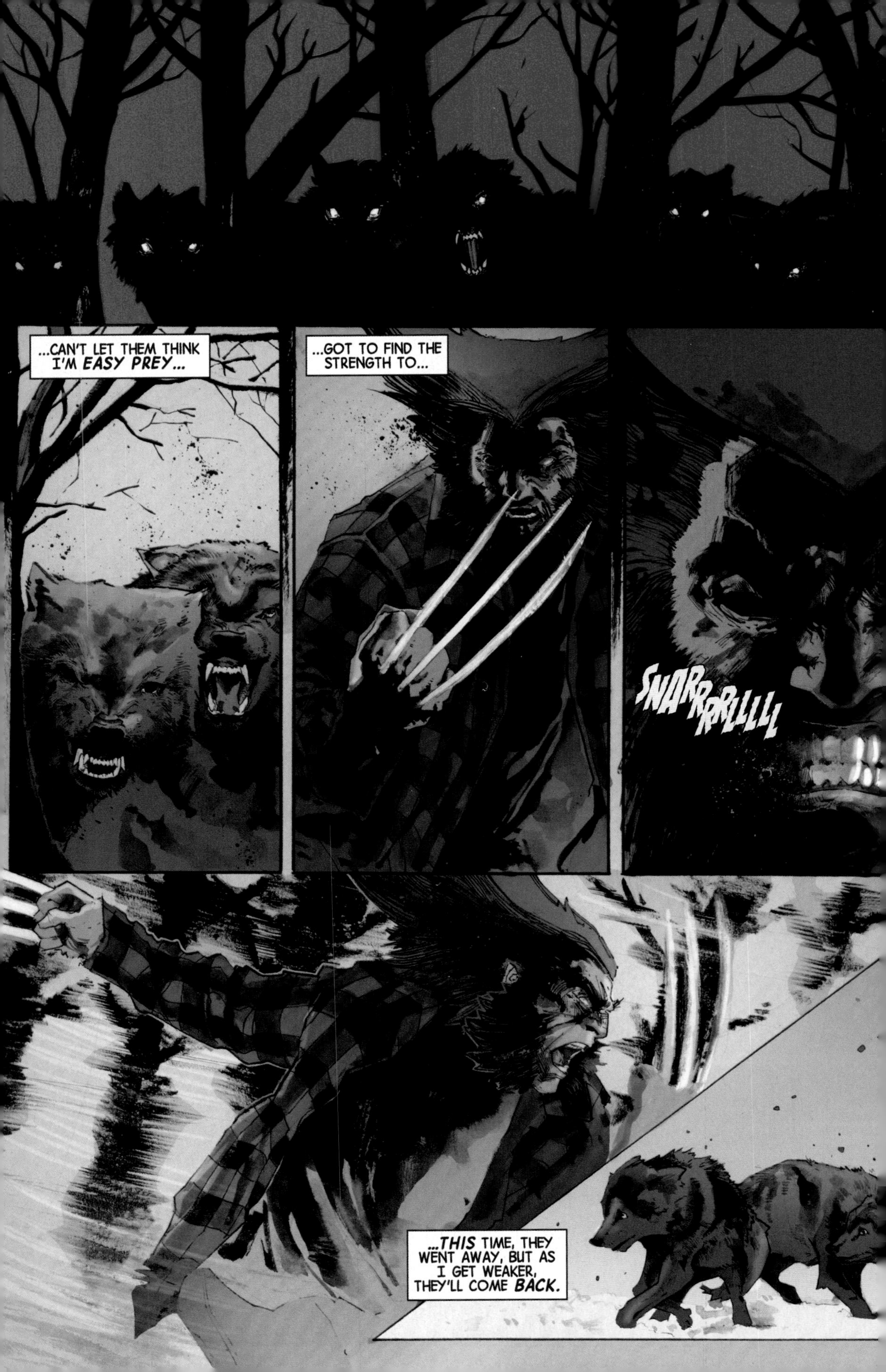
...CAN'T LET THEM THINK I'M EASY PREY...
...GOT TO FIND THE STRENGTH TO...
SNARRRRLLLLL
...THIS TIME, THEY WENT AWAY, BUT AS I GET WEAKER, THEY'LL COME BACK.

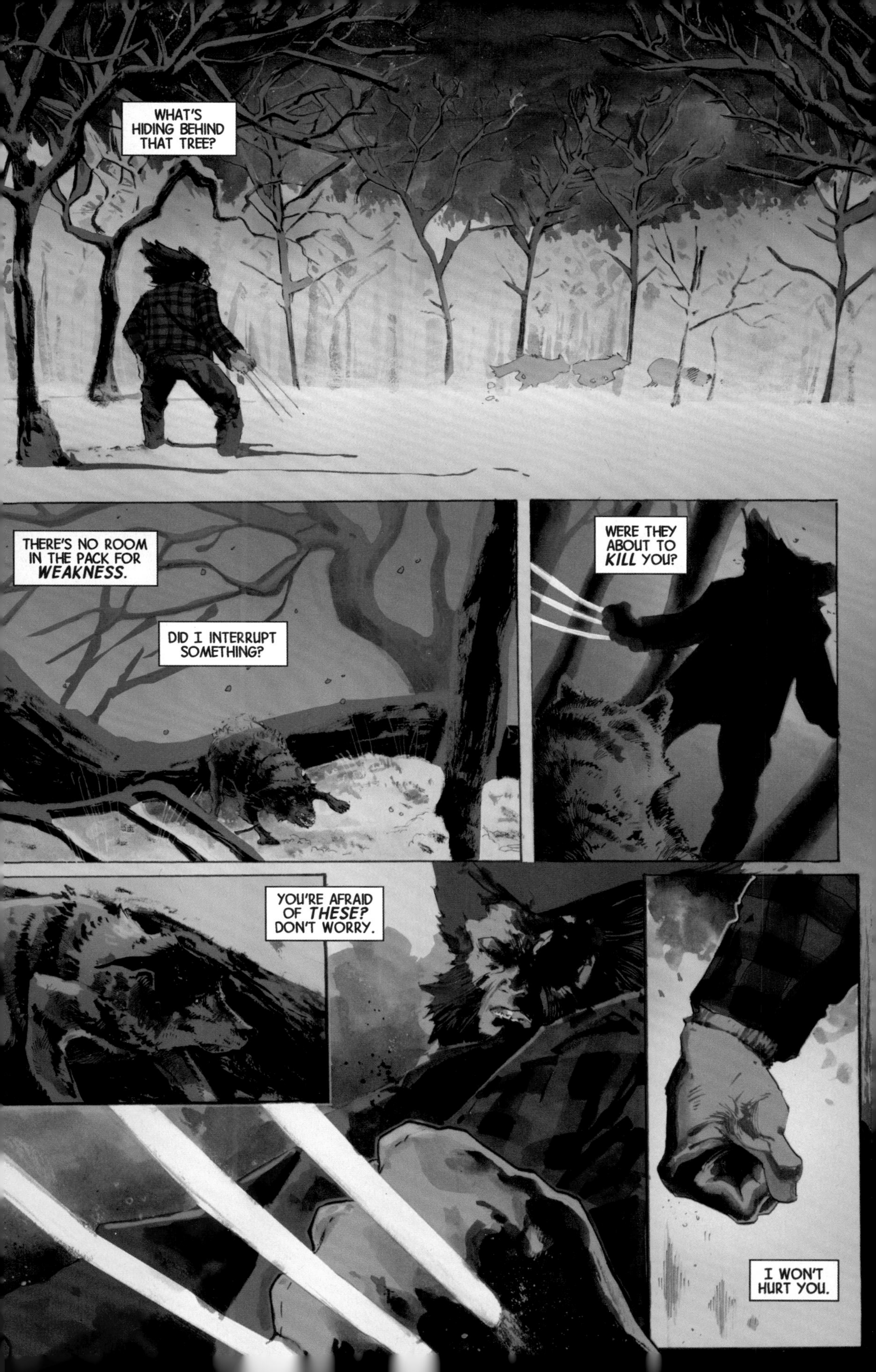
WHAT'S HIDING BEHIND THAT TREE?
THERE'S NO ROOM IN THE PACK FOR *WEAKNESS*.
DID I INTERRUPT SOMETHING?
WERE THEY ABOUT TO *KILL* YOU?
YOU'RE AFRAID OF *THESE?* DON'T WORRY.
I WON'T HURT YOU.

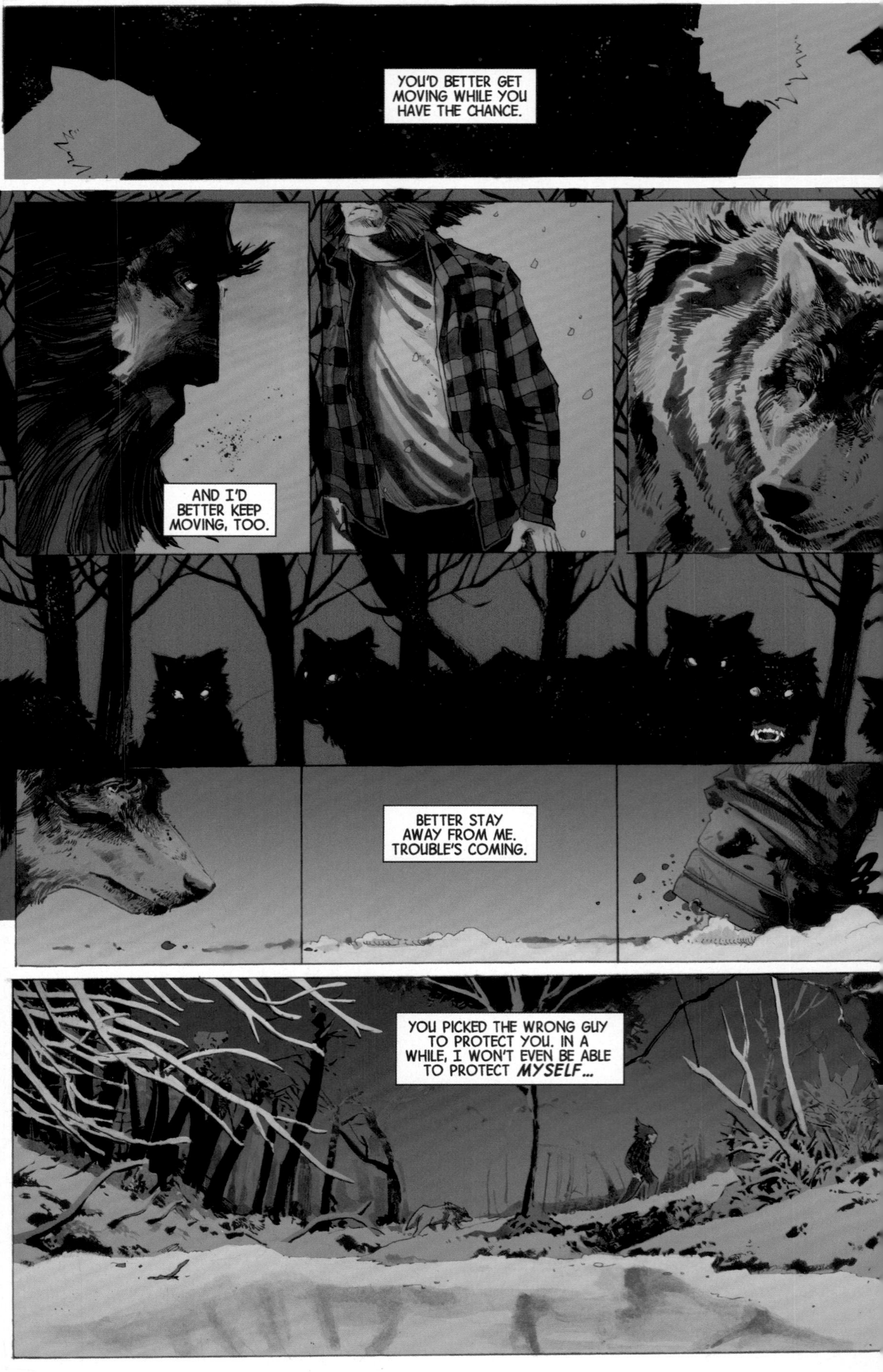
YOU'D BETTER GET MOVING WHILE YOU HAVE THE CHANCE.
AND I'D BETTER KEEP MOVING, TOO.
BETTER STAY AWAY FROM ME. TROUBLE'S COMING.
YOU PICKED THE WRONG GUY TO PROTECT YOU. IN A WHILE, I WON'T EVEN BE ABLE TO PROTECT *MYSELF*...

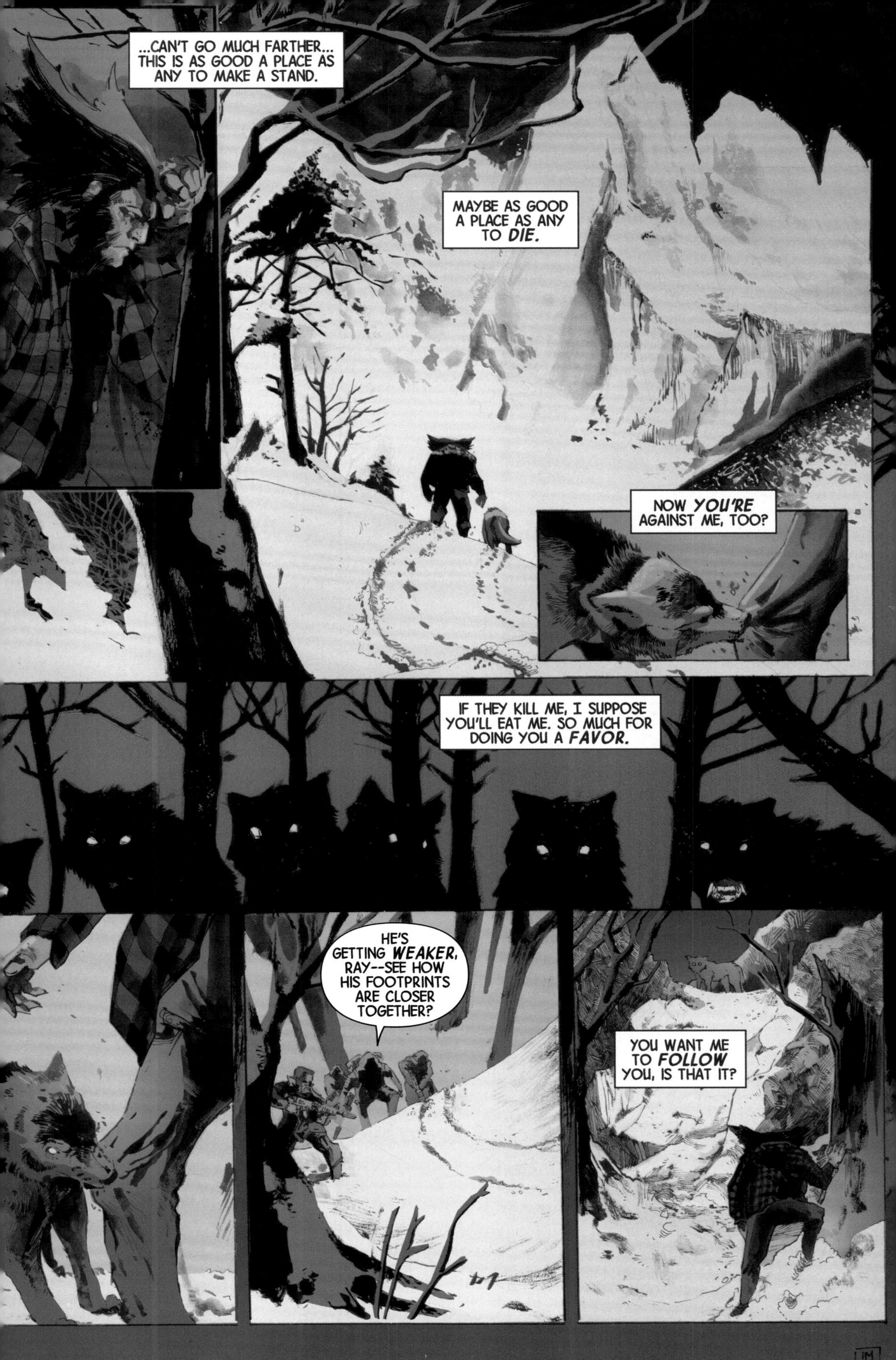
...CAN'T GO MUCH FARTHER... THIS IS AS GOOD A PLACE AS ANY TO MAKE A STAND.
MAYBE AS GOOD A PLACE AS ANY TO *DIE.*
NOW *YOU'RE* AGAINST ME, TOO?
IF THEY KILL ME, I SUPPOSE YOU'LL EAT ME. SO MUCH FOR DOING YOU A *FAVOR.*
HE'S GETTING *WEAKER,* RAY--SEE HOW HIS FOOTPRINTS ARE CLOSER TOGETHER?
YOU WANT ME TO *FOLLOW* YOU, IS THAT IT?
JM

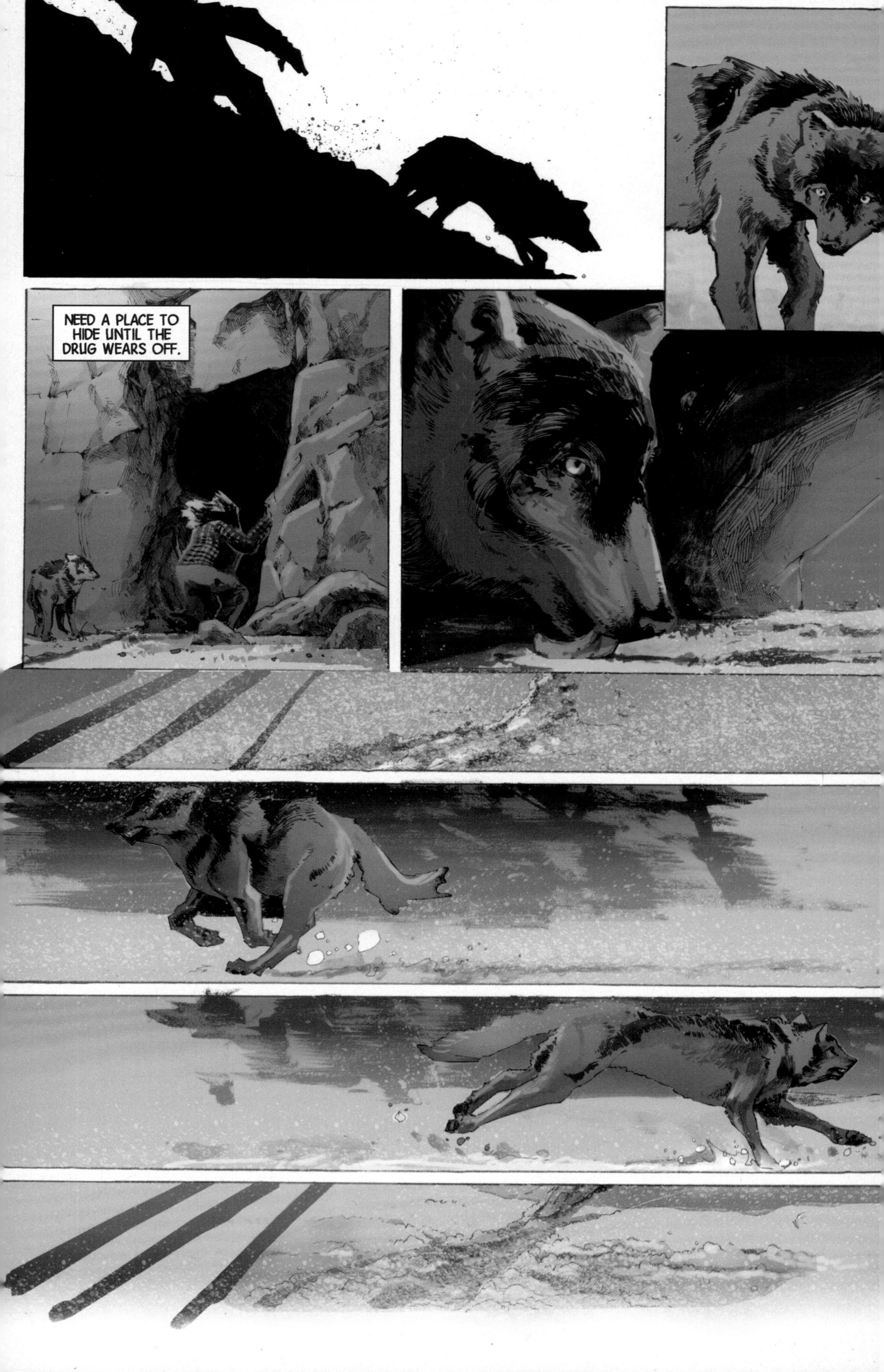
NEED A PLACE TO HIDE UNTIL THE DRUG WEARS OFF.

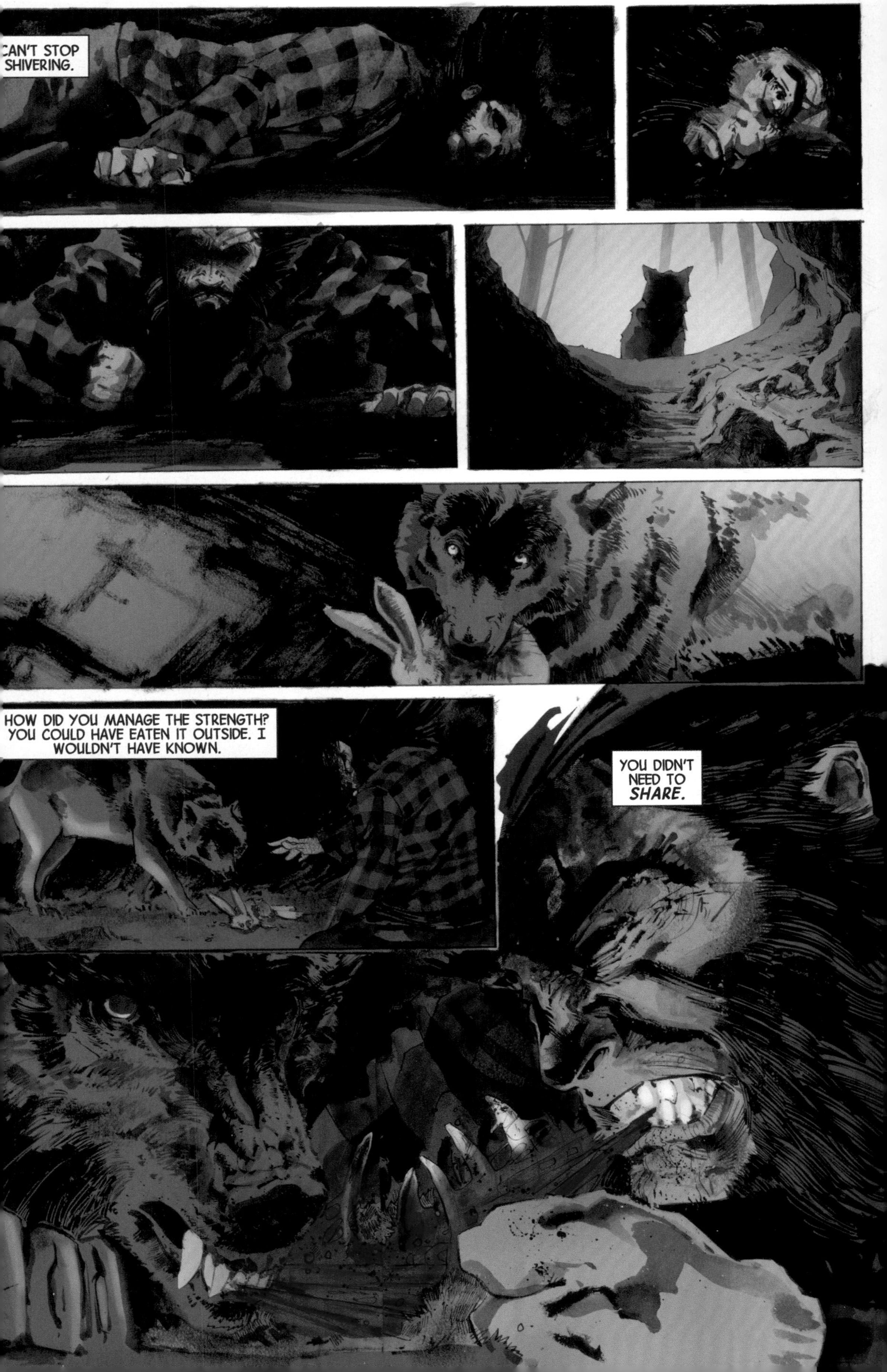
CAN'T STOP SHIVERING.
HOW DID YOU MANAGE THE STRENGTH? YOU COULD HAVE EATEN IT OUTSIDE. I WOULDN'T HAVE KNOWN.
YOU DIDN'T NEED TO SHARE.

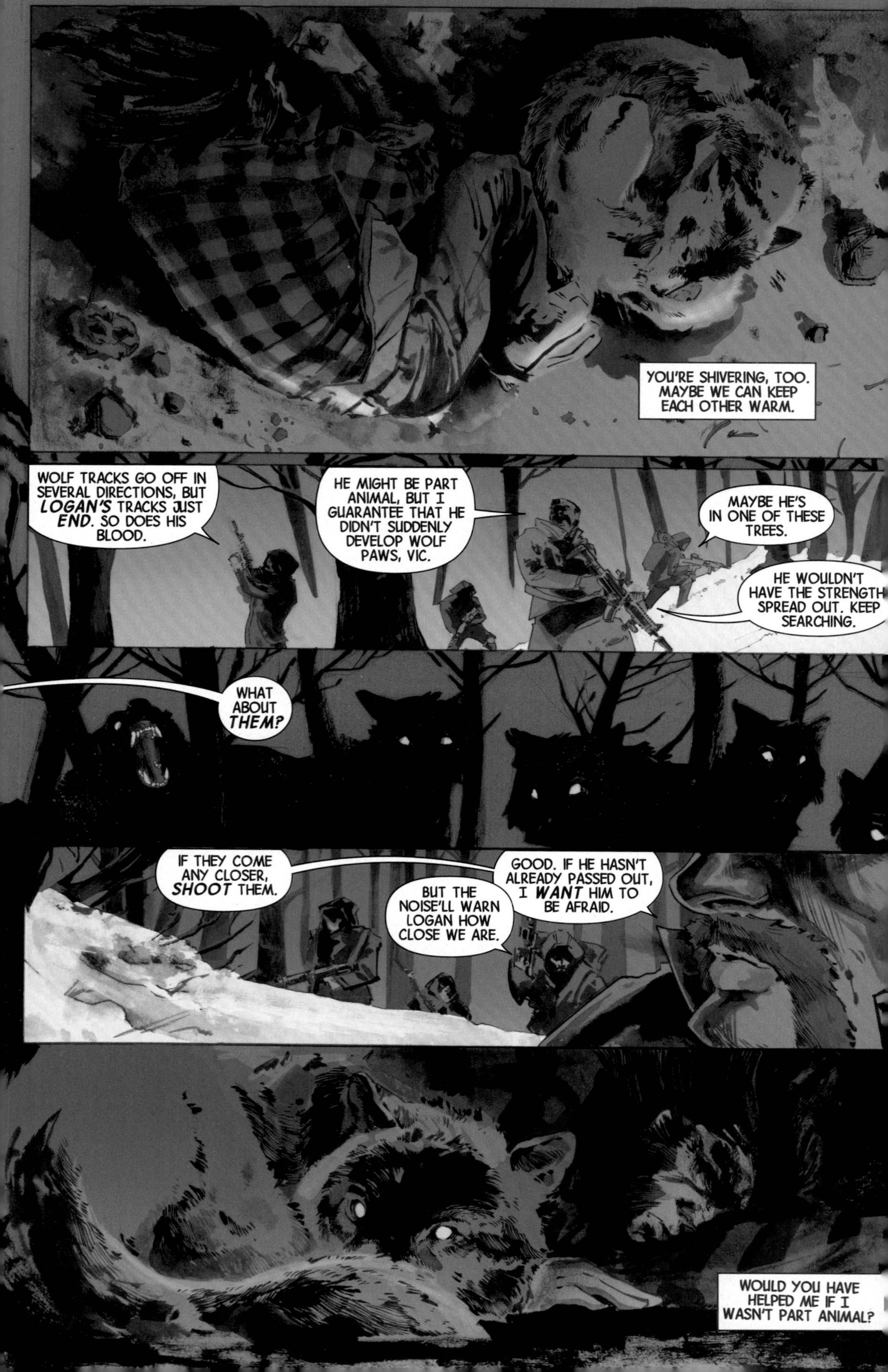
YOU'RE SHIVERING, TOO. MAYBE WE CAN KEEP EACH OTHER WARM.
WOLF TRACKS GO OFF IN SEVERAL DIRECTIONS, BUT LOGAN'S TRACKS JUST END. SO DOES HIS BLOOD.
HE MIGHT BE PART ANIMAL, BUT I GUARANTEE THAT HE DIDN'T SUDDENLY DEVELOP WOLF PAWS, VIC.
MAYBE HE'S IN ONE OF THESE TREES.
HE WOULDN'T HAVE THE STRENGTH. SPREAD OUT. KEEP SEARCHING.
WHAT ABOUT THEM?
IF THEY COME ANY CLOSER, SHOOT THEM.
BUT THE NOISE'LL WARN LOGAN HOW CLOSE WE ARE.
GOOD. IF HE HASN'T ALREADY PASSED OUT, I WANT HIM TO BE AFRAID.
WOULD YOU HAVE HELPED ME IF I WASN'T PART ANIMAL?

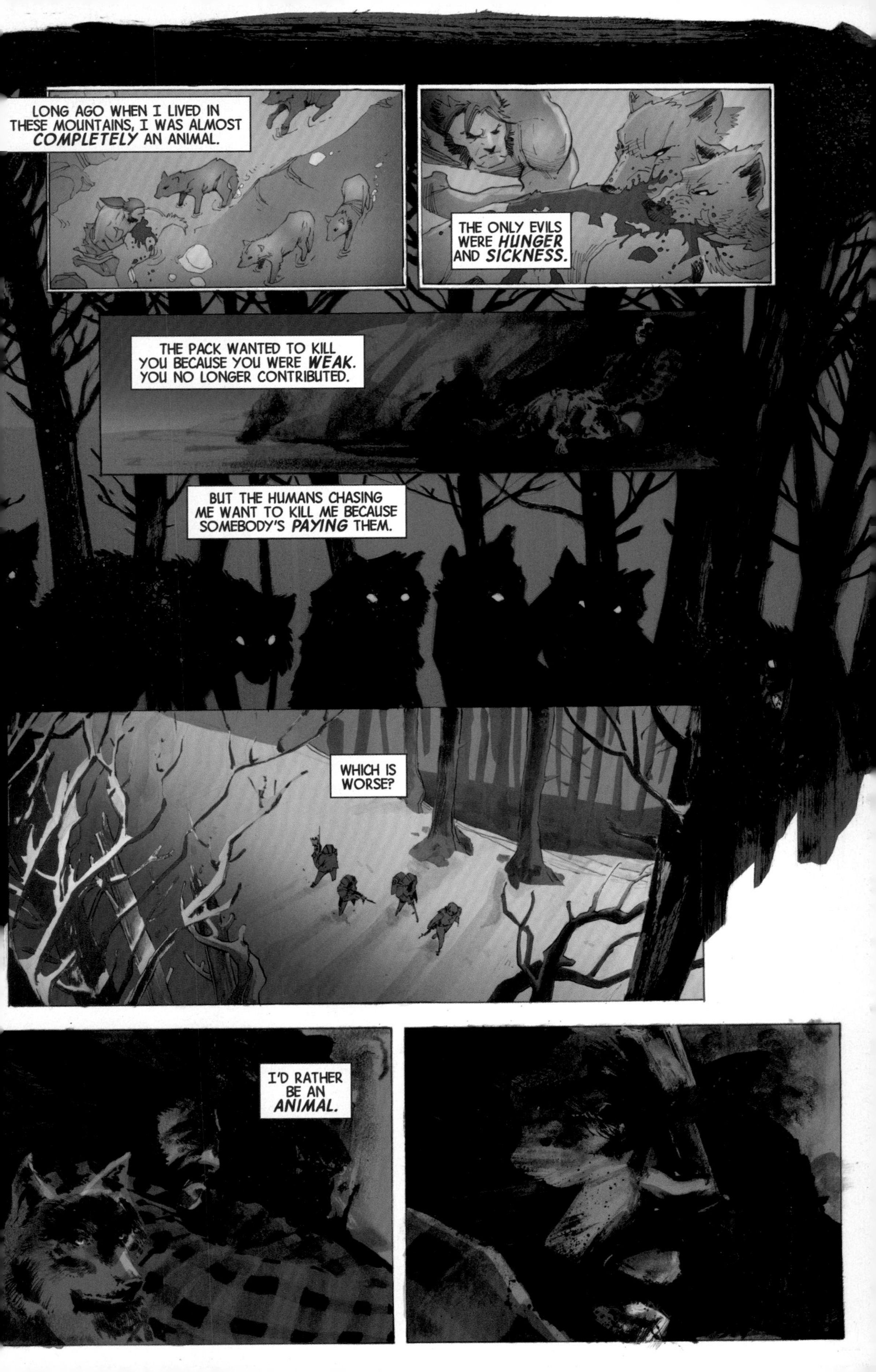
LONG AGO WHEN I LIVED IN THESE MOUNTAINS, I WAS ALMOST *COMPLETELY* AN ANIMAL.
THE ONLY EVILS WERE *HUNGER* AND *SICKNESS.*
THE PACK WANTED TO KILL YOU BECAUSE YOU WERE *WEAK*. YOU NO LONGER CONTRIBUTED.
BUT THE HUMANS CHASING ME WANT TO KILL ME BECAUSE SOMEBODY'S *PAYING* THEM.
WHICH IS WORSE?
I'D RATHER BE AN *ANIMAL.*

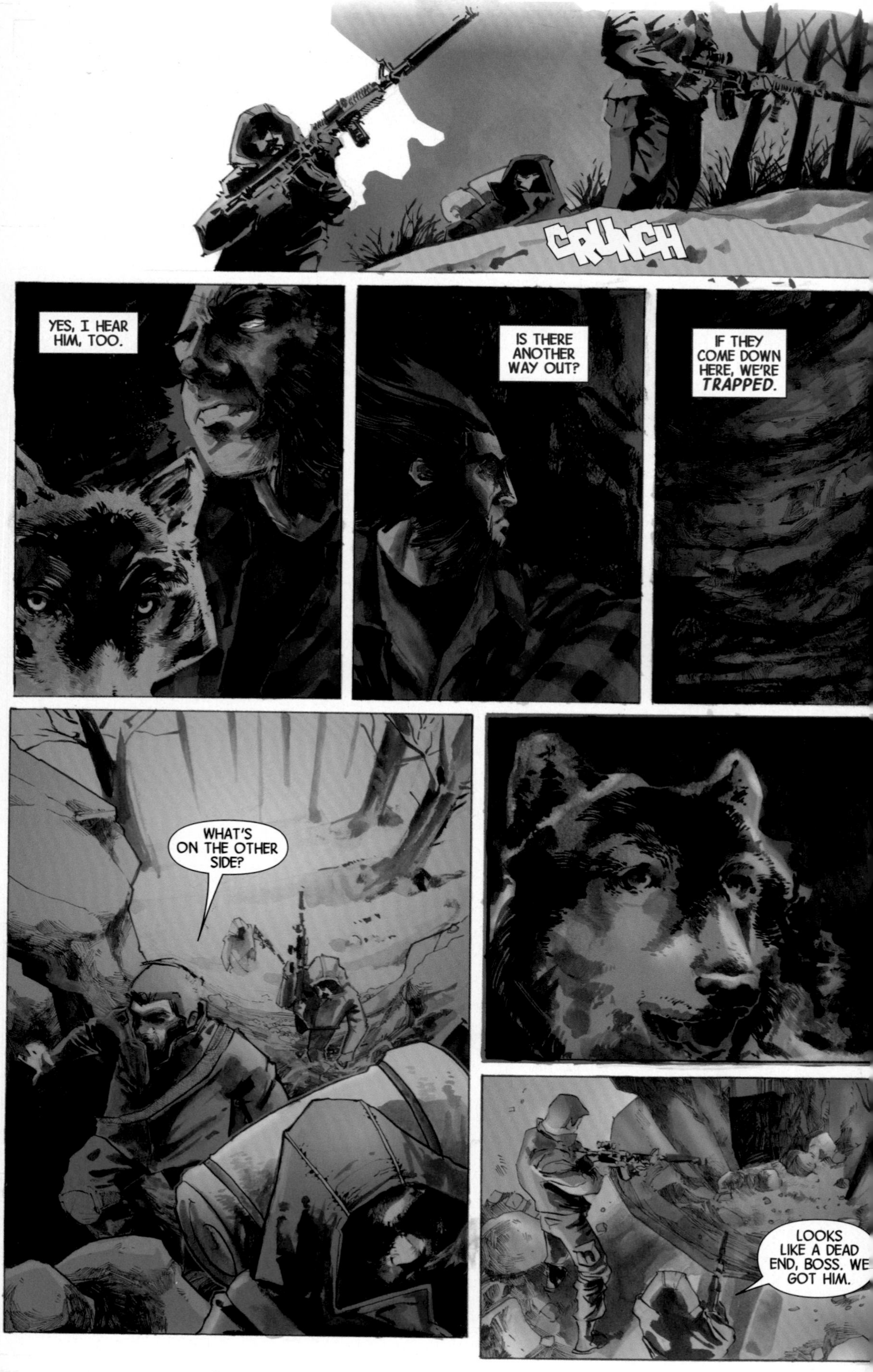
CRUNCH
YES, I HEAR HIM, TOO.
IS THERE ANOTHER WAY OUT?
IF THEY COME DOWN HERE, WE'RE *TRAPPED*.
WHAT'S ON THE OTHER SIDE?
LOOKS LIKE A DEAD END, BOSS. WE GOT HIM.

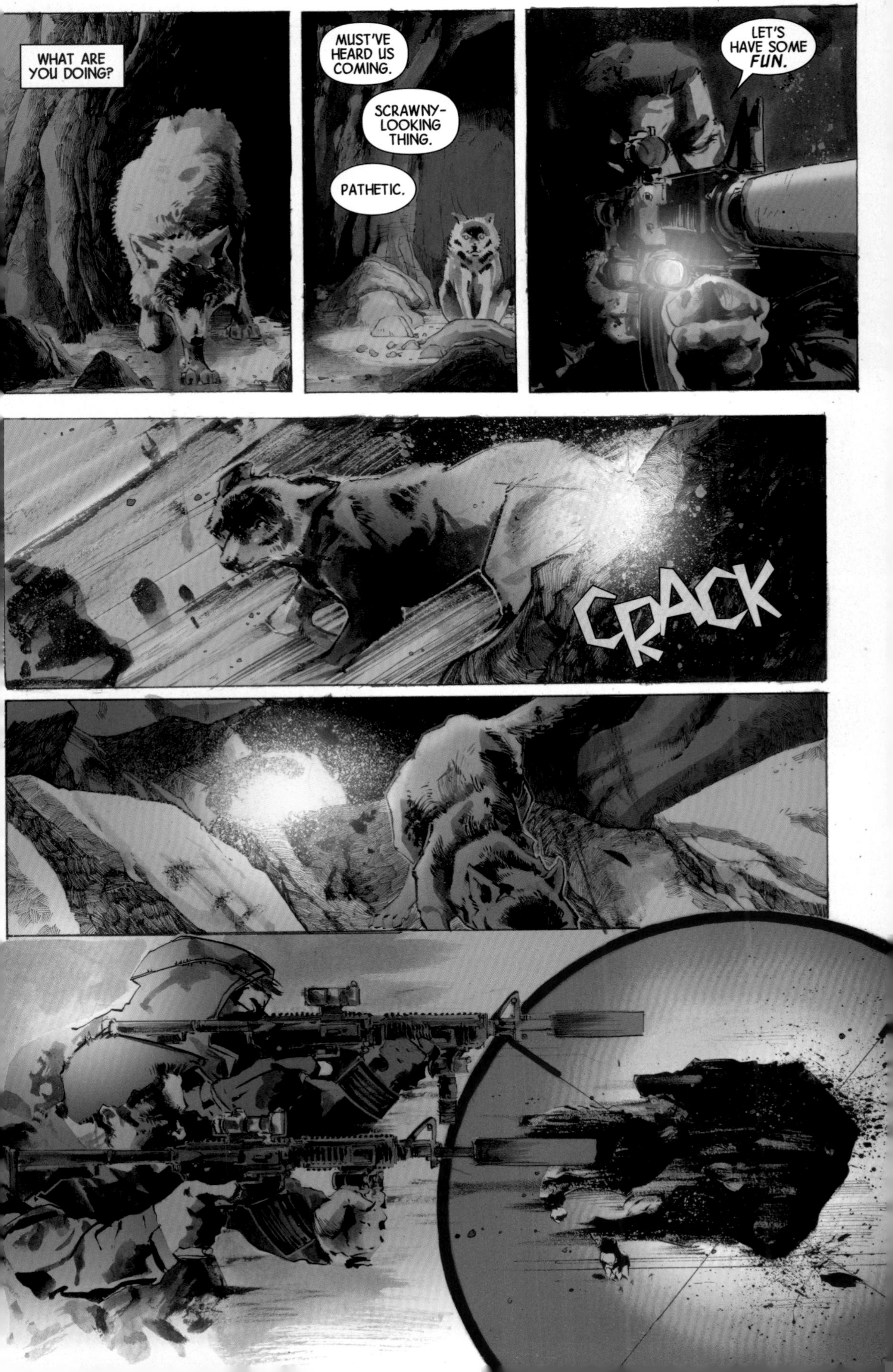
WHAT ARE YOU DOING?
MUST'VE HEARD US COMING.
SCRAWNY-LOOKING THING.
PATHETIC.
LET'S HAVE SOME *FUN.*
CRACK

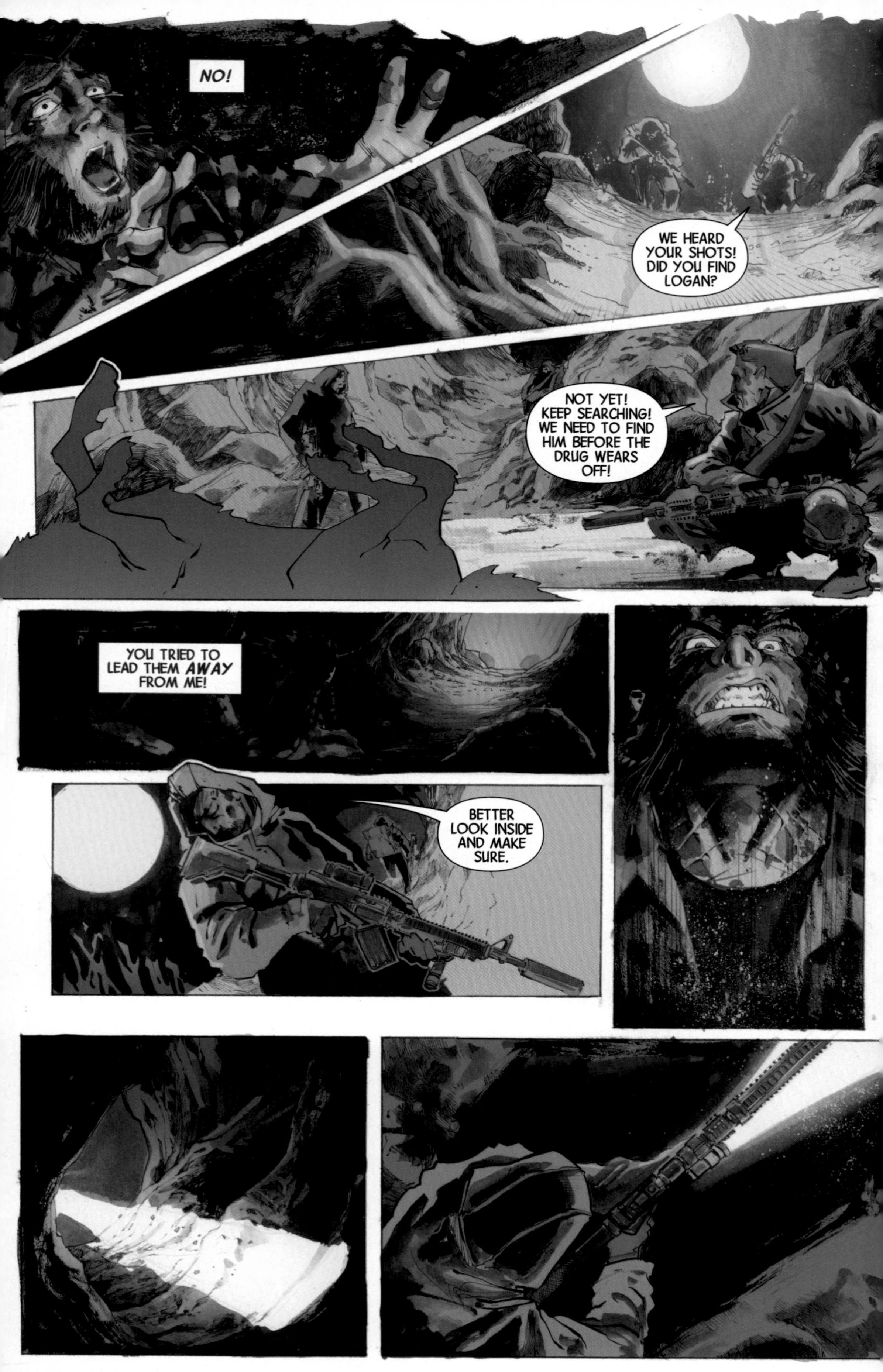
NO!
WE HEARD YOUR SHOTS! DID YOU FIND LOGAN?
NOT YET! KEEP SEARCHING! WE NEED TO FIND HIM BEFORE THE DRUG WEARS OFF!
YOU TRIED TO LEAD THEM AWAY FROM ME!
BETTER LOOK INSIDE AND MAKE SURE.

GRRRRRR

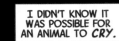

I DIDN'T KNOW IT
WAS POSSIBLE FOR
AN ANIMAL TO *CRY.*

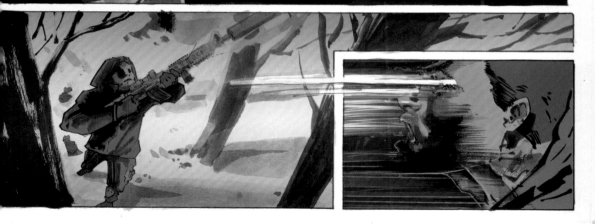

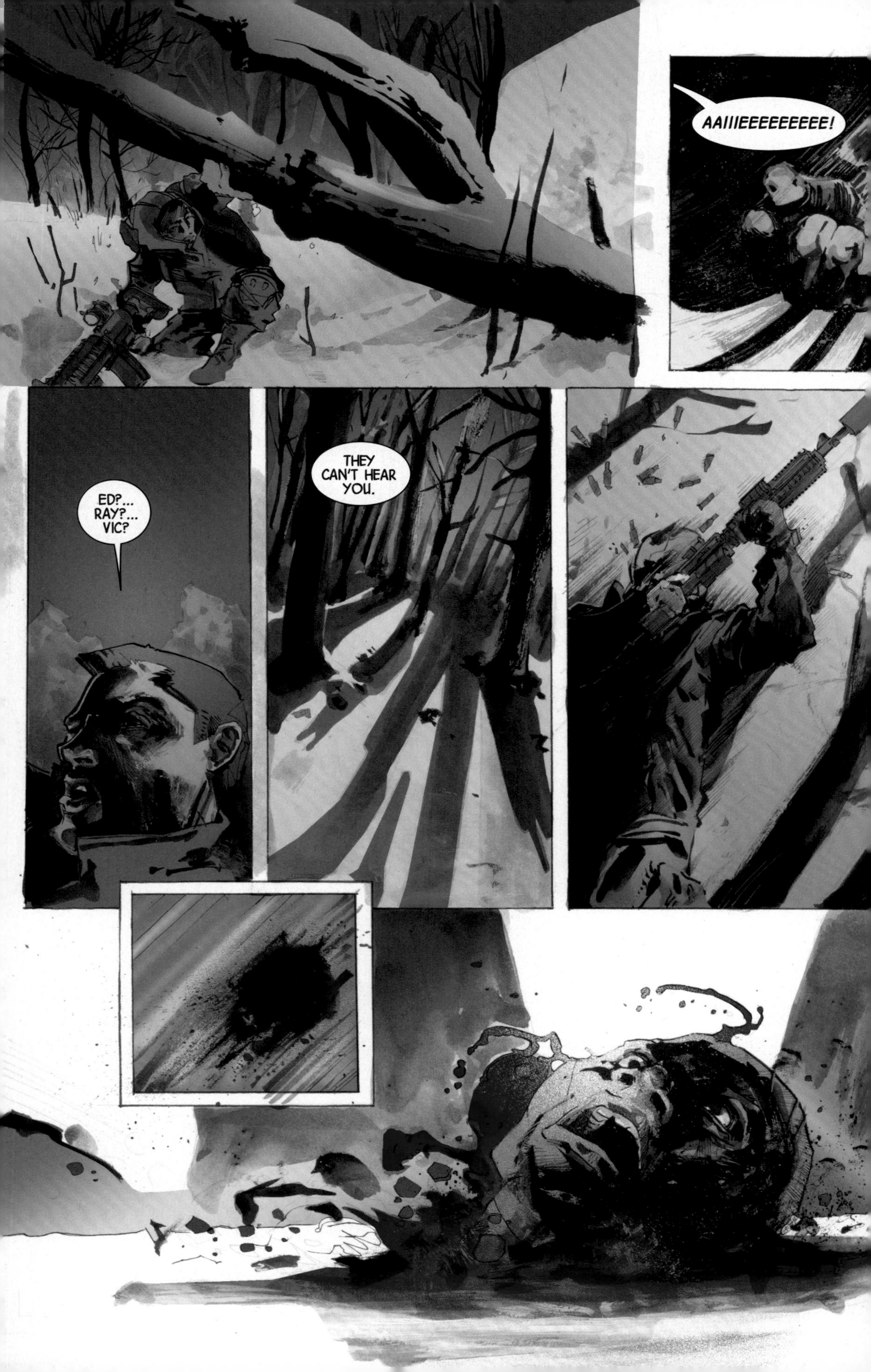
AAIIIEEEEEEEEE!
ED?... RAY?... VIC?
THEY CAN'T HEAR YOU.

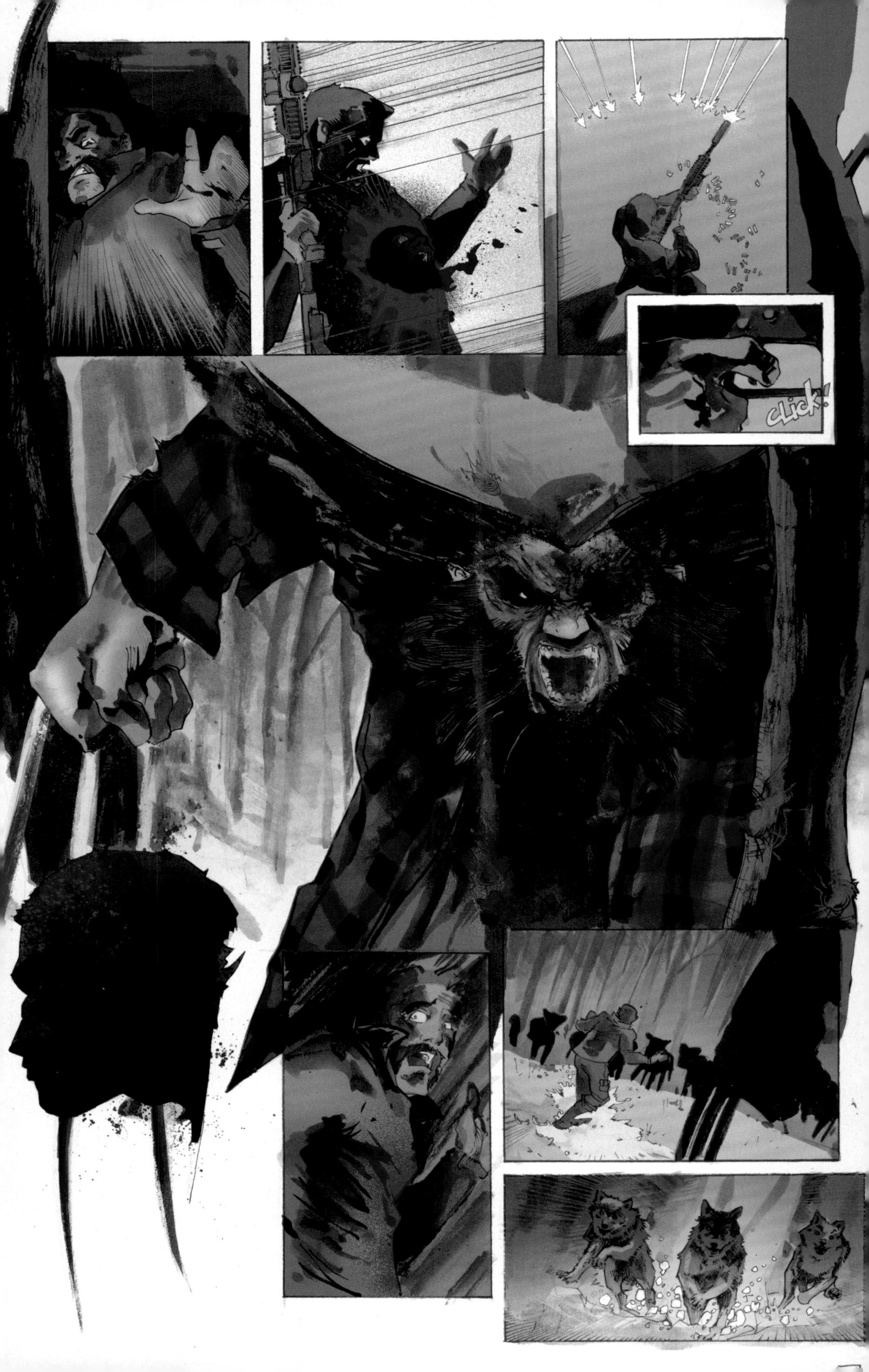
CLICK!

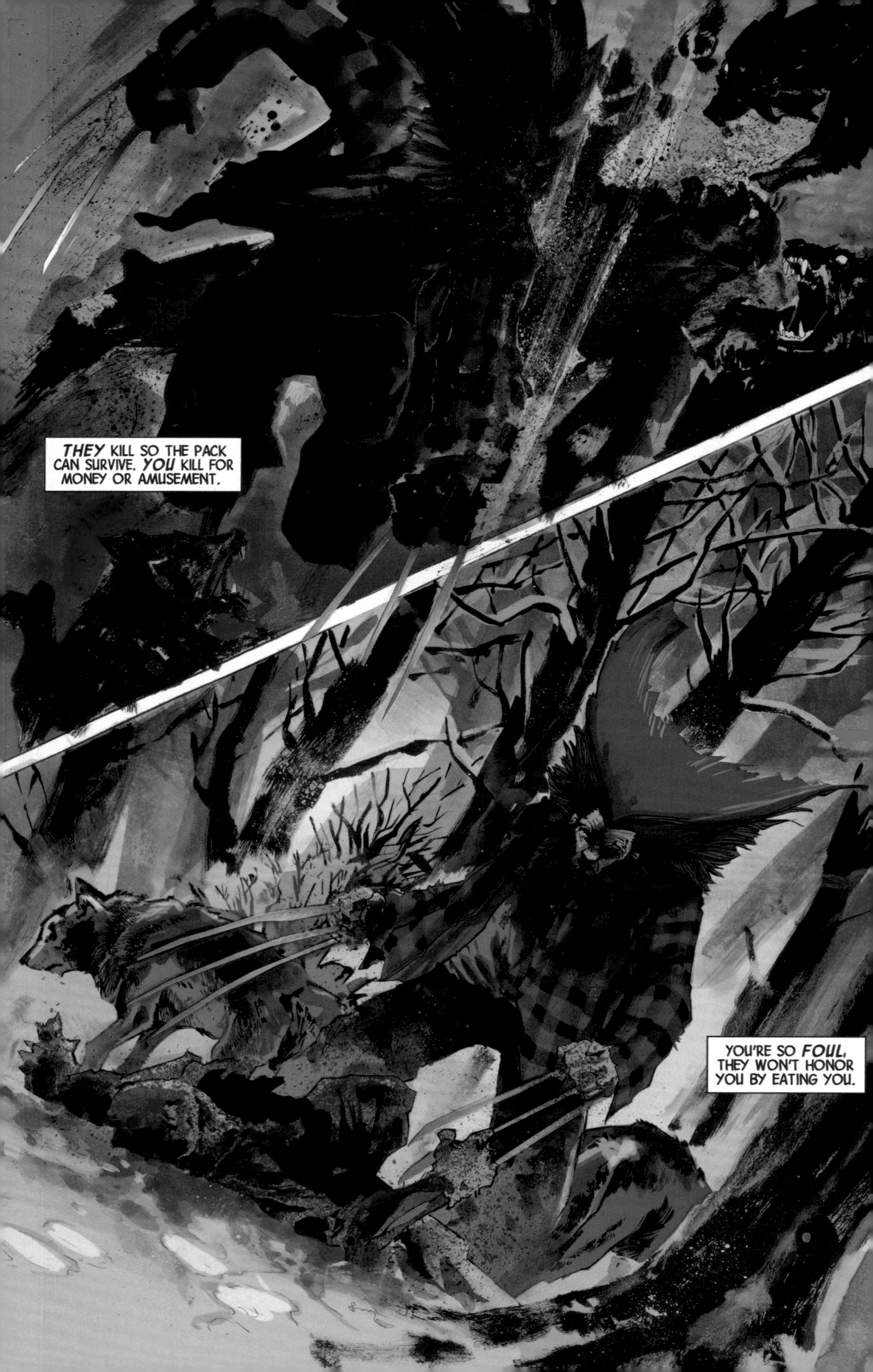
THEY KILL SO THE PACK CAN SURVIVE. YOU KILL FOR MONEY OR AMUSEMENT.
YOU'RE SO FOUL, THEY WON'T HONOR YOU BY EATING YOU.

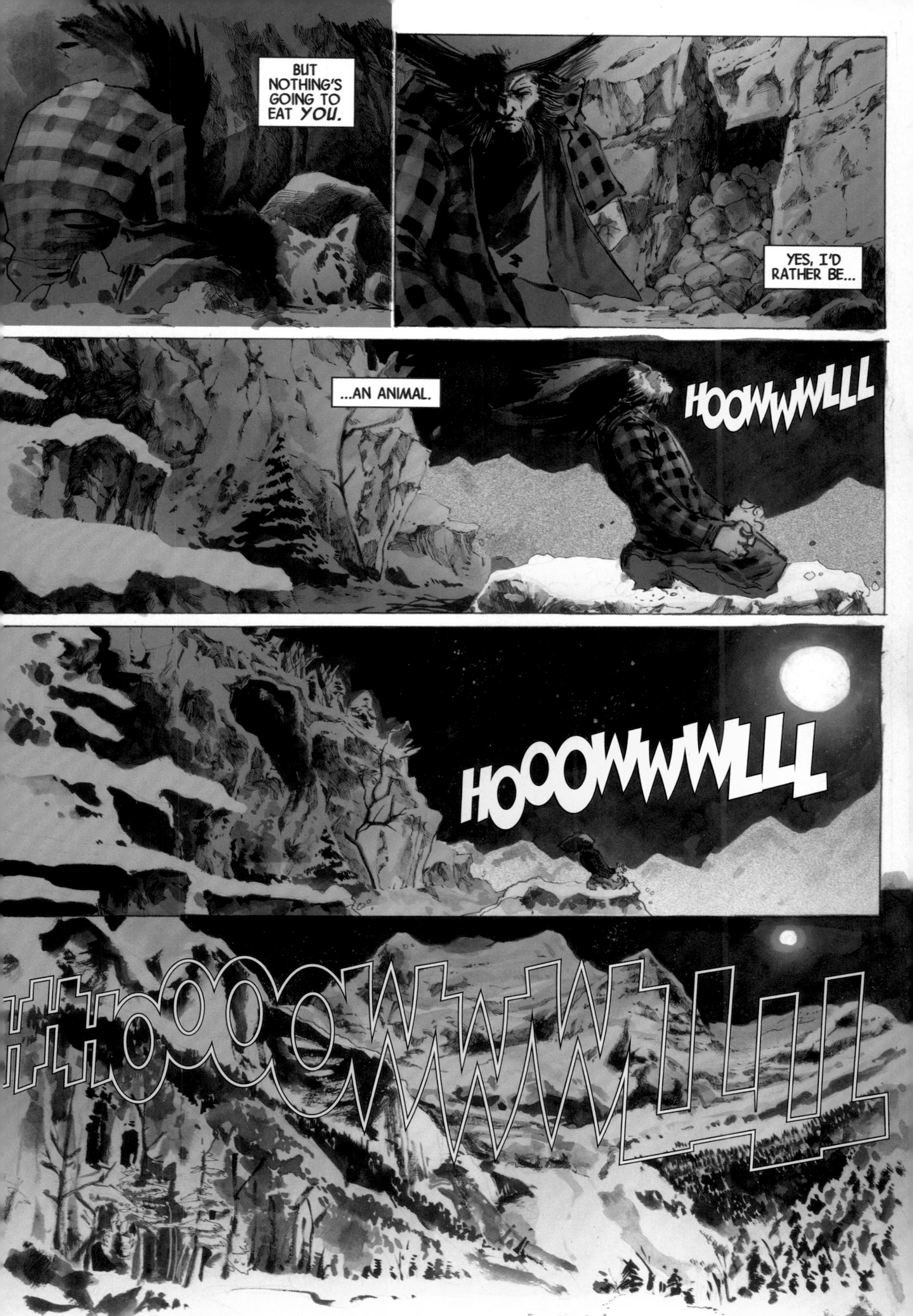
BUT NOTHING'S GOING TO EAT *YOU*.
YES, I'D RATHER BE...
...AN ANIMAL.
HOOWWWLLL
HOOOWWWLLL
HHOOOOWWWWLLLL
JM 14

THE END

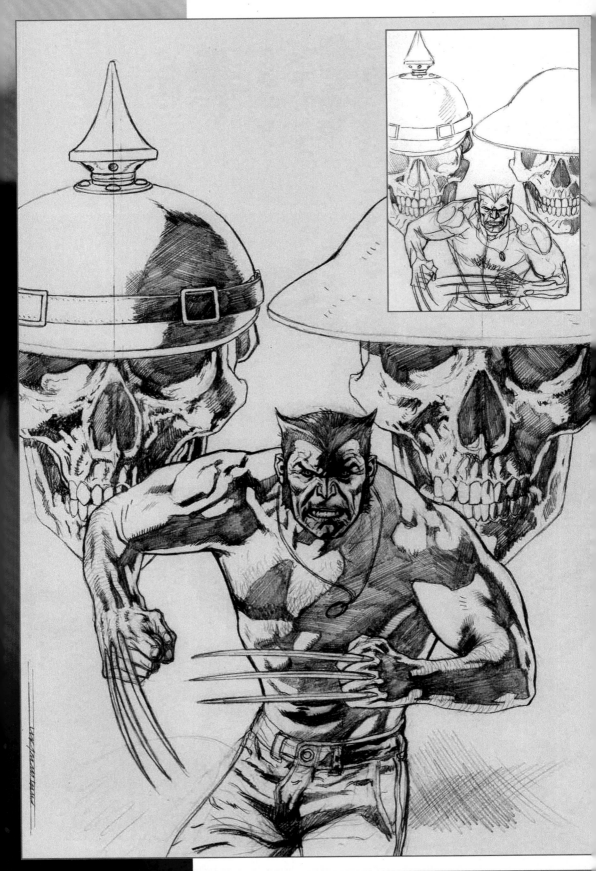

COVER SKETCH AND PENCILS BY KEVIN NOWLAN

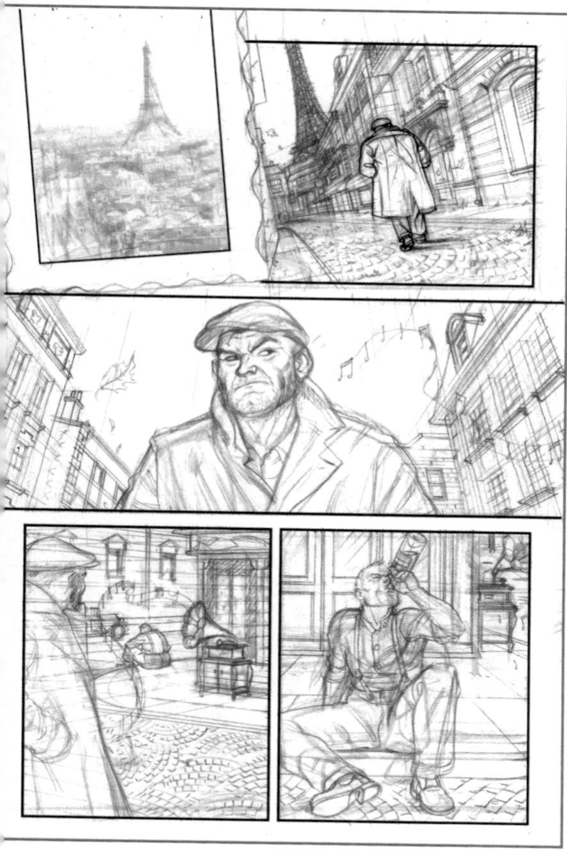

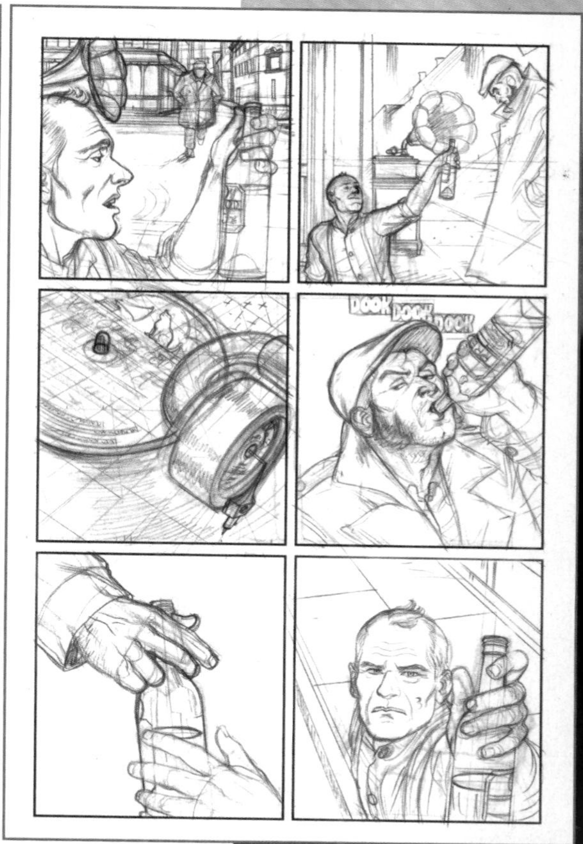
DOOK DOOK DOOK

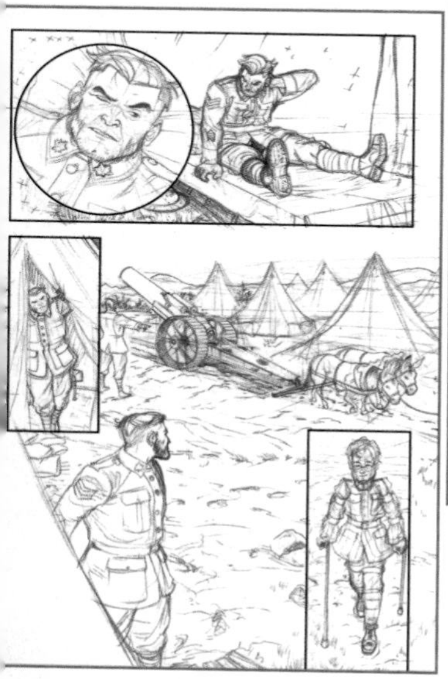

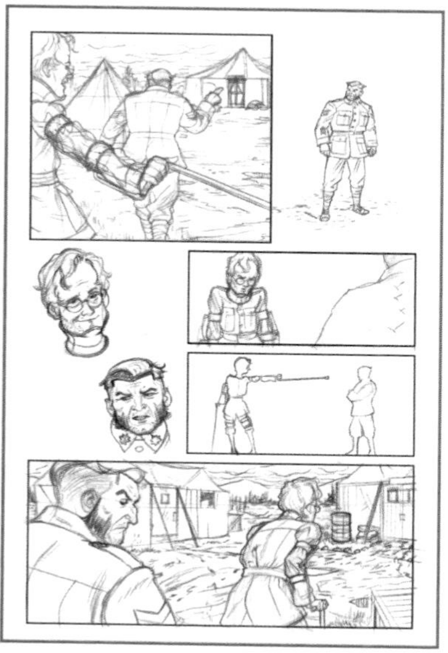

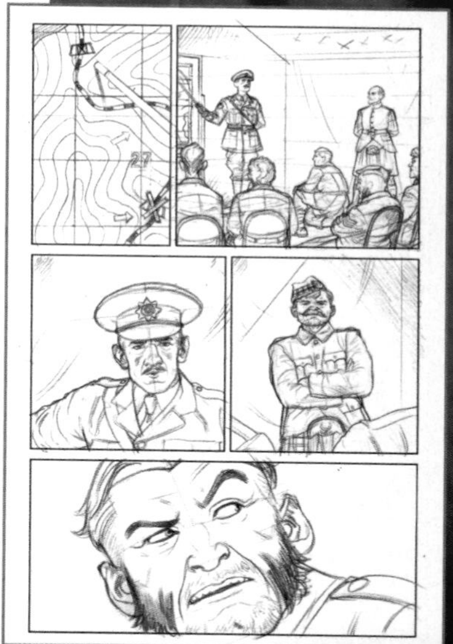

PAGES 1-5 PENCILS BY JOE QUINONES

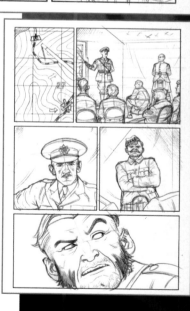

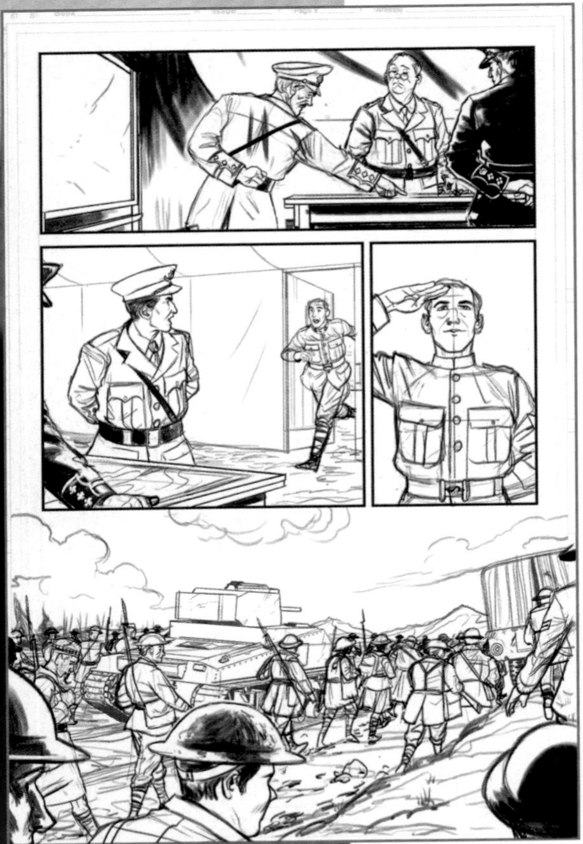

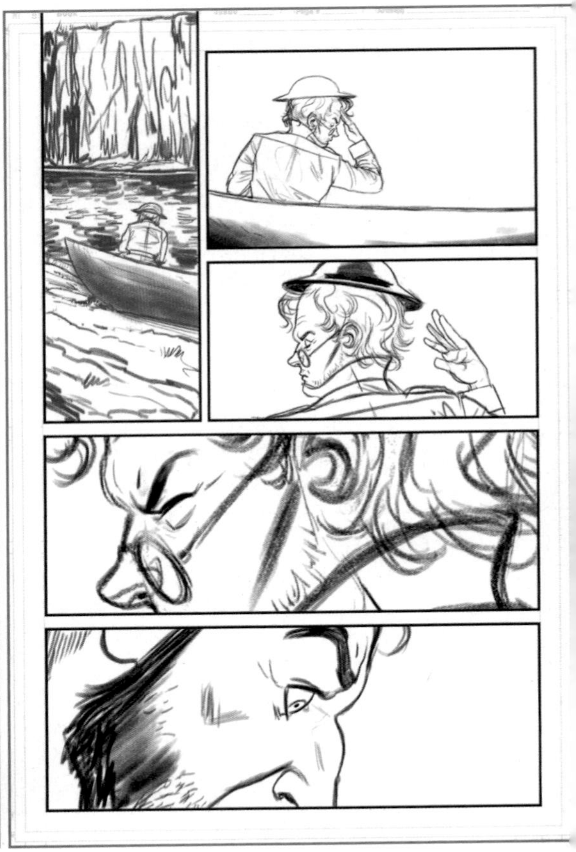

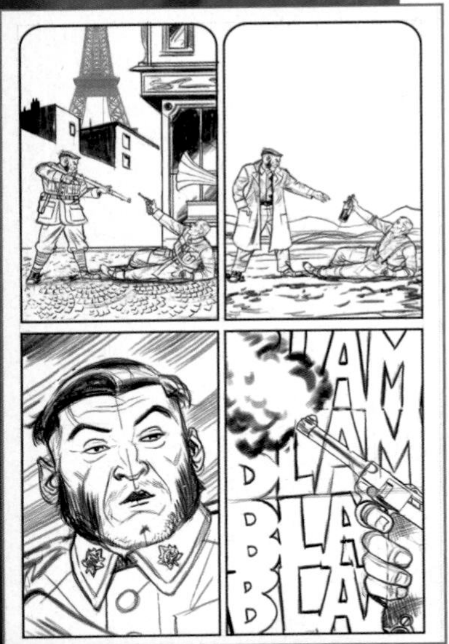

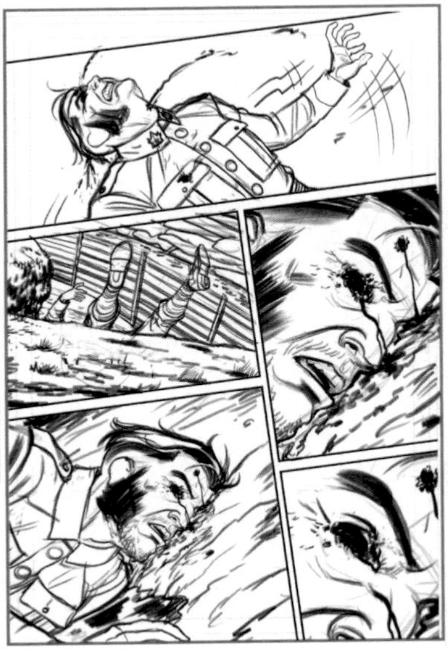

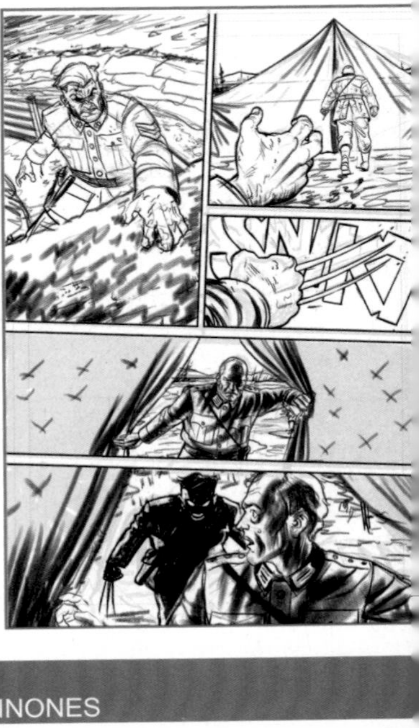

PAGES 1-5 PENCILS BY JOE QUINONES

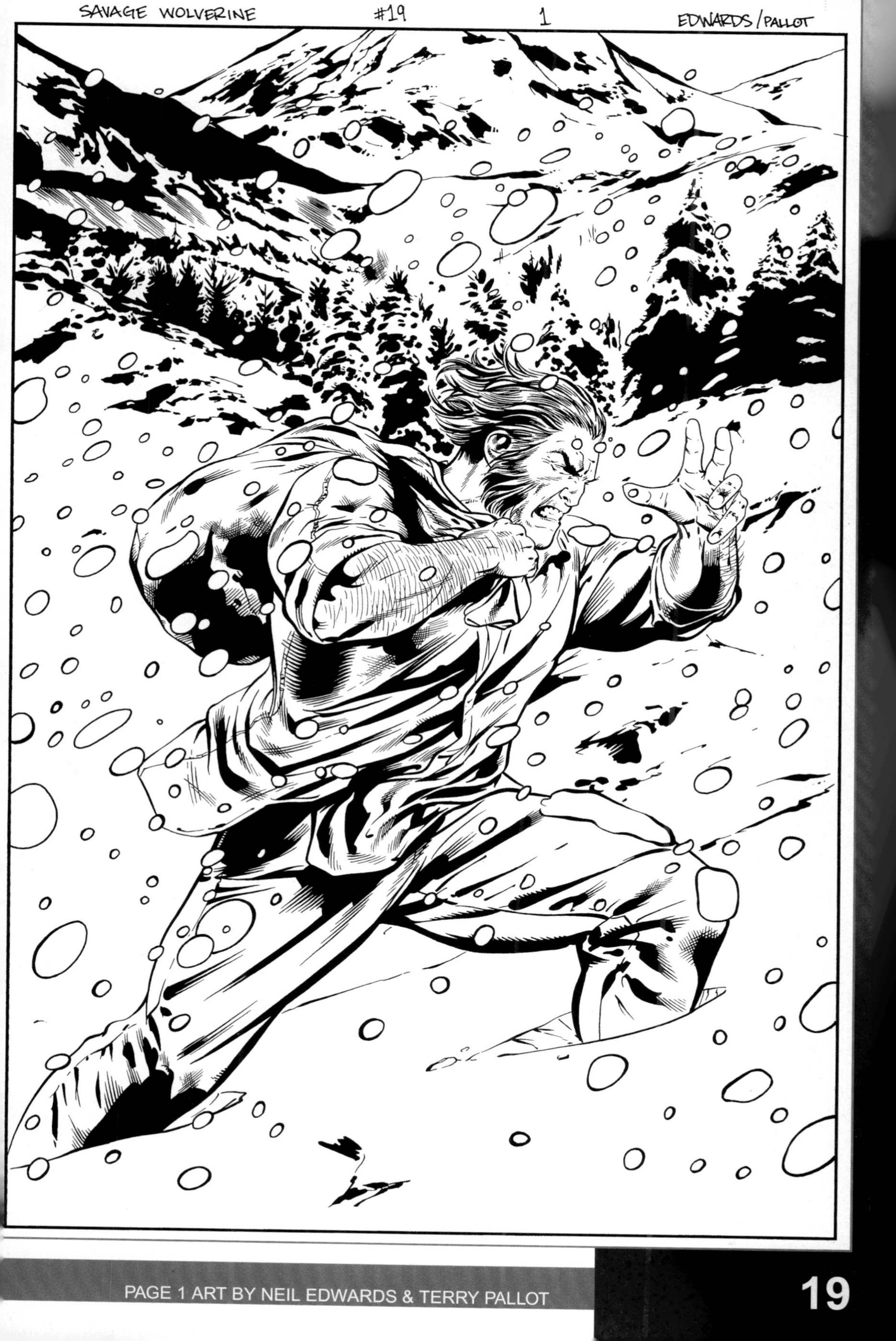
SAVAGE WOLVERINE
#19
1
EDWARDS / PALLOT

PAGE 1 ART BY NEIL EDWARDS & TERRY PALLOT